The Mayflower

In ye name of god Amen. We whose names are underwriten,
the loyall subiects of our dread soueraigne Lord King Iames
by ye grace of god, of great Britaine, franc, & yreland king.
defendor of ye faith, &

Haueing vndertaken, for ye glorie of god, and aduancements
of ye christian faith, and honour of our king & countrie, a voyage to
plant ye first Colonie in ye Northerne parts of Virginia. doe
by these presents solemnly & mutualy in ye presence of god, and
one of another, Couenant, & combine our selues togeather into a
Ciuill body politick; for ye our better ordering, & preseruation & fur=
therance of ye ends aforsaid; and by vertue heerof. to Enacte,
constitute, and frame shuch just & equall Lawes, ordinances,
Acts, constitutions, & offices, from time to time, as shall be thought
most meete & conuenient for ye generall good of ye Colonie: vnto
which we promise all due submission and obedience. In witnes
wherof we haue hereunder subscribed our names at Cap=
Codd ye .11. of Nouember, in ye year of ye raigne of our soueraigne
Lord king Iames of England, franc, & yreland ye eighteenth
and of Scotland ye fiftie fourth. An: Dom .1620.]

Part of the *Mayflower* Compact.

The Mayflower

Vernon Heaton

MAYFLOWER BOOKS · NEW YORK CITY

A *Webb&Bower* BOOK

Edited, designed and produced by
Webb & Bower (Publishers) Limited
33 Southernhay East, Exeter, Devon, England EX1 1NS

Designed by Vic Giolitto

Library of Congress Cataloging in Publication Data
No. 80–13532

ISBN 0–8317–5745–0

Manufactured in Hong Kong
First American Edition

Typesetting and monochrome origination
by Keyspools Limited, Golborne, Lancashire, England
Printed and bound in Hong Kong
by Mandarin Publishers Limited

Contents

To
my granddaughter
Gillian Dorothy Jane Bruce

A Note on Dates

In the 17th century dates were reckoned in what is now known as the Old Style – that is, since then ten days have been cut out of the calendar to give us the New Style used today. For instance, the Pilgrim Fathers first set sail from Southampton on 5th August 1620, which we reckon as 15th August; they landed at New Plymouth on 11th December of that year, which day we now reckon as 21st December.

The Old Style has been retained throughout this book as a matter of convenience; however, the present fashion of dating New Year's Day as 1st January has been followed rather than the old practice of celebrating the event on 24th March.

1 Introductory

The Pilgrim Fathers formed one of very many "splinter groups" of deeply religious people which rebelled against the authority of the Anglican Church in England towards the end of the 16th century. None of these groups had any quarrel with the generally accepted concept of God as understood throughout the Christian world, but they did, in one degree or another, reject the various artificially and politically established "chains of command" imposed between them and their God.

The major sects, such as the Roman Catholics, regarded the hierarchy of their church as God's sole representatives on Earth – with the rights of intercession, forgiveness and retribution. The Anglican Church differed from the Roman Catholics only in that it was national rather than international and because it recognized the English Sovereign rather than the Pope in Rome as the final link with the Almighty. But the Puritans took a very different view of the authority of the church; they permitted no man the right to assume the dignity of being God's appointed agent on Earth, nor would they accept that any church had the sole privilege of interpreting the word of the Lord.

Both the Catholics and the Anglicans preferred dogma, richly endowed churches and brilliant ceremonial as an integral part of the worship of God, and both claimed for themselves absolute authority over their clerics and their congregations – and the unassailable right to order their services in the manner established by their "princes". The Puritan concept of worship, however, included no dogma, no ceremonial, no statuary and no formal Book of Prayer. It despised the panoply, the preferments, the dignities and the rich emoluments of the self-appointed bishops and archbishops and resented fiercely their claim to infallibility and their rejection of the right of any man to worship in accordance with the dictates of his own conscience. It disdained the vestments of the clergy and their ritualistic services, and utterly rejected the use of symbolism in the form

of Holy Mass, Communion, Baptism, the Enthronement of Bishops and the Solemnization of Marriages. They claimed the right to elect their own teachers and objected strongly to being compelled to support the magnificent edifices of church and cathedral through tithes, levies and taxes – preferring to worship solemnly in humble surroundings and in direct communication with God.

But the state religion of England had the advantage, as far as King and government were concerned, of forming a vast network of communication that reached into every corner – and every home – of the realm. Through it ran the authority of the law, the injected fear of the hereafter and the certainty that the vast army of priests employed by it must, inevitably, note the slightest reluctance on the part of anyone to comply with its ordinances. Compulsory attendances at church services ensured that the "Big Brother" technique of surveillance was total; mysticism at those services created fear, the brilliant ceremonial awe – and the parish rolls prevented the citizens from dispersing and so evading taxes, military service and their "duty" to their masters. For those who failed to conform, the penalties were severe and summary.

Those who saw fit to oppose the Anglican form of worship were unfortunately not wholly agreed among themselves. Their religious scruples varied considerably and were often the cause of outspoken and even abusive arguments. Nor were the dissenters all prepared to sacrifice their freedom, and perhaps even their lives, in defence of their beliefs and in defiance of the state church. There were groups which ran with the hare and hunted with the hounds rather than risk the wrath of the established church – and yet continued, lukewarmly, to make some show of nonconformity. Other groups proved to be as fanatically devoted to the worship of God in their own way and as outspoken in their illegal meetings as had been the Christians who had been condemned to the arenas of Rome.

Dr. Taylor rebuking a Popish Priest who was about to say Mass in Hadley Church.

Religious intolerance in sixteenth-century England. Rowland Taylor (*above*), who had been domestic chaplain to Cranmer, was burnt at the stake as a Protestant in 1555. Less than thirty years later, the boot was on the other foot (*below*): in 1581 these two Jesuit "conspirators" were discovered, Parsons escaping but Campion being put to death.

F. Parsons & Campian   F.H. fecit.

Rebellion the effect of Monasteries.

In 1580, when our story really begins, the general body of Puritan opinion preferred to acknowledge the overlordship of the Anglican Church and to accept the dictates of the Queen through her bishops, while yet, in private, worshipping under the guidance of dissenting priests. From this body the more scrupulous and extremist elements broke away as "Separatists", to worship in accordance with their own consciences.

The Pilgrim Church was one such group. It did not hesitate to accept the dangers implicit in holding secret and illegal meetings, and in heeding the teachings of unlicensed, Nonconformist pastors.

Heroic people: men, women and children who refused to recognize the carefully prescribed services imposed on them by the established church and performed by priests whose mock-humility conveyed to them little of the teachings of Christ. They had to be brave to flout the law in that intolerant age.

Failure to attend the services of the Anglican Church might well be penalized by a heavy fine, a spell in the stocks or even with long terms of imprisonment. For some excommunication was the sentence – and the everlasting hell that that implied. For a few, it was execution.

But these sombre horizons, judgements and visitations were a way of life in that era, not to be altered or openly questioned for centuries – despite the surge of conscience among many Englishmen and their growing preoccupation with the form of their worship of God. For generations to come the schism between the Anglican and the Puritan was to continue in bitterness – although basically the sole differences between them lay in the channels of communication between man and his God. Vast though this explosion of differences proved to be, the concept of the authority of the Almighty and of the certainty of Heaven and Hell was never in dispute.

A band of "godly and faythful Christians" under arrest for their religious practices.

2 The Freedom to Worship

Queen Elizabeth ascended the throne of England on 17th November 1558. She was the sister of Mary, her Catholic predecessor; both were the daughters of Henry VIII, founder of the Anglican Church.

From the first, as Supreme Head of the Anglican Church, she needed to step delicately between the claims of the Catholics with their powerful allies abroad and the demands of the Puritans at home; and to stem the flow of the more devout Christians from the Anglican Church into both wings of the

Nonconformists. Both dissenting parties sought to undermine her authority in religious matters, and Elizabeth saw that they posed a threat to the security of her realm, the Catholics insisting on the rule of Rome and the Puritans refusing to defend the established order.

She was well aware that Catholic priests were being infiltrated into England from the continent, pledged to stir up the populace – who were, in the main, at heart Catholics – to rebellion. She was equally alive

Henry VIII who, because the Pope would not allow him to divorce his first wife, Catherine of Aragon, in favour of Anne Boleyn, founded the Anglican Church.

Mary Tudor (with Philip II of Spain), whose rabid Catholicism put many Protestants to the stake all over the country.

to the fact that the Puritans were urging the non-Catholics to refuse to acknowledge her authority as Head of the Church, of the prelates she appointed and through them, in effect, the government of the realm.

The Catholic threat was more easily held at bay as its titular head and most of its leaders were on the far side of the English Channel from their supporters, but the Puritans were an insidious embarrassment in that they had no central authority that she could challenge, no organized cohorts that she could attack, nor even a church building that she could tear down. Queen Elizabeth saw the strict enforcement of discipline on all her subjects, priest and layman alike, within the tentacles of the Anglican Church – which she controlled – as an answer to the problem.

In the year 1559 the Act of Supremacy, making it clear beyond any legal doubt that the Sovereign was to be recognized as the Supreme Head of the English Church, was revived, and almost immediately, the Act of Uniformity reached the statute books, apparently designed to establish the authorized Book of Common Prayer as the only route to the Almighty. Under this Act the detailed ritual of every type of service was laid down, the dogma established as sacrosanct, the vestments to be worn by the priests were made mandatory, and even the precise form of words to be used in the conduct of services was fixed and declared unalterable.

The Marian bishops, almost as one, refused to accept the situation, only to find themselves swept aside by an angry Queen. She appointed the quiet, scholarly and amenable Mathew Parker to the archbishopric of Canterbury with direct orders to reconstruct the Anglican hierarchy using priests who were prepared to accept her pre-eminence in church affairs and to enforce the terms of the Act of Uniformity.

The new Archbishop combed through the lower strata of the clergy and dismissed almost all of those who had received their appointments during the reign of the Catholic Mary – nearly a seventh of the whole priesthood. Those who remained were strengthened by the influx of more than a thousand clergy who had fled abroad during Mary's reign and who were now welcomed back as the stiffening Elizabeth needed to bolster up her authority.

But unexpectedly, and at first unnoticed by the supremos of Elizabeth's church, the returning priests had largely been influenced by the Reformed Church on the continent during their exile, and so came home filled with a quiet but determined spirit of Puritanism. In fact, within a few years they wielded so much power that the lower House of Convocation succeeded in rejecting a motion against the wearing of vestments by only a single vote.

In 1568 Mary Queen of Scots fled to England and sought the protection of Elizabeth; once she had established herself on English soil the Catholic Mary became the focal point around which the newly heartened Catholics rallied. In 1569 the northern Catholics, under the earls of Northumberland and Westmorland, rose against Elizabeth, and the Pope sought to aid their cause with a Bull of Deposition and Excommunication. But the rebellion was crushed easily even before the Papal Bull reached England.

However, Queen Elizabeth was never to be free from the plotting of her Catholic subjects, and Spain

Queen Elizabeth I. In contrast to her elder half-sister Mary, Elizabeth was staunchly Protestant, although her fervour was considerably more tolerant than Mary's.

was from then on to poke a powerful thumb into every pie of Catholic discontent in England. No doubt King Philip II of Spain's interventions would have been more effective if the fractious Netherlands had not kept him out of the North Sea ports; nevertheless, in 1570 he was deeply implicated in the Ridolfi conspiracy, the suppression of which resulted in the Duke of Norfolk losing his head and Mary Queen of Scots being deprived of the little liberty she had been permitted.

England allied herself with France in 1572 under the Treaty of Blois, but in 1580, with the acquisition of Portugal, Philip of Spain decided that he at last held a strategic advantage against Elizabeth. In the following year he completed secret arrangements to support a revolt of the Catholics in England with a powerful invasion of his forces. The plot fizzled out but the enmity between England and Spain sharpened as Philip's involvement in the conspiracy became clear.

In 1586 Anthony Babington, in league with a

Mary Queen of Scots preparing for her execution at Fotheringay. Although Elizabeth had signed the death warrant, she claimed later that she had never intended the execution to be carried out.

Catholic priest named John Ballard, conspired to murder the Queen and her ministers and to organize a general uprising of Catholics in order to free Mary Queen of Scots. The plot was widespread, and Philip of Spain undertook to invade England in its support, but once again it fizzled out. The incautious correspondence between Mary and Babington was intercepted; and the plotters were seized and, eventually, executed. The discovery of the plot provoked a demand from Parliament that the Queen should, once and for all, remove the cornerstone on which rested the endless series of Catholic intrigues: in the following year Mary Queen of Scots was beheaded at Fotheringay.

The death of Mary was, however, to have little influence on Philip's urge to overthrow the English Queen and re-establish Catholic authority in her realm. In 1588 the Spanish Armada put to sea, under

the command of the Duke of Medina-Sidonia, intent on putting an army ashore in England hoping that it would be supported by a massive uprising and so bring to an end the reign of a heretic queen. The force, strong though it undoubtedly was, was totally inadequate for such a venture; and it is probable that the English Catholics, realizing the dangers implicit in the enterprise, would never have risen in sufficient strength. In the event, they were never put to the test: Sir Francis Drake gave the Spanish fleet a severe drubbing in the English Channel, after which a gale from the south-west turned defeat into disaster.

Even that costly failure was not sufficient to dampen Philip's ardour to bring England to its knees. Spanish forces seized Calais and for a time threatened an invasion of England from Brest: the "Invisible Armada" of 1599 caused more alarm in England than had the "Invincible Armada" eleven years earlier.

As Queen Elizabeth staved off the threat from the Catholics, so she struggled to check the growing power of her Puritan subjects. Little notice had been taken of the Act of Uniformity, although it had served to drive the dissenting worshippers underground. They began to meet secretly in private houses and to proliferate into numerous obscure groups.

The defeat of the Spanish Armada, sent in an attempt to impose Catholicism on England and to halt Elizabeth's meddling in the Netherlands.

At first there was little organization about the movement, and never at any time either a general council or even an agreed form of worship. Broadly, the Puritans sought the right to choose their own leaders and to adopt their own form of worship – no more than that, but certainly no less. By 1565 the Anglican clergy, with dwindling congregations and some loss of revenue, began to urge the authorities to enforce the clauses of the Act of Uniformity and steps were taken to discover and to break up the Puritan meetings. In June 1567 the Plumbers' Hall in London was raided and from a congregation of about a hundred worshippers – who claimed they were there for a wedding and that no minister was present – fifteen were arrested and sent to prison. The term was a short one by the standards of that aggressively harsh era; six of them were subsequently arrested for the second time from a meeting of some eighty persons in a private house in March of the following year. The leaders were in this instance imprisoned for a year.

About this time, too, the London Puritans began

to appoint their own body of Elders, consisting chiefly of four or five ministers who had been suspended from the Anglican Church for their refusal to accept the Act of Uniformity in the way they conducted their services. The London Church grew to some two hundred members and it eventually broke away from the general body of Puritans to form an independent church.

In about 1570 the Puritan doctrine was proclaimed in a number of pamphlets, including a manifesto by Richard Fitz entitled *The True Marks of Christ's Church, etc.*, in which he defined the ideals of the "Privy Church in London". The upsurge of such publications caused the Queen to establish a censorship carried out by the ecclesiastical commissioners. As might have been anticipated, such censorship merely resulted in the circulation underground of even more provocative pamphlets and a rising tide of criticism of the established church and its hierarchy.

In 1571 a group of people were imprisoned in the Bridewell, in London, for refusing to obey the Act of Uniformity. They continued to hold their services even in prison, under their freely elected pastor –

(*opposite*) Norwich, where Robert Browne (*c.* 1550–1663) set up his church, on what were later to become known as congregational principles. One of the supporters of this form of worship was to be Oliver Cromwell.

Iconoclasts destroy and remove graven images from the churches. To the iconoclasts, such images were positively blasphemous, and such scenes were not uncommon in the years following the Reformation in England.

Richard Fitz, whom we have mentioned. Another group of Nonconformists was imprisoned in the infamous Clink prison in 1586 and they too held services in prison in accordance with their convictions.

At heart most of the established churchmen were aware of the deficiencies of their church and were anxious enough to do away with much that was purely ornamental and exhibitionist in their services, and many of the lesser clergy cut around, where they could not cut out, many of the ordinances of the Act of Uniformity. In this manner many hoped to achieve freedom of worship by eroding the legislation that controlled the Anglican Church, quietly and without raising a storm of protest and abuse – and without provoking a sudden tightening of the repressive measures already available to the authorities. The precipitancy of the Puritans, by contrast, went far to check the progress of the very cause they wished to forward.

Between 1580 and 1581, Robert Browne formed a church in Norwich in which the first definite scriptural theory of its kind was put forward (it was published in Middelburg, Holland, in 1582). He laid down the principle of a holy people sworn to follow the will of Christ in all things. He asserted that all members of his church had some measure of the Spirit of God in their persons, which gave them equal authority in the conduct of their collective affairs and an equal right to elect their leaders from among themselves in the knowledge that their judgement, in this context, was God-given. Each church of the Brownist persuasion was a separate entity and entirely self-governing, although conferences were held with sister-churches in order to seek counsel and to learn of the progress being made by their movement. Robert Browne was ahead of his time in that he taught tolerance, and he denied the right of any man to "plant churches by power and to force a submission to ecclesiastical government by laws and penalties".

Not many Separatists sought such total freedom, however. Henry Barrowe, for instance, assured his flock that "the Prince ought to compel all their subjects to the hearing of God's Word in the public exercises of the church".

By June 1583 the writings of Browne and his friend

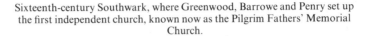

(*left*) Canterbury Cathedral. Successive archbishops of Canterbury led the fight against the growing tide of Nonconformism.

Sixteenth-century Southwark, where Greenwood, Barrowe and Penry set up the first independent church, known now as the Pilgrim Fathers' Memorial Church.

Robert Harrison were circulating so widely that a Royal Proclamation was necessary to make the law's displeasure evident to all – and it encouraged the stepping up of repressive measures against all who sought to evade the law or defied the statutes of the Act of Uniformity.

In August, John Whitgift was appointed Archbishop of Canterbury in succession to the tolerant Edward Grindal, who had shown no enthusiasm for the persecution of the Nonconformists and had even given them some encouragement. Whitgift was a man of a very different calibre. Ostentatious in his ways, he loved high living and on occasions visited Canterbury and other towns at the head of a retinue of eight hundred or more gaily caparisoned horsemen. He had always shown a brusque contempt for Nonconformists and in the vigorous way he opposed them he won the Queen's confidence. Nor did he fail to add the authority of his new office to his prosecution of them. He reinforced the edicts against those who sought to evade the law on uniformity and eventually persuaded Parliament to pass a law that made it an offence even to *be* a Puritan.

Archbishop Whitgift did succeed in suppressing the flood of pamphlets from the Puritan Press. As it happened, the press was discovered quite by accident when it fell from a haycart in a village street. The printers were arrested and imprisoned but the authors were never traced.

Under this pressure, perhaps, Browne decided in 1585 that the time for the full realization of his

Tyburn, where John Greenwood and Henry Barrowe met their deaths in 1593 for refusing to obey the Act of Uniformity.

theories was not yet and to take a more charitable view of the Anglican Church. In October of that year he took the advice of his kinsman, Lord Burghley, and persuaded most of his followers to obey the Act of Uniformity.

In 1592 two of the leading independents, John Greenwood and Henry Barrowe, were temporarily released from prison and, supported by a young and enthusiastic Welshman, John Penry, they founded the first independent church, now known as the Pilgrim Fathers' Memorial Church, in Southwark, London. The majority of the adherents of that "Ancient Church" suffered imprisonment at one time or another. On one sad occasion, out of fifty who were taken sixteen died in prison of jail-fever.

Greenwood and Barrowe met their fate at Tyburn on 6th April 1593, after being condemned on a trumped-up charge of treason. John Penry was executed some few weeks later – on 29th May, near the Old Kent Road, close by the present site of the church – under a warrant issued by Archbishop Whitgift and the Lord Chief Justice.

Many more members escaped to Holland where they reformed the church in Amsterdam; the rest had no option but to go underground or, in a few cases, to abandon their faith altogether.

But it was in a little corner in the north of England that the hardiest plant of the Pilgrim Church took root and began to flourish in secret – until James of Scotland succeeded to the throne of England.

3 The Leaders

In the spring of 1603 King James rode south from his Scottish Kingdom on his way to London and the crown of England. After the royal cavalcade had crossed the border from Yorkshire into Nottinghamshire, the King was conducted to Worksop where he was to be received in style at Worksop Manor, the home of the Earls of Shrewsbury and still dominated by the four-times married, loose-tongued builder of great houses, the Dowager Countess of Shrewsbury – Bess of Hardwick.

It is most unlikely that, as he rode by it less than an hour before he reached that lordly manor, James took any note of the village of Scrooby, the hamlet that was already the centre of an illegal Separatist community and so soon to become the recognized birthplace of the Pilgrim Church and one end of the tenuous cord that was to bind England and America together in perpetual kinship.

At the time that King James rode down the Great North Road, William Brewster held the office of postmaster at Scrooby, a post inherited as was so often the case in that nepotic age, from his father – also named William.

Young William matriculated at Peterhouse College, Cambridge, in 1580 – although, instead of staying on to graduate, he found himself a fine post as an assistant to William Davison, one of Queen Elizabeth's secretaries of state. Davison saw in him someone whom he could trust to help him even in matters of state that required the utmost secrecy. In 1585 he took Brewster with him on a mission to the

Worksop Manor, where James VI & I was received on his journey south.

St Wilfrid's Church, Scrooby.

States General in Holland, where he had been sent to conclude a loan to the United Provinces to assist them in their struggle against Catholic Spain. The astute Elizabeth, however, demanded security for the loan in the form of the possession of three major seaports – to be known as the "cautionary towns". William Brewster was entrusted by his master with

the keys of Flushing – and spent the first night with them under his pillow.

But William Davison was too honest for his time and too naïve for the court of Elizabeth; in his innocent devotion to that lady he was to fall foul of one of her intrigues.

Mary Queen of Scots had been tried and

Site of the Manor House at Scrooby.

condemned for her part in the Babington conspiracy against England and the Queen. Elizabeth was well aware that, whatever the justice of the sentence, this figure, around which so much treachery was persistently plotted, had to die. But she was also aware of the odium that would surely surround her if she ordered the execution of the Scottish Queen to be carried out. With her tongue in her cheek, or so she claimed, Elizabeth ordered the hapless William Davison to draw up the death warrant, and then, when the execution had run its tragic course, she promptly blamed him for being too precipitate, sent him to the Tower of London, and deprived him of his estates.

William Brewster, devoted to his patron, did all he could to help him – then, without employment, he returned a sadder and wiser man to his home in the north of England to assist his father, the Postmaster of Scrooby.

Brewster was a religious man and, no doubt, his experiences at court, and in particular at the hands of Queen Elizabeth, the Supreme Head of the English Church, turned his latent interest in Puritanism into active revolt against the Anglican Church.

He had always preferred the lesser flamboyancy of the Nonconformists to the over-ritualistic and dogmatized practices prevalent in the Anglican Church, as being more in tune with his conscience, and began now to devote much of his time to "preaching" his views in the district where he lived. So deeply did he become involved in spreading the word of God in the fashion that he understood it that, when his father died in 1590, he was occupied with religious affairs to the extent that he was so slow to make the necessary application to be confirmed in the office of postmaster that, for a time, it seemed that he might be displaced. Thoughts of matrimony and its responsibilities were what probably prodded Brewster into securing the post, just in time. He married Mary Wentworth shortly after; they were to have three children, Jonathan, Patience and Fear.

When the ban on dissident forms of worship was reinforced in 1593 and the Puritan Church found itself compelled to pay some sort of regard to the Act of Uniformity in order to protect its members, certain more devoted groups of Nonconformists had the courage to refuse to accept this surrender and broke away from the Puritan mainstream. One such group lay in the Gainsborough/Scrooby district, its membership divided between the two towns. William Brewster encouraged those who lived nearby to use the Scrooby Manor House for their religious gatherings and, being a man of some substance, himself paid to obtain the services of known Nonconformist preachers at their secret meetings.

As the Scrooby Church established itself, Brewster encouraged it to break away from the more "revolutionary" church at Gainsborough, and by

(*above*) A corner of the First Court of Christ's College, Cambridge; (*left*) The college's fine entrance gateway. It was to this college that the young John Robinson went to study: he was to become a Fellow of the College. In later years he returned in unsuccessful attempts to gather new converts to Puritanism.

1602 it claimed an identity of its own as the Scrooby Separatist Church – secret, of course, but with a closely knit, devout following. Brewster nurtured it, gave heart to the fearful, financed it where and when the need arose, and became its Ruling Elder.

The second among the outstanding personalities of the Pilgrim Church in the north of England was John Robinson, who was to become its pastor – but who was never to achieve his heartfelt wish of ministering to his flock in America.

Robinson was born in Sturton-le-Steeple, some twelve miles from Scrooby, in Nottinghamshire, and about five miles to the south of Gainsborough, over the border in Lincolnshire. As there are no parish registers in existence from before 1638, the year of his birth is not known, although it would appear to be about 1576.

As a youth he was sent to Christ's College, Cambridge. He obtained a Bachelor of Arts degree, but stayed on in the hope of obtaining a Master's degree. He was chosen as a Fellow of his College and took Holy Orders – as was usual on election to a fellowship. He gained the coveted degree in March 1599 and then spent another year at Cambridge, during which time he was elected a Reader in Greek and, in 1600, Dean.

A supremely satisfying college career, it would seem, but after ten years of it Robinson resigned his fellowship; on 15th February 1603 he married Bridget White in the Parish Church of St Mary, Greasby, Nottinghamshire, and with the assistance of the one-time Master of Christ's College, Cambridge, now Bishop of Norwich, he gained attachment to St Andrew's Church in that city.

Shortly before, Thomas Newhouse, some five or six years senior to Robinson, had been invited to become the Vicar of St Andrew's and had accepted the living with enthusiasm. But he soon established a dangerous reputation for Nonconformist practices. He refused to wear a surplice and eliminated from his services much of the ritual that was, under the Act of Uniformity, mandatory. Newhouse was popular with his congregation, some of whom enjoyed the thrill of defying authority, but most of whom genuinely preferred the form of worship that gave them the feeling of being in direct communion with God, rather than having to pursue a devious course through a third person, along ceremonious lines and in a precise form of words.

Robinson quickly came under the spell of Newhouse's teachings; with enthusiasm he supported the vicar and helped to swell the deeply interested congregation – until at last the authorities had to take notice of what was happening in St Andrew's Church, and it became evident that Puritanism in the parish would not be tolerated much longer.

In 1604 a proclamation was issued requiring all ministers to conform to the New Book of Canons; the bishops were ordered to take action against those who failed to obey. Both Newhouse and Robinson chose to obey their consciences rather than their bishop, and they were therefore suspended from the Church and deprived of the right to preach or to hold services. Robinson, nothing daunted, gathered his friends together for private prayer – but retribution followed almost at once. Everyone known to attend his services was excommunicated.

He spent three long months in trying to find a solution that would accord with both the requirements of the Anglican Church and his own conscience, concerned for his followers in an age when "excommunication" was considered to be the ultimate penalty – even more terrible than execution. Without doubt he was seriously worried about the effect his attitude was having on the welfare of his family, and not entirely satisfied that he was pursuing the right course.

But steadily, despite the gathering clouds around him, what had been at first a matter of indifference hardened into active disapproval. Yet, deprived of his right to preach or to conduct services, abandoned now by many of his friends and followers and realizing that his wife, however devoted she was to his cause, was finding it almost impossible to provide for their children, Robinson found himself with no alternative but to return to Sturton-le-Steeple, where his parents offered him a home for himself and his family.

At Gainsborough he met John Smith and at Scrooby he came into contact with William Brewster – and others. He found that they and their followers were bitterly and determinedly opposed to any return to the ceremonies of the established church, but fearful of the consequences of their refusal to conform.

Robinson took an active part in giving heart and strength to their determination and took to preaching regularly at their secret meetings. Twice he returned

to his old college at Cambridge to support the cause of Puritanism there, only to find that, however devout and unhappy they might be, no one was prepared to sacrifice possessions or freedom – and perhaps even their life – in support of their beliefs.

Reacting sharply, Robinson returned on each occasion to take an even deeper interest in the Separatist groups near his home – admiring and supporting them in their downright determination not to be diverted from their faith. Gradually, he withdrew from all other activities in order to devote the whole of his time to the groups at Gainsborough and Scrooby, although he soon found that the Gainsborough branch of the Separatist Church was already well served by its pastor, John Smith. Disappointedly, he became aware of Smith's intrigues with the Anglicans and withdrew from them to settle down with the Scrooby independents, although that community also had an active pastor, Richard Clifton.

William Bradford, destined to become Governor of the Plymouth Settlement, was much younger than the others. He was born in March 1590 in the village of Austerfield, Yorkshire, the son of a wealthy yeoman family, and baptized in the Chapel of St Helen, Austerfield, on 19th March of that year. His parents

(above) the chapel of St Helen's, Austerfield, where William Bradford was baptized in March 1590; *(opposite)* a view from the porch of the church into the interior. Bradford was to become one of the most important figures in the early years of the settlement at Plymouth.

died while he was young. A sickly youth who could take little part in active pursuits, devoted to his books and with a religious bent, he was, at first, inclined towards a solitary (though contented) way of life. But the religious controversies of his day soon attracted his attention, and he probed everywhere in the neighbourhood of his home for the views of the various factions – and gradually came to prefer the teachings of Pastor Richard Clifton, the leader of the Scrooby Separatists.

Earnestly and with growing enthusiasm, Bradford began to spend more and more time listening to the teachings of the Nonconformist preachers and, between persistent bouts of illness, he studied their words with avid interest. Thirsty for knowledge and quick to learn, he delved into the mysteries of the French language, and then added a masterly command of Greek and Hebrew so that he could study, in greater depth, the ancient manuscripts that told the stories of the Passion of Christ and of the religious background to the many churches that claimed superiority, in His name, over all others.

Although William Bradford was naturally serious and often buried himself deeply in his studies, he was always sufficiently alive to all that went on around him to take so full a part in the activities of the Scrooby Separatist group that he was soon to become one of its Elders.

John Carver, who was to become the first Governor of the Plymouth Colony, like Robinson was born in Sturton-le-Steeple; he was to become the second husband of Catherine White, sister of Bridget White, who married Robinson. But he leaves little impact on the early history of the Pilgrim Church.

Miles Standish was a member of an ancient family of that name. One of his forebears, John, wounded Wat Tyler after that revolutionary had been felled by the Lord Mayor of London in front of his king in 1381 – and was knighted for it. Another, Sir Ralph Standish, fought at the Battle of Agincourt in 1415. Sir Alexander was knighted for his bravery at Hutton Field in Scotland in 1482 and Henry Standish, a Franciscan friar, became Bishop of St Asaph in 1519.

From these ancestors Miles Standish was born loaded with hereditary wealth and honours – most of which were to elude him, before he came of age, through the actions of less honourably inclined members of his family. A soldier by inclination and training, he served Queen Elizabeth in Holland, supporting the Dutch Protestants against the Catholics from Spain. And it was in Holland that he first met members of the Pilgrim Church who had emigrated there from Scrooby.

Although not a member of that, or any other church, he was strangely attracted to the cause of the Scrooby Separatists. That and, no doubt, his spirit of adventure caused him to accompany the members of the church to America, when the time came. There he was to become their military leader; redoubtable, courageous and something of a military genius.

There are others who take their part as the story of the Pilgrim Fathers progresses, but none can claim, so surely and so early in its history, to warrant the major honours that surrounded its beginnings.

(*opposite above*) The Standish Chapel and Pew in Chorley Old Church. Miles Standish was one of the few Pilgrim Fathers to come from a distinguished and noble family, several of his ancestors having achieved renown.

(*opposite below*) James VI & I enters London on the last stage of his journey south to receive the crown of England in 1603.

4 The Pilgrim Church Survives

King James had little time to settle down on his English throne before he was almost overwhelmed with church affairs.

Fortunately for him, his accession came at a time when the political situation appeared more peaceable than it had for generations – and would again for even more generations. Naval supremacy had been established in the war with Spain and the threat of invasion had been eliminated. The Union with Scotland had ensured peace in the north, and after the Elizabethan conquest of Ireland that island lay quiescent – at any rate for the time being. Trade too was booming, and the wealth of the nation was spreading over a broad front so that almost everyone in the land felt some benefit from the rising prosperity.

Even England's religious independence had been asserted beyond further effective dispute from abroad . . .

But at home religious matters loomed darkly over everything.

The Anglican community – the established church

– lay quietly on the shoulders of the majority of the population, most of whom found it easier to put up with the requirements of the established church than to embroil themselves in the fanaticism of the extremists who dissented from it. The Catholics, however, looked forward almost with eagerness to the protection and even aggrandizement they could surely expect from the only son and heir of the Catholic Mary Queen of Scots – while the Puritans were equally certain of the sympathy of a Scotsman who had been brought up in the Calvinist faith. So James found himself caught up in the middle of a three-way fight between Anglicans, Catholics and Puritans – each of them hostile to the other two and each determined to root out every opinion other than their own.

He made an immediate though ill considered gesture of peace to the two non-established parties, Catholics and Puritans. He remitted the fines that were levied on all who refused to attend worship in an Anglican church, although he did not grant them the right to hear the word of God through preachers of their own persuasion. But, despite his new-found wealth, he had too many favourites in need of his bounty to permit him to sacrifice so profitable a "tax" for long. Even in the first year of his reign in London, 1603, he began to feel the need for more and more money: instead of keeping his promise to remit the fines he strengthened the hands of his collectors.

But, perhaps because of his Protestant upbringing, it was the Puritans who were the most clamorous for the king's attention to their grievances. Only a few months after his coronation about a thousand ministers, in a petition that was to become known as the Millenary Petition, urged him to institute reforms: the main target was the Book of Common Prayer, the main aim the freedom to disassociate themselves from it without incurring penalties.

King James, under the gleaming shield of the Divine Right of Kings, summoned a conference of all

(*left*) James VI & I seated in Parliament.

(*above*) Hampton Court, where James held conference during June 1604 in order to discuss religious practices.

Richard Bancroft, who became Archbishop of Canterbury in 1604: he sternly opposed Puritanism.

the established church should be fined.

Then he turned his attention to the Puritans. In roughest terms he made it clear that he was going to permit no divergence from the dictum of "one doctrine and one discipline, one religion in substance and in ceremony", and his constantly reiterated phrase, "no bishop, no king", made it clear that the one was dependent on the other. And for those who chose not to conform he stated that he intended to "harry them out of the land".

Some small measure of good did come out of the conference, however: a new translation of the Bible was put in hand and a number of relatively minor alterations to the Book of Common Prayer were authorized. But none of these were designed in any way to meet the wishes of the Puritans: indeed, it soon became evident that the king was pressing the enforcement of the Anglican code of worship in exchange for the bishops' adoption of the theory of the Divine Right of Kings – which suggested that opposition to the established church meant opposition to a divinely appointed King. Blasphemy!

The end result of the Hampton Conference was that it served only to stiffen the opposition of king and Anglican hierarchy to those who refused to conform to the canons of the state church.

Archbishop Whitgift died within a month of the conference and Richard Bancroft was appointed in his place. The change boded no relief from persecution for those who refused to conform: the new archbishop had been a ruthless opponent of Puritanism for years. Moreover, it seems likely that his downright and outspoken condemnation of them had done much to promote his career in the church.

He immediately set about drawing the attention of all churchmen to the Book of Canons that he had himself formulated, in the previous year, while serving as Bishop of London. It contained thirty-nine articles and required that every priest should formally acknowledge them as representing the Word of God – that, among other regulations, every priest must wear a cope and surplice during divine services and must insist that the congregation receive communion on their knees.

parties to be held at Hampton Court during June 1604. In the early sessions, probably with a wary eye on the power of Spain, James was polite to the Catholics; but to the Puritans, who posed no physical threat either to himself or to his kingdom, he was downright rude. He lectured all parties endlessly, until it gradually dawned on everyone present that, although James was the son of a Catholic queen, he had been brought up in the Calvinist tradition and was no Catholic – and, having for too long endured the starkly gloomy atmosphere of the Calvinists, he was also no Puritan.

The Catholics had hoped that the Pope would allow them to accept the secular authority of the king in exchange for the right to worship under the rule of Rome, but the Pope refused even to recognize a heretic. In the face of such a slight on his person and his crown, it was to be expected that James would retaliate sharply. He promptly banned Catholic priests and ordered that everyone of that faith – priest and layman alike – who failed to attend the services of

A requisition had been sent to Cambridge by Archbishop Whitgift demanding that a certificate be returned assuring him of the conformity of its fellows, scholars and students. It is interesting that the reply from Christ's College, dated 8th January 1604, did not include the name of one of its fellows, John Robinson – as he was not in residence there over the Christmas period. It could be that this tightening of control in matters of religious conformity within the university caused Robinson to resign his fellowship, although it is more probable that his wish to marry and settle down as a minister of the gospels was more potent in making his decision.

As we have seen, John Robinson took up his ministry in Norwich – a city filled with churches, with no fewer than twenty parishes and little enough to offer in the way of financial rewards to its preachers. He soon found that there was an incipient tendency towards reform in the city, particularly in St Andrew's Church where he was appointed an assistant. But at first he did no more than listen, learn and sympathize with those who prayed so earnestly for the right to worship in accordance with their own convictions.

Francis Mason, something of a peacemaker among the dissident elements within the established churches, delivered a sermon on the subject in June 1605 – and published it subsequently. As a Nonconformist within the Anglican Church, he resented the way the various disputes within the church highlighted the Catholics on one hand and the followers of Robert Browne, the leader of a breakaway movement, on the other. He argued: "As you rejoice the Papists, so you encourage the Brownists, who build their conclusions upon your premises and put your speculations in practice." He urged the Anglicans to meet the Puritans in some commonly acceptable form of worship – or at least mutual tolerance – but the Anglicans, firmly under the control of king and bishops, were adamantly opposed to the slightest compromise.

John Robinson was one of those who supported Mason's views, but as these were met with no favour by the authorities he tended to drift further and further away from the established church in his thoughts – although he was slow to take up a deliberate stand against the established order. On the other hand Thomas Newhouse, the Vicar of St Andrew's, was more downright in his views than Robinson, having little patience with compromise and finding a good deal of support from a section of his parishioners. Slowly at first, Newhouse's

influence made itself felt with Robinson, who began to become equally outspoken from the pulpit, until the actions of the two priests became such a scandal in Norwich that the authorities could no longer tolerate it.

Despite this, Robinson at heart was not as fully committed to the Puritan cause as he professed himself to be, although when at last he and Newhouse were suspended from the church he convinced himself that his views were by then irreconcilable with those of the church he had served. It is probable too, that Robinson had overestimated his influence with the Bishop of Norwich – his patron, under whom he had studied when the latter was the Master of Christ's College, Cambridge. It is even possible that, if he had foreseen the consequences of his outspoken criticisms of the church, he would have been much more cautious in what he had to say and where he said it.

Robinson's suspension from the ministry came as a shock, but he recovered quickly enough when he found that he had an unexpectedly large body of supporters ready to follow him into exile from the church – although, for their own sakes, their meetings with him had to be held in secret. As with most secrets, within a matter of weeks a number of Robinson's flock were named and excommunicated from the church by an indignant bishop.

As an assistant at St Andrew's Church in Norwich, Robinson had lived with his wife and family at only a little above subsistence level; when his suspension from office became effective even his tiny stipend ceased to be paid. He applied for the mastership of one of the Norwich hospitals, where he would at least have a roof over his head and some support from the charity to support his family – and, he believed, a place where he could continue his clandestine ministry in privacy and without the knowledge of the bishop. But his application met with no success. No doubt the sponsors of the charity were aware of the applicant's dispute with the Bishop, equally well informed of the sentence of excommunication that had been imposed on some of his followers, and unwilling to leave themselves open to similar penalties.

He tried also to lease some property from the Norwich Corporation, in the hope of achieving a home plus some little income from sublets – but again he failed, very probably for the same reason.

Robinson had reached the end of his resources. He returned to Sturton-le-Steeple, his birthplace, and

Emmanuel College, Cambridge, one of the colleges where Robinson
endeavoured to stir up support for the Puritan movement.

there found a home for himself and his family with his parents, John and Ann Robinson. But he failed to settle down at once; his conscience was sadly troubled by his suspension from any ecclesiastical office. Although he was now totally opposed to the Canons of the established church, he was a deeply religious man who felt bitterly the deprivation of his right to preach the gospels in an open forum.

He took to wandering about the neighbourhood in the hope of finding both work and some call for his spiritual services. He talked to many and gradually became aware that some thought as he did about church matters: in particular, there were those who had actually formed groups for private worship. He learned there was an important group of Separatists from the established church in Gainsborough, being held together by John Smith; that William Brewster had organized religious "conferences" in the Manor House at Scrooby, in which he lived and worked as postmaster; and that Richard Clifton at Babworth, and even the Vicar of Worksop, Richard Bernard, were beginning to take an independent line of their own.

Still unsure of himself, he sought some answer to his religious scruples in a return to Cambridge; even then, in talks with some of his old friends and colleagues, he denied that he had renounced Holy Orders, or indeed that he had finally severed all connection with the Anglican Church. But he did admit that he spent much of his time at home with Separatists, and preached to them at their meetings.

It was almost certainly during his second visit that he finally abandoned the established church as a corrupt body, and the mainstream of Puritanism as being too ready to compromise with conscience rather than face the persecution of the state church.

He returned to Sturton-le-Steeple refreshed in both mind and body by the decision, and determined to give his full-time attention to the Separatist groups near his home. Almost at once he and John Smith, of the Gainsborough Separatist Church, formally broke their association with the Anglican Church, hoping at the same time to draw other clergymen from it to their side.

Their action created a great deal of argument and discussion among dissenting preachers, but few of them actually followed their example. Richard Clifton and Hugh Bromehead joined them, but they were bitterly disappointed by the Vicar of Worksop's unexpected refusal. Later, in fact, Bernard, the Vicar of Worksop, was to become a fanatical opponent of the Separatist movement.

John Robinson soon learned that the members of the Gainsborough group of Separatists preferred the Bible-thumping of John Smith to his own more reasoned and less inflammatory teachings and, with some reluctance, gradually came to adopt the Scrooby group for his full-time ministrations.

Which quietly drew together Brewster, Bradford and Robinson, to be joined later by John Carver, to form the backbone of the group that was to become known as the Pilgrim Church.

THE SEIZURE OF GUY FAWKES.

The Gunpowder Plot discovered: (*left*) Guy Fawkes is dragged from the cellars of the Houses of Parliament, where he had been discovered among his barrels of gunpowder; (*below*) the conspirators are arrested, Catesby and Percy being slain.

Under the hammer of a rising persecution – being harried from every side, subject to blackmailing threats, spied upon even in their own homes and imprisoned when they were caught – the larger body of Puritans, understandably, surrendered to the pressure of events and resumed their association with the Anglican Church. Prisons in the 17th century were places to dread, and a man had to be devout indeed if he were not to sacrifice his conscience to avoid the bodily discomfort of stone-cold floors, iron bars, filth, starvation and the contemptuous manhandling of the criminals who shared the overcrowded cells.

But there were those who persisted in their nonconformity, even though employers were unwilling to give them work in case they should be classed as sympathizers: these stalwarts often had to travel far and wide to find the means of earning a living for themselves and their families – and to find somewhere they could be in close contact with the comfort of a secret meeting place at which they could worship in accordance with their convictions and where the authorities were not so rabidly engaged in rooting them out.

The Catholics, often wealthy landowners and aristocrats, and having more to lose than the Puritans, were generally either quiescently evasive or, on occasion, prone to secret plots of violence. One small group of bitter Catholics, led by Robert Catesby, conspired to blow up the Houses of Parliament – with King James in it. They hoped that, in the confusion and breakdown of government that must inevitably result, the Catholics at home would rise, Spain would promptly come to their aid – and the Roman Church be re-established in England. As might have been expected, the discovery of the Gunpowder Plot merely served to strengthen the hands of the king and his bishops, and the persecution of those who visibly rejected the Canons of the established church was stepped up and prosecuted more vigorously than ever.

Hounded, afraid for their freedom and of their neighbours, and deprived so often of spiritual comfort, the time had come for those whose consciences would not allow them to conform to seek security in some foreign land – the Catholics in France and Spain and the Puritan Separatists in Holland, the only place in Europe where their opinions and their practices were freely tolerated.

The conspirators in the Gunpowder Plot meet their barbaric deaths.

5 Escape to Holland

In 1606 the Separatist groups at Gainsborough and Scrooby, in a desperate effort to shore up their sorely stretched determination not to conform, formed themselves into a Church Estate in the Fellowship of the Gospel, by a Covenant of the Lord. Almost immediately afterwards the Gainsborough group decided to escape the persecution at home and to seek security in Holland, despite the strict enforcement of regulations against illegal emigration – a strange prohibition, in the face of the king's avowed threat to harry all Nonconformists from his kingdom. Silently and anxiously, they sold their homes and everything else that they could not take with them; with the help of a ship's captain and for a stiff price they were secretly picked up in the mouth of the Humber and taken across the North Sea to Amsterdam.

In the following year William Brewster and John Robinson decided that it was time that they made their preparations to lead the Scrooby group to the Netherlands. But by now the ports were even more securely closed to illegal emigrants. Even within their own villages spies abounded, and because of the penalties exacted from those who were caught aiding them – and the rewards to be earned by those who betrayed them – much time had to be spent in secret negotiations to dispose of properties and to obtain a ship.

William Brewster resigned his office as "Post of Scrooby" in September 1607, which in itself caused some suspicion. In October a large party including

The Old Guildhall, Boston. Puritans attempting to sail from Boston to Amsterdam, were thwarted by a dishonest ship's captain.

the eighteen-year-old William Bradford, under the leadership of William Brewster, succeeded in bribing a ship's captain – at exorbitant rates – to ferry them from Boston in Lincolnshire to Amsterdam in the Netherlands. All was ready, the day came at last, and in absolute secrecy the emigrants made their way on foot to Boston – in small, inconspicuous groups and by differing routes – to reach the waiting ship.

The moment they boarded it the captain battened them down below decks without even giving them time to stow their possessions. He and his crew then ransacked the whole cargo and divided the proceeds up between them. He then brought the passengers up on deck in twos and threes and robbed them of everything they possessed – searching them bodily to find the very last coin. After that he sent a runner ashore to inform the authorities. The shocked and now penniless Pilgrims had no option but to wait to be arrested. In a body they were thrown into prison.

Unexpectedly, the magistrates of Boston showed a degree of sympathy for the prisoners and their desperate plight, but it was beyond their powers to free them until the church authorities had dealt with them. Most were held in the cold, hard and hungry discomfort of an English prison in midwinter for a month before they were released but Bradford, as a mere youth, was released before the others. William Brewster and Richard Jackson were released on bail to answer to a charge of "Brownism" at the Collegiate Church of Southwell on 1st December. Neither put in an appearance and each was fined the sum of £20 in their absence; their rearrest was ordered. £20 in the 17th century was a considerable amount of money.

On 15th December 1607 Blanchard, who had the duty of arresting the pair, certified that he had not only failed in his purpose but admitted that he did not even know where they had hidden themselves. The records do show, however, that in due time the fines were collected, although from whom or when is not clear.

Further attempts were made to cross to Holland by the Scrooby Pilgrims, but after being robbed of all they possessed in their previous escapade they were badly in need of money, and it was some time before they could raise enough to make a second serious bid for freedom.

This time Brewster was the organizer and he succeeded, in the spring of 1608, in hiring a Dutch ship to take off a large contingent of emigrants to the Netherlands. It was to stand off the mouth of the Humber, between Grimsby and Hull, and was to pick up the party from a small boat. Unfortunately the ship was delayed by bad weather for a full day and, with many of the men, and almost all the women and children, suffering from exposure and seasickness, this small boat had to return to the shore to offload its passengers and to wait there for the Dutch vessel to put in an appearance.

When the ship finally arrived, it was the men who boarded it first, determined to reconnoitre the situation aboard the vessel, wary of the treatment they had received during their earlier venture, and prepared to defend themselves, unencumbered by the women, if the need arose.

It was a lengthy pull to the ship as it needed to stand well out because of the falling tide. The boatmen, who might have been expected to know these waters well, were careless enough to run their boat aground on some mudflats and were unable to refloat it. The ship's master, unlike the English captain of a few months earlier, did all he could to assist his passengers. He put his own longboat into the water and sent it to pick up the stranded men. The Dutch sailors showed themselves far more skilled than the English boatmen. They skirted the mudflat warily until they found a spot where they could approach the stranded boat closely enough to allow its passengers to scramble aboard; then they headed directly back towards their ship – hurriedly, because of the rough water and the fitful wind.

As the longboat ran alongside the Dutch vessel, William Brewster led his men over the bulwarks, already feeling assured of the Dutch master's honesty. They conferred for a moment or two, but the captain, with an anxious eye on the darkening horizon, cut it short. He leaned over the rail to order the longboat to pull for the shore to pick up the women, the children, the remaining men and their luggage as quickly as possible.

But a hail from one of the lookouts checked him. The man was pointing towards the shore – and every eye aboard the vessel turned in that direction as they heard the urgency in his voice. A wail of despair rose from the decks as the passengers saw a raiding party of horse and foot bearing down on those who waited at the water's edge for the boat to pick them up.

The women's screams were thrown across the water by the wind and the men aboard the vessel cried their own dismay as the captain ordered the longboat to move smartly astern and to remain in tow. He ignored the shocked protests of the Pilgrims, guessing anxiously that, as a land party had been sent to arrest the illegal emigrants, it was probable that a ship-of-the-line had been sent to intercept him; knowing the penalty for being caught aiding such an enterprise in English waters, he knew that he must abandon the scene as fast as he could. The men aboard the vessel argued angrily and even threatened to use violence if the captain did not put about for the shore again – but it was driven home to them at last that it was beyond their powers to aid those they had left behind, and to return merely meant that they themselves would suffer the same fate.

Before the land dropped away below the horizon, the unhappy Pilgrims saw their families being rounded up, their baggage hoisted onto a wagon and the whole party being escorted away. And, almost before they understood what had happened, a sudden squall of wind and rain struck their vessel and they could do no more than watch, worriedly, as a massive black cloud rolled overhead and the rain turned into a deluge.

The series of storms that followed were some of the worst to be encountered in those waters in many years; with only the clothes they had to stand up in, and distressed in mind and in body, the Pilgrims had to endure fourteen days of storm-tossed waters before they sighted land again – the Norwegian coast, some four hundred miles from their starting point and as many more to go before they could reach Amsterdam, instead of the two hundred miles of sea that lay between their departure point and their destination.

William Bradford was among the passengers from Scrooby who reached Holland with that unhappy and destitute band; then, for some reason, somebody aboard the vessel complained to the authorities at Amsterdam that he was a fugitive from English justice, and he was taken into custody. Fortunately, however, the magistrates were quickly satisfied that he was not a criminal but had fled from religious persecution, and he was freed to join his colleagues again.

Of the few men left on the beach in England to face the advancing "horse and foot" sent to arrest them,

A Dutch ship was to pick up a large group of Puritans on the Humber. The arrival of a party of "horse and foot" to arrest the illegal emigrants forced the captain to abandon the women and children.

Amsterdam in the seventeenth century.

only those who could be of help to the women and children stayed at their side while the rest fled. Why they should have deserted the helpless women and children we do not know. We must assume that they saw no point in joining them in prison, that they anticipated that the women and children would be much more leniently treated than the men – and perhaps because they realized that, having disposed of their homes and their possessions, the women and children would at least have a roof over their heads in prison while the men did what they could to find new homes for them.

The authorities showed themselves helpless to deal with so many unfortunates who, being deprived of their menfolk, were destitute. The magistrates passed them in a body from one court to another in the hope of getting rid of the embarrassing problem, as it was impossible to find room for them all in any of the local prisons. Nor could they discharge them on some pretext of leniency: the unfortunates had no homes to go to. Their desperate plight soon became the scandal of the neighbourhood as they were moved from place to place for trial, with no place to sleep or rest except among the sand-dunes and in the ditches, on their way from one court to another – endlessly begging for food for themselves and their children, collapsing on the roadside from hunger and sickness and with their children on the verge of starvation.

A sudden, unexpected upsurge of admiration and sympathy for the abandoned, desperate women and children was aroused by the sight of such helpless misery. Food began to be donated, and shelter was offered in barns, cowsheds, derelict buildings and, in some cases, even within the homes of those who understood and secretly held the same religious views as they did. And then, with the authorities not daring to risk the contempt and possible anger of the people of the district by interfering, the Pilgrims were gathered up in small parties and slowly, as the occasion and the means arose, they were shipped out to Amsterdam to join their desperately worried menfolk.

Of the Scrooby contingent, William Brewster and the two pastors, Robinson and Clifton, had been left behind in England to see to it that everyone from their group eventually sailed for Holland. They had to negotiate the sale of property, organize the movement of the emigrants, bribe ships' captains – and in so doing had to act often in the open, at great risk to themselves.

Nevertheless, in August 1608, they crossed to Amsterdam with their wives and families to complete the exodus of the Pilgrim Church from Scrooby and its reassembly in Holland.

When Robinson, Clifton and Brewster arrived in Amsterdam they were shocked to find the state of the immigrant church in that city.

It had been founded perhaps as early as 1594 but by 1600 it had come under the joint pastorship of Francis Johnson and Henry Ainsworth. From the very beginning it seemed to have been the target for the relief of the pent-up emotions of those who had suffered persecution at home. Dissension was rife and almost any excuse was enough to trigger off a dispute, which quickly developed into arguments that were debated too freely before a native population, which, however tolerant, soon came to despise those who were behaving so badly among a community that had welcomed them from their distress and given them security from persecution. When John Smith had arrived in Holland with the Gainsborough Separatists, he had joined himself and his group to what had become known as the "Ancient Church" under Johnson and Ainsworth, but had very soon broken away from it to form the second exiled English Church in the city.

Ainsworth and Johnson had already begun to disagree between themselves, violently and publicly, about the government of the Ancient Church; when the elderly, grey-haired patriarchal Richard Clifton arrived, he found that the pair had reached such a degree of bitterly opposed views that Francis Johnson had arrogantly assumed an absolute authority in the face of the more reasonable attempts of Ainsworth to find a peace formula with which to settle their discord.

Johnson deposed Ainsworth from his post as teacher, appointed Richard Clifton in his place, and selected his own officers. Thereupon, Ainsworth retaliated by appointing his own nominees to the posts of Ruling Elders and Deacons, forcing a split between the two factions that outraged the members of the Dutch Church in Amsterdam. Even the schism that followed brought no peace to the twin Ancient churches. Francis Johnson's church became such a hotbed of internal bickering that it finally reached the stage where that "absolutist" actually excommunicated both his father and his brother.

So publicly disgraceful did the church, its officers and its affairs become, and so violent were the disputes over the merest trifles, that the Dutch authorities found it necessary to step in, and the Ancient Church found itself in utter disrepute among the incensed population of the city.

The Pilgrims from Scrooby, after only a brief association with the Ancient Church, withdrew from it and held themselves aloof from the unseemly discord that ravaged its membership – in any event, they needed to concentrate on their own grim and growing poverty. Most of the Scrooby Separatists had sold all they possessed before they left England – although it is to be noted that there were one or two relatively wealthy men among them who, at this early stage in the development of the church, made no offer to form a "community of property".

A number of the Pilgrims lost heart and returned,

A view of Leyden where the Pilgrims made their temporary home.

An engraving, based on an early seventeenth-century drawing, of Leyden University,
one of the most illustrious seats of learning in Europe at the time.

sorrowfully and in defeat, to their homeland. In due time, refreshed and with new savings and better reports from Holland, some gathered up their courage and once again emigrated to join the Pilgrim Church.

But those who remained in Holland, either because of their deeply held Nonconformist convictions that could only lead them to disaster if they returned to England, or because they had not the means to pay for passages home for themselves and their families, found that Amsterdam failed to offer them the life for which they had hoped and prayed. That they had found freedom to worship in accordance with their own consciences was not enough: poverty, the pressures of a wrangling Ancient Church that turned the Dutch against them, and even the way of life of the local people caused them bitterness and distress.

Unexpectedly, it was the Dutch children that did most to unsettle the English. English children had always been brought up in strict obedience to their parents, were permitted few opportunities to engage in "foolish" games, had to work long hours for formidable employers or for their parents, and had to spend much of their time in religious exercises. They were dressed "soberly" and were expected to go about in a "dignified" manner, to have a true appreciation of the need to "honour" their parents – and to "be seen but not heard". The Dutch children, on the other hand, were allowed a great deal of

freedom, were subject to much less discipline and were given ample opportunity and encouragement to indulge in childish and youthful pastimes.

The "stiffer" English parents protested that such freedom bordered on licentiousness and, as it was almost impossible to keep their children apart from the Dutch, found it a serious handicap to the "proper" education of their offspring. They learned too, perhaps with some envy, that their children were quick to pick up the strange language and to accustom themselves to the Dutch way of life – and, despite the fact that the citizens of Amsterdam had given them a home and considerable freedom that they were denied in their homeland, they still preferred to regard themselves as English and to bring up their children as such.

Restless and unhappy, the leaders of the Scrooby community began to look around for a place where the tensions would be less disturbing and the influences on their children less pernicious – and where they could hope to create a settlement of their own within the tolerance of the Dutch government.

Leyden, not more than twenty-five miles to the south of Amsterdam, attracted the attention of both Robinson and Brewster because of its fine new university. A town of some 100,000 inhabitants and reputed to be one of the most salubrious resorts in Holland, it also had the merit of being uninfected by the scandals of the Ancient Church. Robinson and Brewster, after some protracted discussions with the Elders of the Pilgrim Church – and encouraged by the mothers, in particular – wrote to the Burgomaster to ask him if he would allow them to settle there. They explained that there would be about one hundred of them, all from England originally, and that all they asked was to be allowed to live, work and conduct their services in peace.

On 12th February 1609 the secretary to the Burgomaster replied, welcoming them on behalf of the whole community of Leyden.

On 9th April a truce was signed between Holland and Spain, a happy augury for the Pilgrims as they made their way toward their new homes in the city that had defended itself heroically from the invading Spaniards during the sieges of 1573 and 1574 – only fifteen years earlier. Few had even handcarts on which to transport their possessions, the elderly and the sick; and the journey had to be undertaken by families and in small groups as the opportunity, the weather and circumstances permitted. But the move was completed by 21st April 1609.

Fortunately there was a need for workers in Leyden, in particular for skilled weavers and those who could dress cloth. Happily, there were vacancies for unskilled workers too and, although there were craft guilds restricted to the citizens of Leyden which controlled the more highly skilled occupations, they offered no serious hindrance to English craftsmen. It was necessary only to find two or more residents in the town who would act as sureties, to take the oath of loyalty to Holland and to promise to uphold the rights and privileges of the citizens of Leyden to become eligible for membership of a guild. Thereafter it was merely a matter of paying the admission fee: within a year six members of the Pilgrim Church had joined one or other of the guilds.

Rapidly the grinding poverty of those long, weary months in Amsterdam became no more than an unhappy memory and with it there passed away much of the discontent and misery that had bedevilled the group ever since it had left Scrooby. As they settled into the new surroundings, so they became a cohesive whole again: William Pontus was betrothed to Wybra Hanson on 13th November

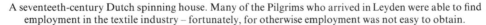

A seventeeth-century Dutch spinning house. Many of the Pilgrims who arrived in Leyden were able to find employment in the textile industry – fortunately, for otherwise employment was not easy to obtain.

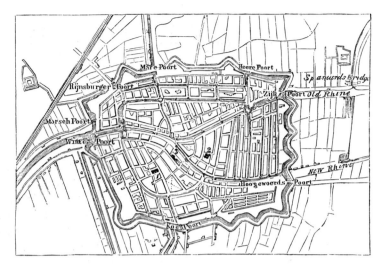

A map of seventeenth-century Leyden.

1610, and they were married three weeks later; John Jennings and Elizabeth Pettinger followed suit and married on the 31st December; and in the following year another six couples married – some of these marriages bringing together members of the church with new recruits to it from England. (Unhappily for William Brewster, however, a child of his died, being buried in Leyden on the 20th June 1609.)

This new contentment checked the steady fall in the membership of the church, caused by families drifting back to England. Now, with word of the much improved circumstances in Leyden, some of these began to return and to bring with them fresh contingents of eager Separatists – until within ten years the original hundred had increased threefold.

Pastor John Robinson settled down happily to his teaching and proved himself ever ready to listen to the arguments of those who disagreed with his views – although it seems that he was generally sufficiently convincing to convert his listeners. He also wrote and published his defence of the Separatists and answered the criticisms of his one-time friend Richard Bernard, Vicar of Worksop. But by 1611 he had become worried by the dispersal of the church community in houses throughout the city and the persistent search for a meeting room as the need arose. Robinson put the problem to the Elders of the Church, and they began to look around for suitable premises.

In the same year a substantial property known as the Groene Port (the "Green Door"), facing the Kloksteeg ("Bell Alley"), came onto the market. It had a sizeable garden behind it and was secluded by a canal on one side, the grounds of the Commandery on another, and the grounds and tenements of the Veiled Nuns on the third. There was a large room suitable for meetings in a house that seemed ideally suited to accommodate John Robinson and his family, and the grounds were large enough to suggest the development of a small housing precinct for members of the community.

Fortunately, there were two members of the Church who were men of some substance – William Jepson, a house-carpenter, and Henry Wood, a draper – and with a little help from Robinson and his wife's sister, Jane White, they were able to offer to meet the purchase price of 8,000 gilders by a 25 per cent deposit and a further 500 gilders each May Day until the transaction was completed. The contract was signed and the deposit of 2,000 gilders paid on 5th May 1611. In the years that followed, no fewer than twenty-one tiny tenements were built in the enclave.

In March 1612 William Bradford was granted citizenship of Leyden, and in November 1613 he married Dorothy May of Wisbech, Cambridgeshire, England.

6 Unhappy in Holland

In 1603 England did not possess a single colony in America, although Sir Humphrey Gilbert had landed at St John's, Newfoundland, in 1583, hoisted the English flag and claimed it in the name of Queen Elizabeth. Gilbert paid a second visit to Newfoundland later that year, but on the 9th September, in driving seas, he was lost together with his ship, the *Squirrel*, and all aboard her. Sir Walter Ralegh made an attempt to follow Gilbert's lead and in 1585 he established a small colony on Roanoke Island, off what is now North Carolina, but the settlement was abandoned within a year. Other attempts were made to colonize the area under Ralegh's direction but without success, and he resigned his rights in the venture to a company of merchants in 1589.

No one knows when the first Europeans made

Sir Humphrey Gilbert, who in 1583 claimed Newfoundland for Queen Elizabeth. A half-brother of Walter Ralegh, he lost his life on the way home from this expedition, when his ship went down with all hands.

Captain John Smith, responsible for the exploration of much of
the eastern seaboard of North America.

contact with the shores of what was to become known as the state of Massachusetts, although it is almost certain that the region was visited regularly by European fishing vessels from early in the 16th century. The first recorded visitor was Bartholomew in 1602, when he gave Cape Cod its name. Two years later Samuel de Champlain explored the coast and the use of those waters by fishing fleets increased as the hazards were charted.

John Smith explored the region further in 1614 and gave names to many topographical features. Others followed at almost regular intervals, but no permanent settlement was attempted along that northern coast before 1620.

The first colony to be founded in America was in Virginia. In 1606 two Virginia Companies were incorporated, one in London and the other in Plymouth, with King James' authority to form settlements in that part of America that lay between latitudes 30° and 45°. They found no shortage of eager colonists in England, many intent on finding freedom and wealth, many others – perhaps the greater part – seeking escape from the law, creditors or their families . . . and quite a few attracted by the sheer adventure of it.

The English financiers gladly provided funds to establish what they hoped and expected to become highly profitable ventures, although during the 17th century few of them ever saw the land they owned. the king encouraged the flow of emigrants as the basis of his own enrichment; the government, as far as it had any say in the matter, foresaw in it the means by which England could gain strength to stand up against a Europe dangerously poised against her; a land-hungry middle class saw themselves as "persons of consequence" owning and operating their own plantations; and those who suffered the weight of persecution by the Anglican Church hoped for freedom in a new land where they could worship as they pleased.

As in all population flows there was, too, a substantial current of those who could find no regular employment at home; and by 1617 the king and government decided that these new lands were ideal dumping grounds for convicted criminals and their unhappy families – and the prisons were emptied to join the exodus.

The actual locality of the first attempt at a settlement was in South Maine, with 120 emigrants from Plymouth, but it proved a failure and was soon

(*above*) Map of America dating from 1550; (*below*) map of
part of Virginia (now North Carolina) in 1585.

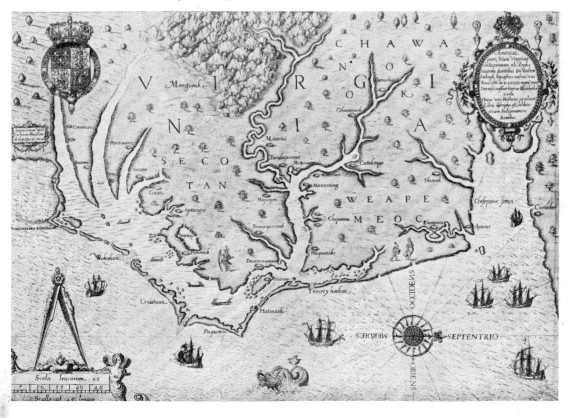

Sir Walter Ralegh, one-time favourite of Elizabeth, goes to his death in 1618, the conclusion of one of the shabbiest episodes of James' reign.

SIR WALTER RALEIGH.

beheaded in Old Palace Yard.

abandoned to occasional fishing fleets. A second party of 143 emigrants followed, this time from London. They entered Chesapeake Bay, penetrated the James River and disembarked on the site that is now Jamestown, Virginia.

It was a miracle that this settlement survived at all. Made up of the less worthwhile citizens of England – some packed off by despairing relatives, some idlers, some escaping their just deserts – they proved themselves to be a shiftless lot in the main; more than half died within a year through indolence and lack of determination. The Virginia Company did its best to save the situation – and its own stake in the venture – by sending a further batch of colonists, better chosen this time. But by the summer of 1610 most of these made up their minds to quit.

Lord Delaware's powerful injection of no fewer than 650 fresh colonists in the following summer turned the scale and, although the settlement was to endure some severe setbacks during the years to come, there was never again any talk of abandoning the project. Sounder management, safeguards for the ownership of land and adequate supply facilities were to do much to establish firm foundations for it, but it was tobacco that was to found the prosperity of Virginia.

Smaller settlements began to proliferate along the James River as an ever-increasing flow of colonists poured in from England; in 1619 no fewer than 1,200 arrived to stake out their land grants.

But the more northerly region that Captain John Smith had named "New England" was having a much more difficult time and, although the coastal areas from Cape Cod to Newfoundland were used regularly by fishing fleets from Europe, even as late as the summer of 1620 no real attempt had been made to found a colony there since the abortive venture to settle 120 planters at the mouth of the Kennebec River, in August, 1607.

In faraway Holland, as in the rest of Europe, the colonization of Virginia was a well-established topic of eager conversation and speculation from about the middle of the second decade of the 17th century – but it was the exploits of Sir Walter Ralegh in the New World that captured the imagination and stirred the blood of the adventurous.

Ralegh had long been enthralled by stories of the legendary El Dorado – the "gilded man" reputed to cover himself in pure gold from the fabulous goldmines of Guiana (this was only one of the many sites attributed to the legend). In 1595 Ralegh had penetrated deep into the country in search of the mines, sailing up the Orinoco, but hostile Indians and the climate defeated him. In the following year he sent one of his captains, Lawrence Keymis, to make a second attempt to discover El Dorado, but despite a determined effort he had no better fortune.

Imprisoned in the Tower of London, Ralegh revived the story of El Dorado in an attempt to procure his release. He assured the greedy King James that he could find the gold mines, given a sufficiently well equipped force of ships and men, and the king made a discreditable bargain with him.

Ralegh was to be released and, if his venture proved to be successful, his estates would be restored to him and he would be pardoned. If, however, he failed or fell foul of the Spaniards who were in effective control of the region and who had made it plain that they would protect it against anyone, he would be re-arrested on his return, charged with piracy and executed.

Ralegh's release was on 17th March 1617, but James did little to support the expedition and he had to sail with a poorly equipped force. He reached the Orinoco on 31st December, but fever compelled him to return to Trinidad, just off the mainland. Too poorly supplied to stay long away from an English port, yet too sick even to stand up, Ralegh sent his son and five small ships from the tiny fleet, under the command of Lawrence Keymis, back to the Orinoco.

Unexpectedly, they came across the Spanish settlement – all prepared to defend itself from behind stout barricades. The battle was short, sharp – and tragic. Ralegh's son was killed and Keymis was forced to return to Trinidad with the story of his defeat. Keymis committed suicide and mutiny broke out among the ships' crews. Ill and heartbroken, Ralegh had no alternative but to return to England – to arrest and execution on 29th October 1618.

The members of the Pilgrim Church in Leyden took a deeper interest than most in the stories of those faraway lands.

Even as early as 1616 they were again becoming unsettled by the conditions under which they lived in Holland – although they had little genuine cause for complaint. They were respected and well liked by the Dutch and had, in general, established themselves in the commerce of the city, found homes of their own

and had a regular place for worship. But they were unable to come to terms with life as it was lived by Hollanders. The old differences of outlook between the stern, parental attitude of the English towards their children and the almost unchecked freedom of the Dutch youngsters persisted, leading to endless disputes between the families. Nor could they, like their children, let themselves become absorbed into the Dutch way of life: too many of them holding themselves in isolation from the rest of the community constituted a colony and a "state within a state". Similarly, the closed membership of the Pilgrim Church meant that too few of the immigrants took the trouble, or succeeded, in learning Dutch – which was bound to place certain restrictions on integration, to set limits to the types of employment available to them, and to debar close, neighbourly relations with the Dutch.

On 20th May 1616 Richard Clifton died in Amsterdam, an elderly, over-burdened man, admired by most and pitied by almost as many because of his devotion to the Separatist Church. No one would have blamed him if he had abandoned the cause and remained at home in England, to spend his declining years in peace. His loss cast a gloom over the community.

In the autumn of that same year William Brewster set up the Pilgrim Press in Leyden – financed by Thomas Brewer. Only Pilgrim books were printed on it, but their circulation in England was to cause a furore in that country, and in Holland, within the next two years.

And overall the Pilgrims were inescapably aware that the truce between Holland and the mighty Spain was due to lapse in 1619 – and there was every indication that war between the two would be resumed. Persecution in England had been a serious and painful burden for the Nonconformists to bear, but the thought of the Spanish Inquisition was far too dreadful a matter for even the most heroic and devoted heretics to stomach.

In the face of all these unsettling problems, John Robinson began to put forward the possibility of a further move – this time to the only place in the world left to them in which they could worship God in freedom and after their own fashion: America.

Solemnly and endlessly he discussed the prospects of such an enterprise with Brewster and other Elders of the church. There were those in Leyden who recalled the stories of the early disasters, knowing that of the 143 that first settled there, only 38 survived to see the next year's harvest – in 1609 – and shook their heads in solemn disapproval. Others, of course – particularly those who had failed to integrate with the local population, the few who had failed to make a satisfactory living for themselves and their families, the ambitious who saw wealth beckoning to them from over the horizon and the frankly adventurous – took the opposite view and pointed out that the growing trade between England and the New World almost certainly guaranteed the success of such a venture. And between the two schools of thought there were those Elders of the Pilgrim Church who could not see where their duty lay.

Common greed found its place in the discussions. El Dorado – limitless gold, however fantastic the stories about it might be – brought Guiana more and more to the forefront of the thoughts of many; they salved their consciences by reminding their fellows

that Captain Leigh, who had been in touch with the Separatists at Amsterdam, had returned from that rich and sunny continent to urge on King James the need to send "able preachers" out there to give religious instruction to the heathen Indians.

It all sounded, on the lips of the enthusiasts, like a land of vast opportunity, far away from the unsettled conditions in Europe. But there were three obvious defects in the proposal. The first was chiefly in the minds of those whose religion overrode everything else: the prospect of gold would inevitably corrupt many of them and distract their attention, long before the settlement could be thoroughly organized, and while it was still their sole source of sustenance. Secondly, the more sober were aware that it was beyond their financial resources to buy or charter ships, to accumulate the provisions and stores they would require to support them until the colony became self-sufficient, and to have sufficient reserves

A party of Virginia Indians (*left*), as seen in the late sixteenth century, waving rattles while praying. Not all accounts of the Indians were as unbiased, and many unsavoury characteristics were attributed to the "naked savages", among them cannibalism (*right*).

of general equipment to keep them going until they had put down roots in a land where civilization had never been known. Thirdly, it was known that a Spanish settlement existed in the region, and this raised the prospect of a bitter religious war.

A wave of disappointment and even defeatism swept over the Leyden Pilgrims as it gradually dawned on them that the venture was beyond their financial strength and their probable physical endurance – and the Elders quietly thanked God that the Pilgrim Church was not to be dragged into an enterprise that suggested no real desire to make the highest priority the need to create a compact community in which to worship God freely.

But their fears were quickly dissipated as they turned their thoughts instead towards Virginia. There was no gold there to tempt the weaker members of the community, and the soil was said to be rich and fruitful. There were two known commercial enterprises, the London and the Plymouth Virginia Companies, already in existence and prepared to finance colonies in America – on terms, of course. (The former, the Virginia Company of London, was reorganized in 1609 and again in 1612 as the Treasurer and Company of Adventurers and Planters of the City of London; the Plymouth Company, organized in 1605, was superseded in 1620 by the Council for New England.) English settlements already prospered on the James River, but there was no reason why the Leyden Pilgrims should be compelled to join up with others – in that vast region they would be able to carve out a settlement for themselves – but it would be comforting to know that others of their nationality were within reach to help them in an emergency. Nor would they be within range of Catholic armies from Spain, or so close to England to cause anxiety about the Canons of the Anglican Church.

The discussions became eager as this new prospect pleased all shades of opinion, except the very few who had sunk themselves contentedly into the Dutch scene. Towards the end of the summer of 1617 – even before Sir Walter Ralegh had returned to England to announce the failure of his third and last voyage to find El Dorado – the decision was made to open negotiations with the London Virginia Company.

In May, Robert Cushman and John Carver were chosen to make their way in secret to London to sound out the directors of the Company, but it was September before they crossed the North Sea and made contact with them. Their first task was to convince the financiers that, although they were Separatists from the Anglican Church and living in Holland, they were not rebellious subjects of King James and were sufficiently responsible to ensure a profitable return to the Company. They presented seven articles of their faith to the Company to establish the fact that they assented to the doctrines of the Church of England – although in certain features they did not emphasize their nonconformity.

1. To the Confession of Faith (The 39 Articles of Religion of 1562) published in the name of the Church of England, and to every Article thereof; we do (with the Reformed Churches where we live, and also elsewhere) assent wholly.

2. As we do acknowledge the Doctrines of Faith there taught; so do we, the fruits and effects of the same Doctrine, to the begetting of saving faith in thousands in the land [of England], Conformists and Reformists, as they are called: with whom also, as with our brethren, we do desire to keep spiritual communion in peace; and will practice in our parts all lawful things.

3. The King's Majesty we acknowledge for Supreme Governor in his Dominions in all causes, and over all persons: and that none may decline or appeal from his authority or judgement in any cause whatsoever: but that in all things obedience is due unto him; either active, if the thing commanded be not against GOD's Word; or passive, if it be, except pardon can be obtained.

4. We judge it lawful for His Majesty to appoint Bishops, Civil Overseers or Officers in authority under him in the several Provinces, Dioceses, Congregations, or Parishes, to oversee the Churches, and govern them civilly according to the laws of the land: unto whom, they are, in all things, to give an account; and by them, to be ordered according to godliness.

5. The authority of the present Bishops in the land, we do acknowledge so far forth as the same is indeed derived from His Majesty unto them; and as they proceed in his name: whom we will also therein honour in all things; and him, in them.

6. We believe that no Synod, Classes, Convocation, or Assembly of Ecclesiastical Officers hath any power or authority at all but as the same [is] by the Magistrate given unto them.

7. Lastly, we desire to give unto all Superiors due honour, to preserve the unity of the Spirit with all that fear GOD, to have peace with all men what in us lieth, and wherein we err to be instructed by any.

The seven articles had been drawn up in Leyden and they were signed by John Robinson and William Brewster as the leading authorities in the Pilgrim Church at that time.

But it was not enough to satisfy the directors of the London Virginia Company alone; the settlements already established in Virginia existed not only as belonging to the trading company, but were also subject to the authority of the crown – which included all Acts of Parliament, not least the Act of Uniformity.

This setback was not enough to defeat the Pilgrims of Leyden: they decided to mobilize the assistance of their most powerful and influential friends. Brewster referred the two negotiators, Carver and Cushman, to a very old family friend, Sir Edwin Sandys, one of the Council for Virginia. A statesman and a Member of Parliament, knighted by the King, son of the one-time Archbishop of York and connected with the old Scrooby Manor House, he had the ear of King James. In November 1617, he wrote to William Brewster in Holland stating that he had recommended the application of the Leyden Pilgrims to the "Gentlemen of His Majesty's Council for Virginia", but pointing out that a great deal was still required in the way of information and proposals before a final decision could be expected.

Brewster and Robinson replied in the following month setting out their application in detail, and Cushman and Carver were encouraged to learn that the Council for Virginia was prepared to welcome the proposals. They even began to assume that the king would "rubber stamp" the Council's advice.

The king, in fact, being satisfied with the rather vague explanation that the colonists were to live in the New World by "fishing", seemed prepared to approve the application – but he hesitated, and finally referred the matter to the Archbishop of Canterbury and the Bishop of London for clarification of the religious content of the proposal.

Sir Edwin Sandys threw his powerful influence into the scales and succeeded in persuading George Abbot, the Archbishop of York, and Robert Naunton, one of His Majesty's principal Secretaries of State, to promote the cause of the Pilgrims. Quite unexpectedly, the Archbishop suddenly found himself accused of helping the adventurers "to make a free, popular state, in Virginia" in defiance of the laws of England and the established church – with himself as their leader.

The matter was passed to the Privy Council but the Anglican authorities were unwilling to accept any assurances suggested by the Pilgrims, nor were those pleading their cause as honest as they might have been, creating confusion rather than promoting the application. The weeks of 1618 passed into months as the negotiations over matters of dogma, the freedom of elect Elders, baptism and the Oath of Allegiance followed one another endlessly – until, in the end, the king grew tired of the constant petitions, each one differing only in detail from its predecessor, and made his decision – one of those disturbingly garbled rulings that was to satisfy nobody. He undertook to "connive at them and not to molest them; providing they carried themselves peaceably" – but he refused to give any public authority, or to add his seal to his ruling.

The king's vague and somewhat uncertain decision caused a great deal of dismay and unhappiness to the Pilgrims in Leyden. But the Elders pointed out that the biggest seal on the finest parchment in the world meant little to a king who had made so very many promises in the past and kept so few of them. The way was open to the Pilgrim Church to makes its bid to settle in America – beyond that they were in the hands of God, and subject to the whims of King James.

Sir Edwin Sandys, who helped to promote the cause of the Pilgrims.

7 Thoughts of America

Although it would be impracticable to wind up all their affairs on a given date, or to find shipping to carry every man, woman and child in a single, mass exodus, the Pilgrims made up their minds to set about making the final preparations to cross the Atlantic to Virginia as fast as they could. They sent Robert Cushman, with this time William Brewster, to England to reopen negotiations with the London Virginia Company, and in the Spring of 1619 the pair arrived in London, ready to settle for the best possible terms they could obtain for the granting of a patent to make the venture.

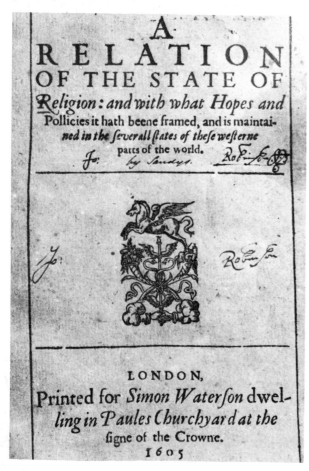

But matters were not to run as smoothly as the representatives of the Leyden Pilgrims had hoped. They found the Virginia Company in the throes of internal strife and were, for the time being, in no position to negotiate. Sir Thomas Smith had tendered his resignation from the offices of Treasurer and Governor of the Company because of the burden of his outside interests – and, for some strange reason, he was promptly dismissed by his fellow directors. On 28th April 1619 Sir Edwin Sandys took his place but Smith, incensed by such treatment, retorted by opposing the election of Sandys and demanding that he himself should be returned to his old offices.

Unable to make any headway while the dispute in the boardroom of the Virginia Company remained unsettled, Robert Cushman made a trip to Kent to have a talk with Captain Sir Samuel Argall, who had recently returned from Virginia, to learn at first hand of the progress being made in that colony.

Argall's story was an unhappy one. He told Cushman of how Francis Blackwell had contracted to carry the last of the members of the Ancient Church in Amsterdam to Virginia and had packed aboard the vessels he had chartered no fewer than 180 passengers – far more than the ship could possibly accommodate in safety during an Atlantic crossing in winter. Blackwell's handling of the situation had been so scandalous that there had been a bitter outcry from the emigrants at the sight of what had been provided for them. Even those who watched the loading of the vessel from the quay at Gravesend were appalled by the brutal overcrowding and added their own violently expressed objections to the distress of the passengers.

The voyage started at the beginning of September 1618. The ship, low in the water, had wallowed its way to the Thames estuary, beaten slowly and

Frontispiece of Sir Edwin Sandys' book *A Relation of the State of Religion*, with John Robinson's autograph.

Part of the Scilly Isles, the last sight of land before the Atlantic crossing.

hazardously through the Straits of Dover, down the Channel and eventually, in the teeth of a rising gale, the passengers and crew saw the Scilly Isles drop astern – the last sight of land they were to have for many a long day. Driven far to the south of its course in continuously heavy seas and with no sight of the stars to pinpoint their position, it was only a matter of time before the ship's master lost all sense of direction. Weeks turned into months as the unhandy, wallowing, partially dismasted and badly strained vessel fought to survive the incessant gales – while the crew, overworked and running short of food and water, weakened and despaired.

Captain Maggner, the master, and six of his crew died in those dreadful conditions – and shortly afterwards Francis Blackwell suffered the same fate and was buried at sea. For further weeks the undermanned vessel was blown about the ocean as the passengers did what they could to help the sailors to maintain some sort of a course. But scurvy, shortage of food and water, and the lack of warmth, dry clothing and rest gradually took their inevitable toll, and as the days went by more and more died and had to be committed to the raging Atlantic.

It was March 1619 before that hell-ship sighted Chesapeake Bay – with only 50 survivors from the original 180 passengers.

Sir Samuel Argall's news, when it was received in London, resulted in a heightening of the tension in the boardroom of the London Virginia Company, and Cushman reported to the Leyden Separatists that it would undoubtedly cause even further delay in their negotiations with the directors of that Company. (He mentioned in his letter, too, that William Brewster was sick.) But, sooner than expected, the patent was granted although, on the

The title page of David Calderwood's *Perth Assembly*, the pamphlet which did so much harm to the Pilgrims' attempts to persuade James of their loyalty.

advice of some of Cushman's friends, it was agreed that it should not be taken out in the name of any member of the Pilgrim Church but in that of John Wincob, who intended to sail with them – he was a member of the household of the influential Countess of Lincoln.

On 9th June 1620 the Virginia Company ordered that its seal be attached to the patent, which provided all the authority the Pilgrims needed to proceed with their venture. (Although, as it happened, Wincob did not sail with them and the patent which had cost them the loss of so much time, labour and expense was never to be of any use to them. In any event, the patent was not actually signed until 3rd November of that year, by which time the emigrants were within a week of sighting Cape Cod.)

The whole enterprise was to be put in jeopardy because of the publication of a pamphlet called the *Perth Assembly*, printed on the Pilgrim Press in Leyden at the beginning of 1619.

Separatist or any other publications that provoked opposition to the Established Church in England were prohibited throughout King James' realm, but William Brewster was by no means averse to badgering the Anglicans by printing such literature, on the press that Thomas Brewer had financed for him, for that very purpose – and found a wide demand for it in both England and Scotland.

At first it did little more than annoy the authorities in Britain, but eventually some very good reprints were run off in Leyden and returned to the United Kingdom for circulation; this began to achieve a notoriety that attracted the attention of the king.

James in those years was striving to persuade the Scottish Presbyterians to accept his Supremacy of the Church, and in August 1618 he did his utmost to enforce his views on the General Assembly of the Church of Scotland at Perth.

David Calderwood was the Scotsman who was chiefly responsible for the outspoken protest from the Presbyterians and expressed his opinions in no uncertain manner in an "essay" entitled *Perth Assembly*. Having difficulty in getting it printed, he sent the manuscript to his friend William Brewster in Holland. Brewster approved of it and immediately issued it in pamphlet form.

PERTH ASSEMBLY.

CONTAINING

1 The Proceedings thereof.
2 The Proofe of the Nullitie thereof.
3 Reasons presented thereto against the receiving the fiue new *Articles* imposed.
4 The oppositenesse of it to the proceedings and oath of the whole state of the Land. *An.*1581.
5 Proofes of the unlawfulnesse of the said fiue Articles, *viz.* 1. Kneeling in the act of Receiving the Lords Supper. 2. Holy daies. 3. Bishopping. 4. Private Baptisme. 5. Private Communion.

EXOD. 20. 7.
Thou shalt not take the name of the Lord thy God in vaine, for the Lord will not hold him guiltlesse that taketh his name in vaine.

COLOS. 2. 8.
Beware lest there be any that spoyle you through Philosophy & vain deceit, through the traditions of men, according to the rudiments of the World, and not of Christ.

MDCXIX.

The copies were smuggled into Scotland in April 1619, without regard for the prohibition against such publications or the penalties exacted of those caught engaged in such traffic. They were transported in vats that would normally have been filled with French wines to Burntisland, on the north bank of the Firth of Forth, near Kirkcaldy and opposite the port of Leith to where they were subsequently shipped.

There could be no doubt about the identity of the author: the very style in which it was written proclaimed it as coming from the pen of David Calderwood and, inevitably, it was brought to the attention of the authorities who promptly ordered his arrest. King James, angry at this blatant opposition to his authority, demanded that all steps should be taken to find and punish the author and everyone else connected with the offending publication.

In July the press was traced to Holland. It was Sir Dudley Carleton, King James' Ambassador at the

Sir Dudley Carleton, employed by James to track down the originators of the *Perth Assembly*.

Hague, who came across a copy of the publication, traced it back to the environs of the city of Leyden and sent the pamphlet, with a report on it, to Secretary of State Sir Robert Naunton in London, adding the information that he had succeeded in persuading the States General of the Netherlands to issue an edict against the printing of unlicensed publications, and promising to stir the Dutch authorities into enforcing that prohibition once he had succeeded in pinpointing the whereabouts of the offending press.

Carleton proved himself to be an efficient detective for by 22nd July he had traced the publication to William Brewster. He wrote to Naunton at once to tell him of his discovery and of the fact that Brewster was known to be in London at that very moment, although at a secret address.

In fact, as we have seen Brewster had accompanied Robert Cushman to London as early as May. But, despite a full-scale search, he was not to be found there, and at the beginning of August Naunton wrote to the Ambassador in Holland to warn him that Brewster had probably returned to Leyden – and to stress the king's over-riding demand for the arrest of the printer and the suppression of his press.

David Calderwood escaped to Holland with a number of his accomplices, *via* Newhaven, but although this move was known to the authorities it failed to lead them to Brewster's hiding place.

In growing anger, James ordered his Ambassador to "deal roundly" with the States General of the Netherlands in the matter of the arrest of Brewster. Nor was Carleton slow to implement his master's wishes. He traced the printer to Leyden and then urged his king's demands on Jacob von Brouckhoven, the representative of the city of Leyden in the Council of the provincial State of Holland.

But, as he was a matriculated member of the University of Leyden, only that body had the right to examine Brewster: they ordered him to attend before them on 19th September. All they learned when they met on that day was that Brewster was sick "somewhere in the city". They then ordered that he be brought "voluntarily" into the Debtor's Chamber.

The City Council took the matter as one of little importance and Brewster was not in fact detained – although Carleton understood that he had been

Sᵗ Dudley Carleton Kᵗ
SECRETARY OF STATE.

Sturt Sc.

taken into custody. When that misunderstanding had been cleared up, James used his influence to send Brouckhoven back to Leyden to seize the printing press and any of its publications he found there. On 11th September a bailiff of the University applied for the services of an assessor and a magistrate to help him with the seizure. They raided Brewster's house, seized the press and nailed up the door – but Brewster succeeded in making his escape, and Thomas Brewer, who had financed the Pilgrim Press, was taken in his stead.

Brewer was not easily cross-questioned by the University authorities. Even though Carleton provided a list of the questions that should be put to him, and although Dr Cornelius Swanenburg was assigned to the task of conducting the interrogation, the Ambassador had to report exasperatedly on 18th September that Brewer gave hopelessly vague and unsatisfactory replies, and that in consequence he

A sixteenth-century printing shop in Holland. At a distance from the English forces of law and order, the self-exiled Nonconformists were able to publish dissenting pamphlets in comparative safety.

had used the authority of the Prince of Orange to detain the man – even although the whole "Company of Brownists" offered to go bail on his behalf.

Carleton also stirred up the city of Amsterdam and pressed the authorities there to make a search for Brewster, but no trace of him was to be found within its limits. James, angrily unwilling to be baulked of some prey, demanded – in the stiltedly polite manner of the day – that Thomas Brewer, an Englishman resident in Leyden, should be sent to England for examination.

The Ambassador made a formal request for the extradition of Thomas Brewer, but he came up against the jealously guarded privileges of the University and the County Council of Leyden. Although the Curators of the University convened a meeting together with the Burgomaster of Leyden on 11th October, they agreed with reluctance only to subject Brewer to further examination themselves, although in the presence of anyone the Ambassador cared to nominate; to send him for examination by

Part of Newgate Prison, where Thomas Legate died.

his brother Thomas, had been imprisoned in London on a charge of heresy. Thomas Legate died in Newgate gaol, but Bartholomew had been taken before James to argue his views. He had then been tried before the Consitory Court, and in March 1612 was burned at the stake as a heretic – as it happened, the last person ever to go to the stake in London because of his religious convictions.

Brewer's conditions were that he receive assurances that the king had personally asked him to present himself before him; that he go as a free man and not as a prisoner; that he receive no punishment, either bodily or in the loss of any of his possessions, during his stay in England; that he be allowed to return to Holland within a reasonable time; and that his journey be made at the expense of the State.

Sir Dudley Carleton agreed the demands, but it seems that even then Brewer was in no hurry to leave the safety of Holland, particularly after meeting some of his friends in Middelburg who advised him strongly to be very wary of any promise made by James. He sailed on 28th November from Flushing, in company with Sir William Zouche, and after a week's delay through bad weather the pair arrived in England.

James was furiously angry that Brewer should have come to England under the shelter of such pledges and pettishly attempted to evade paying the cost of the journey from Holland. Brewer was questioned by Sir John Benet and Sir Henry Martin, both of them experienced examiners of those whose religious beliefs differed from those of their king and the Anglican Church; but, as at Leyden, very little information of any value was obtained from the wily Brewer and he was discharged.

He returned to Leyden in due course – at his own expense – but, although King James had failed to muzzle the Pilgrim Press directly, the States General in the Netherlands published an edict on 13th January 1620 against any further printing of literature of a libellous or licentious nature.

The exact whereabouts of Brewster during those attempts to suppress the Pilgrim Press and to discipline its authors and managers, remain a mystery. Certainly he was never taken into custody for any offence. David Calderwood also was never called upon to face the king's justice.

The whole unhappy episode, however, as could only be expected, changed King James' "passive connivance without public authority" to the Leyden

the Ambassador; or to surrender Brewer in exchange for an undertaking to return the prisoner to Leyden, unharmed, within two months.

A wrangle followed. Carleton refused to enter into a bond for the return of Brewer on the grounds that his king's word should be sufficient, which the Curators ignored, quoting as a precedent their refusal to send a German named Cluverius to Prague to answer to a charge of writing a book in criticism of the Emperor Rudolph.

James, in a fury, ordered his Ambassador to use the whole of his weight and authority with the States General to intervene and to compel the Curators of the University to conform with his demands, but by the time the message reached Holland, a deputation from the University informed Carleton that Brewer had expressed a wish to go to England to settle the matter – on conditions. The conditions were understandable in view of the still bitter memory of a Nonconformist preacher of a sect known as the "Seekers", Bartholomew Legate, who, together with

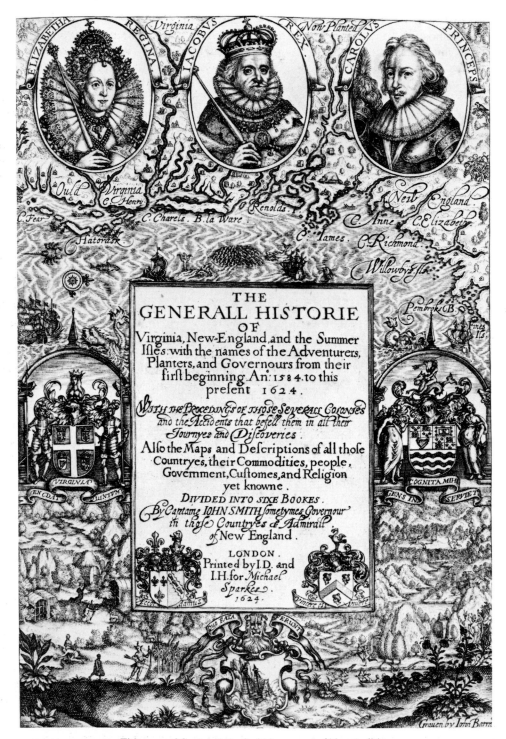

Title page of Captain John Smith's account of his expeditions
in North America. The map in the background shows parts of
Virginia and New England.

Pilgrims' plans to found a settlement in the New World into outright hostility to the enterprise. From the moment the king demanded the arrest of Brewster it seemed to the Elders of the Pilgrim Church that it had become impossible to take advantage of the patent granted to them by the London Virginia Company.

Despairingly, Pastor John Robinson looked elsewhere than to England for financial help, and for a land that was being colonized by some other nation friendly to their religious scruples. There was only one other, of course, and that was the Netherlands. Robinson was aware that the New Netherlands Company was already trading in that latitude in which New Amsterdam was to flourish and in the distant future to become New York – far to the north of the English settlements on the James River in Virginia.

He made contact with the directors of the Company who, after some deliberation, favoured the suggestion that they should provide the means and the land on which the Leyden Pilgrims could establish a settlement of their own. On 2nd February 1620, the Company presented a petition to the Prince of Orange seeking his approval and help in forwarding the enterprise, pointing out that there were about four hundred would-be settlers involved and that the New Netherlands Company was prepared to land them on the shores of the Hudson River and to provide them with sufficient cattle, grain and other supplies to assure them a good start; it hoped that the Prince would authorize the detachment of a couple of warships to accompany them to guarantee the security of the colony as a Dutch settlement.

Twice the petition was presented and twice it was rejected by the Prince of Orange. In the meantime Robinson had met Thomas Weston, a merchant of London who had recently arrived in Leyden and who warned him against becoming too deeply involved with the Dutch, so the negotiations with the New Netherlands Company were dropped. Weston proved to be equally unenthusiastic about the London Virginia Company and, as an alternative, proposed that he and some of his friends and business associates should be allowed to finance the venture. The scheme suggested by him was that the proposed "plantation" should be operated as a joint-stock corporation for seven years. At the end of that time the capital and the accumulated profits were to be divided amongst the backers, to be called the "Adventurers", and the emigrants, who were to be known as the "Planters", in proportion to their shareholdings. But the houses and the land brought under cultivation in the form of gardens were to be excluded from the dividend and left to the Planters as their individual private property. The Planters were to work exclusively for the Company of Adventurers, except for two days a week when they were to be free to improve their houses and gardens. It was proposed that the shares in the Corporation should be fixed at £10 each; and that every Planter aged 16 or over was to be allotted one share free of charge and could buy, for cash or approved goods, as many shares as he pleased and could afford at that price.

Weston assured Robinson and the Elders of the Church that there would be no shortage of money to charter ships and to provision them, and suggested that the Pilgrims should draw up provisional Articles of Agreement along the lines he had indicated.

The details of the articles as agreed between the Leyden Pilgrims and Thomas Weston were initialled in Holland and Weston took them to London for final approval and signature by those who were to finance the enterprise.

The agreement contained eleven articles:

1. The Adventurers and Planters do agree: That every person that goeth being aged sixteen years and upwards, be rated at £10: and £10 to be accounted a Single Share.

2. That he goeth in person and furnisheth himself out with £10 either in money or other provisions, be accounted as having £20 in Stock: and in the Division shall receive a Double Share.

3. The persons transported and the Adventurers shall continue their Joint Stock and Partnership together the space of Seven Years: except some unexpected impediment do cause the whole Company to agree otherwise: during which time all profits and benefits that are got by trade, traffic, trucking, working, fishing or any other means of any person or persons remain still in the Common Stock until the Division.

4. That at their coming there they choose out such a number of fit persons as may furnish their ships and boats for fishing upon the sea; employing the rest in their several faculties upon the land; as building houses, tilling and planting the ground and making

The Old Rhine at Leyden.

such commodities as shall be most useful for the Colony.

5. That the houses, and lands improved, especially gardens and home lots, should remain, undivided, wholly to the Planters, at the Seven Years' end.

6. Whosoever come to the Colony hereafter, or putteth any into the Stock, shall, at the end of the Seven Years, be allowed proportionately to the time of his so doing.

7. He that shall carry his wife and children or servants shall be allowed for every person now aged sixteen years and upward a Single Share: or if they be between ten years old and sixteen, then two of them to be reckoned for a person both in Transportation and Division.

8. That such children as now go, and are under the age of ten years, have no other Share in the Division but fifty acres of unmanured land.

9. That such persons as die before the Seven Years be expired, their executors to have their part or Share at the Division proportionately to the time of their life in the Colony.

10. That all such persons that are of this Colony are to have their meat, drink, apparel and all provisions out of the Common Stock and goods of the said Colony.

11. Secondly. That they should have had two days in a week for their own private employment, for the more comfort of themselves and their families; especially such as had families.

Unexpectedly, however, on his arrival in England with the agreement Weston made two significant alterations to the text without any reference to John Robinson and his associates. Paragraph 5 was amended to read: "That at the end of the Seven Years, the Capital and Profits (viz. the houses, lands, goods and chattles) be equally divided betwixt the Adventurers and the Planters. Which done, every man shall be free from other of them, and any debt or detriment concerning this Adventure." Paragraph 11 had been deleted altogether.

When the new terms became known in Leyden there was an immediate outcry against them and John Robinson voiced the general disapproval. Many of the Pilgrims, believing that the terms they had agreed during Weston's stay in Leyden were final and open to neither dispute nor amendment, had disposed of their property and furniture so as to have money on hand with which to buy shares in the venture, provide clothing, bedding and cooking equipment for the long voyage, and start life all over again in an uncivilized land. Some of them were in the state where further delay, to renegotiate the terms or look around for new backers, would necessitate finding new homes and furniture – and even having to find jobs in place of those they had given up or businesses that they had sold.

A whole series of acrimonious discussions followed and there was a spate of impassioned correspondence with Cushman in England, until it was decided that Samuel Fuller, Edward Winslow, William Bradford and Isaac Allerton should write on behalf of them all to their representatives in England, John Carver and Robert Cushman, protesting at the new conditions and instructing them to insist that the original terms of the agreement with Weston should be honoured.

The letter, written on 31st May 1620, had some little bite in it against Cushman, saying, "Whereas Robert Cushman desires reasons for our dislike, promising thereupon to alter the same; else saying we should think he had no brains: we desire him to exercise them therein ..." The letter stated quite flatly that such unreasonable clauses as "That the Merchants should have the half of men's houses and lands at the Dividend ... And that persons should be deprived of the two days in a week agreed upon, yea, every moment of time for their own particular" should be deleted.

In the meantime a number of Separatists from London and elsewhere expressed a wish to be allowed to join the Pilgrim Church in its move to the New World, and, understanding the persecution under which they suffered in England and feeling that their religious beliefs were much the same as their own, the Leyden Pilgrims gladly accepted them.

At Robinson's suggestion the London Separatists appointed Christopher Martin of Billericay, Essex, to join Cushman and Carver as their representative in the negotiations with Thomas Weston and the London merchants. In practice, however, most of the negotiations took place in London between Cushman and Weston, with Carver joining in by letter from Southampton and Robinson from Leyden in Holland – an awkward arrangement that did nothing to expedite a final settlement.

Cushman became short-tempered at the way negotiations were being dragged out through the long delays in forwarding and receiving letters – and the need for so much correspondence – and complained bitterly. A self-opinionated man and a thorough-going believer in the community of property, he had long been sharply concerned at the failure of the Pilgrim Church to declare its belief in the joint ownership of wealth – regardless of the fact that no such belief had ever been a part of the Church's creed. Now, perversely, he grew irritably critical of the need imposed on him to consult with the Elders in Leyden over the terms of any proposed agreement with Weston.

On 10th June 1620, Cushman wrote to John Carver in Southampton and replied to the letter of the 31st May from Fuller, Winslow, Bradford and Allerton in Leyden.

To Carver he complained bitterly: "I have received from you, some letters full of [dis]affection and complaints: and what it is you would have of me, I know not. For your crying out, 'Negligence! Negligence! Negligence!': I marvel why so negligent a man was used in the business ..." He points out with some justice: "... in now being in three places too far remote, we will, with going up and down and wrangling and expostulating pass over the summer before we will go." But Cushman did provide Carver with the information that "We have reckoned, it should seem, without our host; and counted upon one hundred and fifty persons. There cannot be found above £1,200 and odd monies, of all the Venturers you can reckon: besides some cloth, stockings and shoes; which are not counted. So we shall come short at least £300 or £400."

His letter to those at Leyden complained of the discouragement under which he worked because of the indecisions and disagreements, and declared that he had been on the point of passing the whole affair over to Carver to complete. "But, gathering up myself, by further consideration: I resolved yet to make one trial more ..." He informed them that Weston, if it had not been for his promise at Leyden, would have abandoned the project because of the objections to his alterations to the agreement. Then Cushman went on to make it clear that he was going ahead with matters in agreement with Weston, without waiting for the authority of the Elders of the Church: "... advising together, we resolved to hire a ship; and have took a liking of one till Monday, about sixty last [120 tons]: for a greater we cannot get, except it be too great. But a fine ship it is ..." And the penultimate paragraph berates them with: "If I do such things as I cannot give reason for, it is like you have set a foot about your business; and so turn the reproof to yourselves and send another, and let me come again to my combs. But I refuse not to have my cause judged, both by God and all indifferent men ..."

The aisle of St Peter's Church, Leyden.

And for the first time we find a reference to the *Speedwell* when Cushman asks that Master Reynolds "tarry there, and bring the ship to Southampton", and learn that a Pilot, Captain John Clarke, had been hired.

Unaware of this letter, John Robinson wrote on the 14th to Carver at Southampton complaining bitterly that no shipping had yet been provided to transport the Pilgrims from Holland to England and that no money was available for the purpose, despite the fact that many of the emigrants had already paid over to Weston the monies they had invested in the enterprise – others flatly refused to make their contributions until they could at least see a ship at their disposal. He went on, unhappily, to assure Carver that those who had already invested in the venture now bitterly regretted their haste.

Robinson deplored the fact that Weston seemed set on evading his undertaking to finance the venture – or that he was in fact using the money that had already been subscribed for his own benefit. He accused Robert Cushman of being unfit to represent the members of the Pilgrim Church, being too ready to accept any terms laid down by Weston's Adventurers and utterly careless of advice and orders from the Elders at Leyden.

Robinson's letter leaves no doubt that at that moment the whole enterprise was on the point of disintegration. He himself was most unhappy about the negotiations over the altered terms of the agreement with Weston, doubted Weston's honesty in the matter, resented Cushman's dealings with that man without the full authority of those at Leyden, and saw the discontent that was seething among the members of the Church over the whole sorry business.

So ragged had become the organization that the few wealthy members of the Pilgrim community – in particular, Thomas Brewer and Edward Pickering – on whose resources depended the needs of the colony once it settled in America, were showing a distinct reluctance to continue their support, and as the immediate finances promised by Weston were not forthcoming even the majority of the members, whose purchase of shares was small, were beginning to withdraw any other assistance.

But Thomas Weston was having his difficulties in England, too. A number of damaging reports were circulating in London concerning the Pilgrim Church, rising chiefly from their association with the Ancient Church – however remotely – and tarring it with the same brush of disgraceful conduct and scandalous behaviour in the conduct of their affairs. The Anglican authorities in the Privy Council, out of sheer resentment that the Separatists seemed to be gaining ground throughout the kingdom, fostered such reports.

Robinson did his best to answer these attacks in a pamphlet, *A Just and Necessary Apology*, seeking to stress the points of agreement between the Separatists and the Anglicans rather than emphasize the differences. He tried, too, to refute the charges made against them in the Privy Council and in public. But, perhaps because the *Apology* was printed in Latin, it had very little impact on those who believed the slanders and did little to persuade their backers to fulfil even the terms of the revised version of the agreement – nor were they likely to, Cushman realized, so long as there was no move by the Leyden Elders to accept those terms.

Fearing that the whole enterprise was going to collapse, Cushman and Weston took drastic steps to save the venture, and on 1st July 1620 they agreed and signed the terms as representatives of the two parties. No attempt was made to reach a compromise, so desperate had they become for a decision.

Illustration from a contemporary manuscript showing Queen Elizabeth I,
whose vigorous championship of the Anglican Church made various groups
of Separatists think of emigration to the New World.

James VI and I, the first of the Stewart monarchs of England.

8 They Board the *Mayflower*

Despite the quarrels between Robert Cushman and John Robinson, the impetus to complete the arrangements for the move to America gathered pace, but at no stage was any serious attempt made to form a tightly organized and efficiently administered expedition. The Pilgrims were all amateurs who had never before had the remotest connection with such an enterprise.

Nor were they prepared, probably for financial reasons, to accept outside help. Captain John Smith, who had first sailed to Virginia in 1612 and had spent the succeeding eight years exploring the region and helping to colonize it, hearing of this latest venture, offered to accompany the Pilgrims to the New World, but was turned down. Even less sensibly they refused to listen to his very valuable advice.

Cash was, however, their immediate need. John Robinson, William Brewster and William Jepson mortgaged the property they owned in Leyden, and

Thomas Rogers sold his house in the town for 300 gilders, to create a starting fund, and fortunately some of the monies already invested with Thomas Weston and the Company of Adventurers began to trickle back to Holland.

As soon as they had sufficient funds on hand, and without waiting for the news that Cushman had his eye on a suitable ship for the trans-Atlantic voyage, the Leyden Pilgrims began to look around for an auxiliary vessel that they could purchase outright to carry them to England to join the London contingent. Such a vessel had to be stout enough to cross the Atlantic in company with the mother ship and to be retained in Virginia for use as a fishing vessel.

After a brief search they found a small ship, the *Speedwell*, of 60 tons, lying at Delfshaven some twenty-four miles from Leyden. Without worrying about having it surveyed by an expert they bought it.

A mill on the Maese at Delfshaven, the port from which the Leyden Pilgrims were to embark on the *Speedwell* for England.

The old gates of Delft.

In their enthusiasm the Elders proceeded at once to fit the ship out for the journey to England and America. They wasted no money on consultations with a shipwright, and no time in waiting to appoint a ship's master to oversee the work, before they began to rerig and refit the vessel. Amateurishly, they concerned themselves more with increasing the available accommodation and creating the largest possible sail area than with the essential matter of seaworthiness. They employed cheap, unskilled, incompetent labour where they could not do the work themselves. The result was that the *Speedwell* was seriously overmasted, causing severe strain to the seams under even the minimum of sail in only a moderate wind, and in stormy weather far too much work for the tiny crew that such a vessel would carry.

Reynolds was engaged in London to captain the *Speedwell* and to stay with them in America for the first year. He arrived in Holland at the end of May, before the refit had been completed – yet, it appears, he did little to point out or remedy the ill considered and poorly executed alterations.

In Leyden the Pilgrims were heartened too when they learned that John Carver was making preparations for berthing and loading the mother ship, when it had been procured, and the *Speedwell*, while Christopher Martin was busy in Kent gathering up provisions for the voyage and to sustain them until a follow-up supply ship reached them in Virginia, and Cushman and Weston concentrated on finding the best possible ship to carry them all to the New World.

At last the news reached Leyden that everything was ready in England and waited only for the arrival of the contingent of Pilgrims from Holland.

John Robinson was almost overwhelmed with relief by the progress of events. It seemed that despite all the arguments, recriminations and delays of the past months everything was now ready for the great day. A large enough ship was at their disposal in England, the *Speedwell* was available and had been made ready for its part in the venture, provisions were on hand in Southampton, and they still had the rest of the summer and early autumn before them to make the voyage less hazardous and to give them time to erect shelters in Virginia before the winter storms could take their toll.

The pastor, in an upsurge of thankfulness, decreed they have a "Meeting and keep a Day of Humiliation, to seek the Lord of his direction". It was a day of heartfelt gladness and eager expectation, spent as cheerfully in celebration as in humility and prayer – and, as had happened too often in the past, without waiting to obtain proper confirmation of all that had been promised.

Hardly had the Day of Humiliation gone by before it began to dawn on the Leyden Pilgrims that the arrangements for the exodus were anything but complete. The first failure to make itself evident was the lack of accommodation for them all. The *Speedwell* was far too small to carry the whole membership of the Leyden Pilgrim Church to Southampton in a single voyage, nor was it practicable to run a shuttle-service between Holland and England as, with the addition of the London contingent of emigrants, even the two vessels together could not possibly transport all who had intended to go. Only now did the Elders realize that some three hundred Pilgrims in Leyden and an unknown number from London expected to make the journey in ships that together could not possibly accommodate many more than one hundred passengers.

To complicate matters, the sudden decision to sail found many of the Pilgrims unprepared for the event, generally those who had most to lose through a too early disposal of their assets and most to gain in that they could afford to buy shares in the Corporation.

But the choice had to be made between those who were to sail and the greater number who must be left behind to follow on later – certainly not before the following year. It proved to be a heartbreaking task made none the easier by the knowledge that a number of those who must be left behind had already thrown up their jobs and given up their homes.

It was decided that William Brewster's driving energy could not be left behind, and that John Robinson should stay in Leyden to minister to those of his church who remained there. Families were broken up, in the expectation that they would be reunited within a year; the younger and more adaptable members had to be given some sort of priority; and the Elders were needed in the New World to lend their authority to the enterprise. And then it was felt that there must be a binding declaration between those who sailed and those who did not to ensure that there would be no division between them. A solemn compact was agreed by the two sections of the Pilgrim Church asserting that they were as one community and would have the right to move from one place to the other without hindrance or question.

It was also agreed that if "the Lord should frown upon our proceedings ..." those who needed to return from the New World would receive all assistance when they arrived back in Holland, and if "... God should be pleased to favour them ..." the successful would do everything in their power to help the others to join them.

The signing of the *Mayflower* Compact.

A Dutch seascape, thought to be of the *Speedwell* sailing from Delfshaven.

Confirmation came at last that Cushman and Weston had indeed chartered a ship at Southwark, but there was a further spate of discontent among the Pilgrims when it was learned that it was not the 180-ton vessel that Cushman had indicated in his letter of 10th June but a smaller one of 120 tons – which suggested the need for a further reduction in numbers.

But there could be no further restrictions to the list of passengers without creating serious privations for those who, having now disposed of all they possessed, would be left stranded if they were not permitted to sail – and it was decided that the consequent overcrowding would have to be endured. Nor was there any time to make alternative arrangements; the *Mayflower* was about to sail from London for Southampton with the members of the Southwark Independent Church and a few of their friends in the expectation of being joined almost at once by the contingent from Leyden.

Again John Robinson ordered a Day of Solemn Humiliation and, now that the departure for the unknown world on the far side of the Atlantic

Ocean was imminent, the prayers were urgent and said with fervour.

On 20th July Robinson conducted a farewell service in his home in Kolksteeg, Leyden, in the room that had become their accustomed meeting place. Afterwards there was a feast prepared and organized by those who were left behind. Then came the rush to finish packing and to dispose of the last of their unwanted possessions, and the Pilgrims were all ready to leave Leyden on the start of their long journey.

On 21st July the emigrant Planters set out on the road to Delfshaven where the *Speedwell* and its master, Reynolds, were ready to receive them. They were accompanied on that 24-mile trek by almost all who were to remain behind, many of their Dutch friends and a number of the curious. Some travelled by coach, others in wagons, on horseback and in many cases on foot – their baggage piled onto

A time for prayer during the Day of Solemn Humiliation as the Pilgrims prepare for departure from Delfshaven – "the prayers were urgent and said with fervour".

handcarts or strapped to their backs. Friends joined the procession from as far away as Amsterdam to add their good wishes and goodbyes and others trekked from towns and villages all over the Netherlands.

John Robinson's farewell address was long, full of exhortations to become close friends with the Pilgrims from England when they met them at Southampton, and he expressed the wish, nostalgically no doubt, that in his absence some other pastor would be found to guide them in their worship of God. It must have been in his mind that the spiritual need of the greater part of his flock in Leyden was not the only reason for leaving him behind; he must surely have heard some whisperings of the fact that he and his teachings and writings were not well received by their backers in England, being provocative to both King and leaders of the Anglican Church. Cushman's letter to John Carver mentioned a Master Crabe as a possible replacement for

Robinson, although in the event the opposition to him and his teachings proved even more pronounced than it was to Robinson's and he was left behind.

On the morning of Saturday 22nd July, the wind being fair and the tide full, the captain ordered his crew to prepare to put to sea.

The Pilgrims crowded aboard the *Speedwell* and John Robinson stepped onto the deck among them. He knelt and said a final, heartfelt prayer for the success of the enterprise. Then he shook hands all round and said his last farewells before stepping ashore – while those aboard the vessel and those on the quayside were too overcome by the solemnity of the occasion to do more than call a few parting words of encouragement and prayer.

Edward Winslow, who was one day to be governor of the colony, leaves a record of the last parting. He tells that as the ship slipped from the quay those aboard fired their muskets and three small cannons in salute. They then turned their eyes towards the harbour mouth – and the future.

The Pilgrims with their goods and livestock; in the background can be seen the *Mayflower* and *Speedwell*.

The crossing to England was made in calm, warm and balmy weather with just enough of a summery breeze to speed the passage of the little pilgrim ship, and four days later, on 26th July 1620, the *Speedwell* arrived at Southampton and the Leyden Pilgrims got their first sight of the *Mayflower*.

She was a square-rigged vessel of 120 tons, stoutly built, broad of beam and solid in appearance. She looked to be in sound condition, seamanlike in the way her master kept her and all ready for sea. They were to learn that the vessel was registered at Harwich, the home town of her master, Captain Jones – whose Christian name is thought to have been Christopher. He was part owner of the *Mayflower* and reputed to be a good seaman, proud and confident in his ship. He had had experience of the waters off Greenland in pursuit of whales, was said to be a kindly man, and was an excellent shot.

Of the crew we know little, except that the two master's mates were Robert Coppin the pilot and

John Clarke the second pilot. A third mate, Williamson, was also shipped for the voyage to America. The ship's surgeon was Giles Heale and a master gunner had charge of the ordnance taken to safeguard the Pilgrims in the New World.

Others shipped, besides the passengers and crew, included a cooper, John Alden, and four seamen: John Allerton, Thomas English – who was to be the master of the shallop that they were to use for fishing and communications – and Trevore and Ellis who were to stay with the Pilgrims for a year to help found the settlement. (Trevore and Ellis fulfilled their contract and then returned to England, Allerton and English died during the first epidemic of sickness and John Alden eventually married Priscilla Mullins and remained in New England as one of the colonists.)

As was the custom in the 17th century – and for

King Henry VIII's gun, close to the spot where the passengers
embarked for the *Mayflower* and the *Speedwell*.

some while thereafter – the Pilgrims took with them
their own provisions for the voyage: bedding, toiletry
and every other necessity – besides all the tools,
equipment and seeds they could expect to need when
they landed in America. They took aboard with
them, too, their dogs, and it is probable that they had
a few goats.

It seemed that all the frustrations that had dogged
the enterprise for the better part of three long years
were to be a thing of the past and the Pilgrims foresaw
the end of any further recriminations, petty
squabbles, administrative failures and heartbreaking
indecisions. On that fine warm day their hearts were
high.

But matters were not to go as smoothly as
everybody hoped. There had first to be a distribution
of accommodation in the two vessels between the
Leyden and the London emigrants, by no means an
easily settled affair when the families from London
had already staked out their claims in the larger ship
and were unwilling both to give them up and to
occupy less space. Nor were the two parties as yet on
friendly terms with one another – and to make
matters more difficult Cushman, the organizer on
behalf of those from Leyden, was barely on speaking
terms with Christopher Martin, his opposite number
among the Londoners.

The second problem to arise was the question of
the agreement between the Adventurers and the
Planters, concluded between Thomas Weston and
Robert Cushman – and for long enough the source of
friction beween Cushman and Robinson. The
Leyden Pilgrims had fully expected that the leading
members of the Company of Adventurers would be
at Southampton to meet them and to settle with them
the disputed terms of the agreement. But only
Thomas Weston turned up, intent on getting the
signatures of each of the emigrants to the Conditions
of Agreement as he had worded it, and quite
unprepared to renegotiate it.

And, thirdly, they were shocked to be told by the
master of the *Speedwell*, at so late a stage in the
proceedings, that his vessel was unfit for the voyage
across the Atlantic and needed some considerable
repairs to make it even seaworthy again. The instant
outcry was quelled by Reynolds, the master, who said
that the Pilgrims had only themselves to blame. It was
they who had ordered and carried out the refit to the
vessel in Delfshaven, without seeking any pro-
fessional advice and with the aid of unskilled labour
instead of qualified craftsmen.

There was no avoiding the need to put the vessel in
proper trim, but it meant that many of the Pilgrims
from Leyden, driven ashore to make way for the

carpenters, were stranded without even the means to rent accommodation in the town and had to find what shelter they could among the wharfside buildings.

Yet, even in these disheartening circumstances, they continued to stand firm in their refusal to sign the new conditions to the agreement.

The Elders met Weston in an attempt to assert their claim to a settlement on the original terms. They pointed out that they had been advised by John Robinson before leaving Holland not to agree to anything other than the original terms, and that they had no authority to vary them without the agreement of those left behind in Leyden.

Weston was angry and adamant about their refusal to accept the terms between Cushman and himself, and declared flatly that if they refused to sign "they must then look to stand on their own legs" – and returned to London.

On 3rd August a representative group of the Pilgrims despairingly wrote to the Company of Adventurers in conciliatory terms in the hope of finding some area of agreement that would satisfy both parties and ease their own straitened circumstances. They pointed out that Cushman had agreed the terms without the full knowledge of the community, and referred them to the clauses at issue. They reminded the Adventurers that Thomas Weston had in fact agreed the original terms before leaving Holland to consult with them – and the Pilgrims had accepted that agreement in good faith and as binding to both parties. In that understanding they had paid over such sums of money as they had agreed as being their share of the cost of the enterprise.

The letter then reiterated their complaint that they found themselves saddled with an agreement negotiated without their knowledge or assent. In fact, they claimed that until Weston presented them with the new agreement to sign in Southampton they had seen nothing of it. The letter persisted in making the point that Robert Cushman never had the authority to negotiate beyond the original agreement and that he had merely been sent to England to receive the monies due under it and to set in motion the plans for the move to America.

Such statements reflect little credit on the writers of that letter: there had been much acrimonious correspondence on the subject of the agreement and a lot of discussion; some had refused to leave Holland under the new conditions. Besides, in their talks with Thomas Weston before he left for London a few days earlier, they had told him they had been warned in Holland not to sign the new agreement.

The Pilgrims offered to compromise by undertaking, if the venture was profitable in the seven years of its contracted life, that they would be willing to continue the profit-sharing basis for a longer period – provided the original agreement, on all other counts, was accepted by the Adventurers.

The letter concluded with a plea for some understanding to their plight at Southampton. The delay had already resulted in so much extra expense to the Pilgrims that they had been compelled to sell much of their essential provisions for £60 to clear them of debt before they could leave England. They claimed, pathetically, that they were "scarce having any butter, no oil, not a sole to mend a shoe, nor every man a sword to his side, wanting many muskets, much armour, etc".

The cries of "poverty" are not easily construed centuries later but it cannot escape notice that of the 102 passengers who finally crossed the Atlantic there were no fewer than fifteen servants. John Carver took 3 menservants and 1 maidservant, Edward Winslow 2 menservants, Isaac Allerton 1 servantboy, Samuel Fuller (a Dean and their surgeon) 1 manservant, Christopher Martin 2 menservants, William Mullins 1 manservant, William White 2 menservants and Stephen Hopkins 2 menservants.

We know that there was no set level of wealth in the Pilgrim Church; some had more – some much more – than others, but so many servants suggests that there were still some considerable resources available to the Planters, even if it was likely that some of the servants clung to their masters merely for the sake of their keep, food being the prime and most valuable commodity in such a venture.

9 Setbacks in English Waters

The *Speedwell* was ready to sail by 5th August 1620, only two days after the Pilgrims' letter to the Company of Adventurers in London had been written.

Some satisfactory rearrangement of passengers and their accommodation in the two vessels had been accomplished, although not without some considerable argument – and, we must assume, some speedy compromise concerning the agreement, although it still remained unsigned.

The emigrants and crews boarded their vessels, checked the equipment, hoisted in the longboats, secured the shallop and made ready for sea. Immediately before they cast off, a last letter from John Robinson, their pastor in Leyden, was read to the assembled company. It was, as was usual with 17th-century correspondence, lengthy, loquacious and flowery. Its message was in the nature of a parting sermon, because they had no minister with them, and urged upon them five points in their future conduct. They were to seek the guidance of God, be of good behaviour, be charitable to the strangers with whom they were to mingle, work for the common good, and elect a Civil Government from among themselves. The latter was the most significant exhortation and the Planters acted on it at once. For the duration of the voyage they elected a governor and two or three assistants for each ship with authority over everybody concerned.

Christopher Martin, probably because he was the acknowledged representative of the larger group of emigrants from London, was elected Governor of the *Mayflower* and Robert Cushman as one of his assistants – which meant that Cushman, who had until then controlled the financial affairs of the Planters, had to relinquish the cash in hand and the accounts to Martin. John Carver was appointed Governor aboard the *Speedwell*.

But no organization, however well founded, was going to be effective in a leaky ship – as the *Speedwell* proved itself to be, almost before it turned onto a westerly course in the Channel. In a calm sea with only a light wind, Reynolds shocked his passengers by reporting that his ship was leaking so badly that he dared not face the open sea. Ship's Governor Carver and his assistants rushed below to examine the hull under the waterline and check the damage, and were quickly convinced that the vessel was taking in more water than the pumps could handle.

Carver signalled the *Mayflower* to come alongside; as soon as it was within hailing distance he told Captain Jones the position and asked for his advice. Jones could offer no immediate solution and

The Pilgrim Fathers leaving Portsmouth Harbour; from the colour print by Gustave Alaux.

DARTMOUTH, DEVON, ENGLAND.

This plaque commemorates the time the Pilgrims spent at anchor off Bayard's Cove, Dartmouth.

suggested that the ship would have to put back towards the nearest harbour where a closer examination could be made and, if necessary, proper repairs could be carried out. It was decided to make for Dartmouth as the most convenient haven, and both vessels veered towards it.

A thorough examination of the hull from stem to stern was carried out, this time by qualified shipwrights, while the passengers and crew of the two ships controlled their impatience as best they could. The result came soon enough – and certain enough: until the leaks discovered by the examiners had been efficiently stopped there could be no hope of the *Speedwell* putting to sea again.

This further delay, and the additional expense, did much to dampen the enthusiasm of the emigrants – who had already endured almost too many disappointments and frustrations since the move to Virginia had first been mooted.

Robert Cushman, who had been the cause of so much dissension among the Pilgrims, was already deeply upset because of the criticisms to which he had been subjected from all sides. His failure to win the election for the governorship of the *Mayflower*, and the fact that in consequence he had to hand over the financial control of the enterprise to Christopher Martin, had added sorely to his depression, so that this latest setback brought on a nervous illness and he had to be taken ashore.

From there he wrote to a Separatist friend of his, Edward Southworth, who lived in Duke's Place, Aldgate, London – a district that was strangely free from molestation by the Anglicans because it happened that no church existed in the parish and

The *Mayflower* and *Speedwell* in Dartmouth Harbour, where the
latter vessel was examined yet again for faults in preparation for a
further attempt to cross the Atlantic.

there were no clergy to report on the activities of the
Separatists. He told Southworth of his utter
depression and of how his health and spirits had
suffered because of the series of ill-fortunes that
continued to frustrate the expedition. He explained
that in this latest setback, "... if we had stayed at sea
but three or four hours more she would have sunk
right down. And though she was twice trimmed at
Hampton, yet now she is as open and leaky as a sieve,
and there was a board two feet long, a man might
have pulled off with his fingers, where the water came
in as at a mole hole."

Cushman complained that by the time they left
England they would have consumed half their
victuals and were likely to land in America with less
than a month's provisions to last them through until
their first harvest. Nor was he himself to be free of
further trouble, despite the fact that he was ill and no
longer had any office in the enterprise. His letter went
on to tell of how he had been inundated with
arguments and complaints about the conduct of
affairs, and he wrote bitterly that Martin had spent
£700 during their stay in Southampton – the total
sum invested by the London Adventurers.
Challenged to account for the way the money had
been spent, Martin had become indignant and refused;
careless of the distrust that was instantly aroused, he

declared the Leyden Pilgrims to be a "froward and
waspish, discontented people..." and made no effort
to comply with their request. Cushman claimed,
probably with good cause, that by now many of the
emigrants would gladly have abandoned the journey
if they could have got their money back – but his
emphasis on the fact that Martin would not allow
them ashore in case they deserted must be highly
suspect.

Then he aimed his barbs at John Robinson,
complaining bitterly that the pastor had advised the
Pilgrims not to sign the agreement with the
Adventurers; and, perhaps significantly, he accuses
him also of warning the Leyden Pilgrims not to
choose Cushman for any office in the enterprise – a
most unlikely action on Robinson's part from distant
Holland, and there is no trace of any such suggestion
in Robinson's extant letters to the Elders aboard the
ships. Finally, Cushman warned his friend that it
would be a miracle if they ever established a
plantation in the New World and that violence would
break out among them all before the task was
completed.

Altogether, a deplorable letter from a discredited
representative, an offended Elder and a totally
disheartened man.

There was a resurgence of hope when the *Speedwell*

Dartmouth Castle as it must have been around the time that the
Mayflower and *Speedwell* were in the harbour.

was again fit for sea and some of the bitterness and
frustrations were forgotten, at any rate for the time
being. On 23rd August, with 120 passengers crowded
aboard the two vessels, the *Mayflower* and the
Speedwell cast off and worked their way out into the
Channel, swung their bows towards the west and
breasted the broad Atlantic swell.

But the trials and troubles of the Pilgrim Fathers
were by no means things of the past when the
southernmost and most westerly tip of England sank
from their sight below the horizon. Before they had
sailed the first hundred leagues (300 nautical miles) of
that three-thousand-mile voyage, and just as the
passengers must have been settling down into what
little comfort they could find, Reynolds, master of the
Speedwell, once again raised the cry that his ship was
leaking badly and in danger of sinking.

Again Carver and his assistants made a rapid
survey of the bilges and discovered that, even with the
pumps at full pressure, they could not hold back the
steadily encroaching sea. The decision to put about
and make for land before the ship sank was
inescapable. With the *Mayflower* close alongside,
Carver explained the situation to Captain Jones: a
hurried consultation but the Captain could offer no
alternative solution; it was impossible to examine the

ship from outboard in an Atlantic swell and there
could be no doubt that she was, in any event, making
water faster than it could be checked. Nor, as Jones
explained, even if they could trace the source of the
leaks, was it practicable to make underwater repairs
at sea.

The emigrants watched in frustrated, bitter
despair as Reynolds turned his ship about and as
Captain Jones, worried for the safety of the leaking
Speedwell and all aboard her, altered course to escort
the crippled ship back to England.

The little fleet reached Plymouth after a slow,
wallowing and anxious journey, fraught with the need
to hoist as little sail on the *Spedwell* as possible
to prevent the overlarge masts whipping in the breeze
and opening the split seams further, to manoeuvre so
as to ride the waves lightly and to keep all hands
busy at the heavy task of manning the pumps or
baling out. And it was a thoroughly exhausted and
dejected ship's company that had to be landed at
Plymouth Hoe to make way for yet another
examination of the ship's hull below the waterline.

The examination was more protracted this time
and very thorough, but fortunately the people of
Plymouth took compassion on the stranded Pilgrims
and did what they could to help them in their distress.

Few had the means to pay for accommodation ashore and all of them had to live on the ship's stores, but through the kindness of the citizens none of them were allowed to come to any harm.

The examination of the *Speedwell* revealed little in the way of parted timbers or any other obvious source of leaks, but the bilges *had* been waterlogged, which suggested that the movement of the vessel through the water and the strain from the heavy masts, even in the lightest of breezes, tended to open up one or more of the seams – which closed again as soon as the pressure was eased. The shipwright's report indicated that, for the ship to be made thoroughly seaworthy and fit for an Atlantic voyage, it would require to be rerigged – an expensive and lengthy business that could not be borne by the Pilgrims.

There was the usual outcry against those who had recommended the purchase of the vessel and, at the instigation of Captain Reynolds, against those who had organized the refitting of the ship at Delfshaven. Only later – much later, and after a great deal of thought – was the fault placed squarely with the master. He and his crew had been hired to spend a year in America helping the colonists establish a settlement there; very early in the proceedings they had begun to regret their contract. The wily Reynolds had seen the means to extricate himself and his crew from the expedition and had taken advantage of the inept fitting-out. All he had

had to do was to crowd sail onto the over-large and too-tall masts to strain the hull where they had been stepped, and so open up the seams until he eased the pressure on the planks by reducing sail again.

It is reasonable, however, to consider why Reynolds and his crew had come to regret their bargain. They had seen the way in which their employers had refitted the *Speedwell* at Delfshaven, they were certainly aware of the last-minute chaos over the allocation of accommodation, the extent of the overcrowding when it was realized that the *Mayflower* was smaller than the vessel they had expected to meet at Southampton, seen and heard the protracted and bitter arguments with Cushman and Weston over the agreement to finance the expedition – and had been thoroughly alarmed by the sale of a substantial part of the settlers' provisions to pay their debts in England.

But whatever the real cause of the dangerous state of the *Speedwell*, it seemed at the time that there was no alternative but to leave the vessel behind and to sell it. The funds received from its sale would at least ease the total indebtedness of the Pilgrims to shipwrights, carpenters and harbour masters.

But such a decision was easier to make than to carry into effect. It was obviously impossible to transfer all the passengers from the *Speedwell* to the already over-crowded *Mayflower*. The problem was made simpler, however, by the willingness – the very ready willingness – of eighteen of the Pilgrims to sacrifice their places and remain behind. Not unexpectedly Robert Cushman had again to be

The *Mayflower* and *Speedwell* leaving Dartmouth Harbour.

PILGRIM FATHERS WHO SAILED FROM HERE
THE BARBICAN, PLYMOUTH, IN THE MAYFLOWER, 1620

MASTER WILL BRADFORD	FUSTIAN MAKER AUSTERF D.YORKS
JOHN CARVER	MERCHANT OF DONCASTER.
MASTER EDW'D WINSLOW	PRINTER OF DROITWICH.
MASTER WILL BREWSTER	POSTMASTER, TUTOR, ETC.
MASTER ISAAC ALLERTON	TAILOR OF LONDON.
CAPT. MYLES STANDISH	SOLDIER OF CHORLEY, LANCS.
MASTER STEP'N HOPKINS	WOTTON UNDER EDGE GLOUCS'TR.
MASTER CHRIS MARTIN	GREAT BURSTEAD ESSEX.
MASTER WILL MULLINS	SHOPKEEPER DORKING, SURREY.
MASTER WILL WHITE	WOOL CARDER.
MASTER RICH WARREN	MERCHANT OF LONDON.
EDWARD TILLEY	CLOTH MAKER OF LONDON.
JOHN TILLEY	SILK WORKER OF LONDON.
PETER BROWNE	GREAT BURSTEAD ESSEX
FRANCIS EATON	CARPENTER OF BRISTOL.
FRANCIS COOK	WOOL COMBER OF BLYTH
THOMAS ENGLISH	MARINER.
THOMAS TINKER	WOOD SAWYER.
THOMAS ROGERS	MERCHANT.
JOHN RINGDALE	LONDON.
EDWARD FULLER	REDENHALL NORFOLK.
JOHN TURNER	MERCHANT.
JAMES CHILTON	TAILOR OF CANTERBURY.
JOHN CRACKSTON	COLCHESTER.
JOHN BILLINGTON	LONDON.
RICH BRITTERIDGE	GREAT BURSTEAD ESSEX.
RICHARD GARDINER	HARWICH ESSEX.
MOSES FLETCHER	SMITH OF SANDWICH.
JOHN ALDEN	COOPER OF HARWICH.
SAMUEL FULLER	SAIL MAKER.
JOHN GOODMAN	LINEN WEAVER.
DEGORY PRIEST	HATTER OF LONDON.
THOMAS WILLIAMS	YARMOUTH NORFOLK.
JOHN ALLERTON	MARINER.
JOHN HOOKE	SERVANT BOY.
RICHARD MORE	LONDON.
ROGER WILDER	MAN SERVANT.
WILLIAM LATHAM	SERVANT BOY.
JOHN HOWLAND	LONDON.
WILLIAM BUTTEN	AUSTEREIELD.
RICHARD CLARKE	EDMOND MARGESON
GILBERT WINSLOW	JASPER MORE.
EDWARD DOTEY	EDWARD LEISTER.
JOHN LANGEMORE	ROBERT CARTER.
WILLIAM HOLBECK	EDWARD THOMPSON.
GEORGE SOULE	ELIAS STORY.

The plaque at Plymouth, Devon, commemorating the sailing of the Pilgrim Fathers.

The Pilgrims prepare to board the *Mayflower* in Plymouth Harbour; a drawing by M. J. Jeffries.

taken ashore; he had had enough by now and "volunteered" to be left behind with the members of his family.

The stores were transferred from the *Speedwell* to the *Mayflower*, although much ingenuity was needed to find room for them. There were now 102 passengers aboard the *Mayflower* – 35 from the church in Leyden and 67 from England – besides the crew – crowded almost to the limit of human endurance. They were to become known as the "Forefathers" among the Pilgrim Fathers.

William Bradford, who was in his turn to serve as Governor of the Colony in New England, and as the recorder of much of its history, has left us a complete list of the Forefathers who sailed with the *Mayflower* when it finally left England.

The 1st household:

1. *John Carver*, destined to become the first Governor of the colony. He died at Plymouth, New England, in April 1621.

2. *Catherine Carver*, his wife, who died in Plymouth, New England, two months after her husband.

3. *Desire Minter*, who eventually returned to England and died there.

4. *John Howland*, a manservant who subsequently married *Elizabeth Tilley*, the daughter of John Tilley. From that union ten children were born; the eldest daughter had four children of her own by 1650, and their second daughter one. John Howland died at Plymouth, New England, in 1673.

5. *Roger Wilder*, a manservant who died in the Spring epidemic of 1621 at Plymouth, New England.

6. *William Latham*, a servant boy who, after spending twenty years in the colony, moved away and died of starvation in the Bahamas some time after 1641.

7. *A maidservant* whose name we do not know. The only information concerning her that has come down to us is that she married in Plymouth, New England, and died there a few years later.

8. *Jasper More*, a boy attached to the Carver household. He died in Cape Cod harbour aboard the *Mayflower* on 6th December 1620.

The 2nd household:

9. *William Brewster*, the Ruling Elder. He died at Duxbury, one of the satellite townships that the Pilgrim Fathers eventually established within a few miles of their settlement at Plymouth, on 10th April 1644 at the age of about 80.

10. *Mary Brewster*, his wife, who died at Plymouth, New England, some time before 1627 but, it is believed, at a ripe old age.

11. *Love Brewster*, their son, who died at Duxbury, New England, in 1650, survived by four children.

12. *Wrastle Brewster*, another son who died young and unmarried, although the actual date and whereabouts are not known. It is likely that his death occurred before his father moved from Plymouth to Duxbury.

13. *Richard More*, a boy attached to the family. He married, had four children, changed his name to Mann and died at Scituate, another off-shoot township of Plymouth, New England, in 1656. One of Jasper More's two brothers.

14. *Another boy named More*, brother of Jasper and Richard, whose christian name is not recorded. He died in the Spring epidemic at Plymouth, New England, in the early months of 1621.

The 3rd household:

15. *Edward Winslow*, Governor of the colony 1644–1645. His first wife, whom he married at Leyden, Holland, in 1618, died during the first winter in America, on 24th March 1621. He married again in May 1621, the first marriage to be celebrated in the New England colonies. His second wife was Susannah, widow of William White and mother of Peregrine White, the first English child to be born in New England.

Edward Winslow was often chosen to represent the colonists in England and in 1643 was one of the Commissioners of the United Colonies of New England. He returned to England for the last time in October 1646 and spent nine years holding various offices under Cromwell. He left two children behind him after his death at sea in the West Indies in 1655.

16. *Elizabeth Winslow*, first wife of Edward Winslow. Died during the Spring epidemic, 24th March 1621.

17. *George Sowle*, a manservant who died at Duxbury, New England, in 1680, survived by eight children.

18. *Elias Story*, a manservant who died at Plymouth, New England, during the Spring epidemic of 1621.

19. *Ellen More*, a young girl and sister of the three boys attached to other Pilgrim families; another who died during the Spring epidemic of 1621 in Plymouth, New England.

The 4th household:

20. *William Bradford*, who was to be elected Governor of the colony after the death of Governor John Carver in 1621, which office he was to hold, except for a period of five years, for the rest of his life. He married for the second time in America. He died at Plymouth, New England, on 9th May 1657, in his 68th year, "lamented by all the Colonies of New England as a common Blessing and Father of them all."

21. *Dorothy Bradford*, his first wife, tragically drowned in Cape Cod harbour on 7th December 1620.

The 5th household:

22. *Isaac Allerton*, whose second wife, a daughter of William Brewster, joined the settlers at a later date. He had one son by her before she died. Allerton married for a third time. He died at New Haven, Connecticut, in 1659.

23. *Mary Allerton*, his first wife, who died on 25th February 1621, in the Spring epidemic.

24. *Bartholomew Allerton*, their son, who returned to England where he married and, presumably, died.

25. *Remember Allerton*, their daughter, who married Moses Maverick and died at some date subsequent to 1652 at Salem, New England.

26. *Mary Allerton*, another daughter, who married Thomas Cushman. (No relation, as far as is known, to Robert Cushman.) She died at Plymouth, New England, in 1699, the last survivor of all who sailed to America in the *Mayflower*.

27. *John Hooke*, a servantboy who died in the Spring epidemic of 1621.

The 6th household:

28. *Samuel Fuller*, Deacon and surgeon. His wife followed him to New England at a later date. He died at Plymouth, New England, in 1633.

29. *William Butten*, his manservant, who died aboard the *Mayflower* as it neared the coast of New England on 6th November 1620.

The 7th household:

30. *John Crackston*, who died in the Spring epidemic of 1621.

31. *John Crackston*, his son, who died in 1628 at Plymouth, New England, after an accident when he lost his way in the depths of winter. One of his feet was badly frozen and the subsequent fever brought about his death.

The 8th household:

32. *Miles Standish*, an ex-army captain who had served in the Netherlands. Appointed military captain of the Pilgrim settlement at Plymouth, New England, although he was never a member of the Pilgrim Church. He represented the settlers in England 1625–6 and helped to buy out the Merchant

The Pilgrims being treated hospitably at the Island House, Plymouth, by the local residents; a drawing executed by M. J. Jeffries at the time of the commemoration of the 350th anniversary of the *Mayflower*'s sailing.

Adventurers. He married for a second time and moved to Duxbury in 1632, when it was first settled, and died there in 1656.

33. *Rose Standish*, his first wife, who died in the epidemic at Plymouth on 29th January 1621.

The 9th household:

34. *Christopher Martin*, the Treasurer for the Pilgrim Fathers in succession to Robert Cushman, and appointed as such before leaving England in 1620. He died in the first epidemic aboard the *Mayflower* as it lay off Plymouth, New England, on 8th January 1621.

35. *His wife*, whose name has not been preserved in the records and who died in Plymouth later in the epidemic of Spring 1621.

36. *Solomon Prower*, a manservant who died during the early epidemic at Plymouth on 24th December 1620.

The Old Guildhall and Fydell House at Boston, Lincolnshire.

A modern view of the waterfront at Leyden (or Leiden).

The stone just visible in the foreground bearing the name *Mayflower* marks the site of the Pilgrim Fathers' embarkation.

(opposite above) A house similar to those built by the first settlers at Jamestown, Virginia. Jamestown was the first permanent English settlement in America.
(opposite below) One of the three ships which landed at Jamestown, Virginia, in May 1607.

37. *John Langemore*, a manservant who died at Plymouth during the epidemic of December 1620.

The 10th household:

38. *William Mullins*, died during the epidemic in Plymouth on 21st February 1621.

39. *His wife*, whose christian name is not recorded and who died during the Spring epidemic of 1621.

40. *Joseph Mullins*, their son, still a child; the third member of the family to die in the 1621 epidemic at Plymouth.

41. *Priscilla Mullins*, their young daughter, the only one of the family to survive the winter of 1620–1. In due time she married John Alden, a cooper who had been hired to accompany the Pilgrims to help in the establishment of the settlement. He elected to remain there when his contract expired. By 1650 they had

eleven children, their eldest daughter having five of her own. Priscilla died at Duxbury, New England, at some date after 1650.

42. *Robert Carter*, a manservant who died during the Spring epidemic of 1621.

The 11th household:

43. *William White*, another victim of the epidemic at Plymouth, on 21st February 1621.

44. *Susannah White*, his wife, who afterwards married Edward Winslow. She died at Marshfield, New England, 1680.

45. *Resolved White*, their son, who married, had five children by 1650 and died at Salem, New England, some time after 1680.

(*Peregrine White*, their infant son, who was born on board the *Mayflower* in Cape Cod harbour, in December 1620 – the first English child to be born in New England. He married in due time, had two children before 1650 and died at Marshfield, New England, on 20th July 1704.)

46. *William Holbeck*, a manservant who died at Plymouth during the Spring epidemic of 1621.

47. *Edward Thompson*, a manservant who died aboard the *Mayflower* in Cape Cod harbour on 4th December 1620, the first of the Pilgrims to die in New England.

The 12th household:

48. *Stephen Hopkins*, from London. He died at Plymouth in 1644.

49. *Elizabeth Hopkins*, his wife, died at Plymouth at some date after 1640.

50. *Giles Hopkins*, his son by a former wife. He married and died – at Yarmouth, New England, in 1690.

51. *Constance Hopkins*, his daughter by a former wife. She married Nicholas Snow and died at Eastham, New England, 1677.

52. *Damaris Hopkins*, a daughter by his marriage to Elizabeth, who married Jacob Cooke in Plymouth, New England, and died there some time between 1666 and 1669.

(*Oceanus Hopkins*, a son, born on board the *Mayflower* while it was still at sea, but died at Plymouth in 1621.)

53. *Edward Dotey*, a manservant from London who married, for the second time, in New England, had seven children, and died at Yarmouth, New England, in 1655.

54. *Edward Leister*, a manservant who, once he had served his time with the Hopkins family, made his way south to Virginia, where he died.

The 13th household:

55. *Richard Warren*, left his wife and children behind in London to follow him to America at a later date. Five daughters subsequently joined him with his wife in Plymouth, and two sons were born to them in America. He died at Plymouth in 1628.

The 14th household:

56. *John Billington*, whom Governor Bradford described as "being [of] one of the profanest families amongst them. They came from London: and I know not, by what friends, shuffled into this company." Billington was constantly punished for various offences and was hanged in October 1630 for the murder of John Newcomen.

57. *Ellen Billington*, his wife, who in 1638 married Gregory Armstrong.

58. *John Billington*, their son, as intractable as his father, who died before him.

59. *Francis Billington*, another son, who married and had eight children. He died at Yarmouth, New England, in 1650.

The 15th household:

60. *Edward Tilley*, who died in the first epidemic in 1621 in Plymouth.

61. *Ann Tilley*, his wife, who died during the same epidemic.

62. *Henry Samson*, their cousin but only a child. He married, had seven children by 1650, and died at Duxbury, New England, in 1684.

63. *Humility Cooper*, another cousin and also a child, who "was sent for into England; and died there".

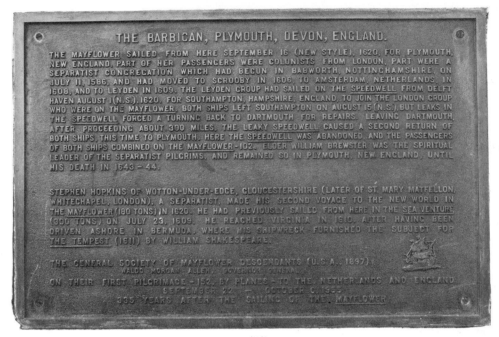

This plaque was erected in 1955 on the 335th anniversary of the pilgrims' voyage by the General Society of Mayflower Descendants.

The 16th household:

64. *John Tilley*, died at Plymouth during the epidemic of 1621.

65. *His wife*, whose name we do not know, and who died in that same epidemic.

66. *Elizabeth Tilley*, their daughter. She married John Howland and died at Plymouth, New England, in 1687.

The 17th household:

67. *Francis Cooke*, who was to be followed by his wife and two of their children at a later date. He was a great-grandfather many times over by 1650 and died at Plymouth in 1663.

68. *John Cooke*, his son, who married, had four children before 1650 and lived until 1694. He died at Dartmouth, New England.

The 18th household:

69. *Thomas Rogers*, died in the epidemic of 1621.

70. *Joseph Rogers*, his son, whose brothers and sisters joined him in New England later. He married, had six children and died at Eastham, New England, in 1678.

The 19th household:

71. *Thomas Tinker*, who died in the epidemic of 1621.

72. *His wife*, whose name is not recorded.

73. *Their son*, whose name too has not been preserved. He and his mother died in that same epidemic.

The 20th household:

74. *John Rigdale*.

75. *Alice Rigdale*, his wife, both of whom fell victims to the Spring epidemic of 1621.

The 21st household:

76. *James Chilton*, who died aboard the *Mayflower* as it lay in Cape Cod harbour on 8th December 1620.

77. *His wife*, whose name has not been preserved and who died shortly afterwards at Plymouth during the 1621 Spring epidemic.

78. *Mary Chilton*, their daughter. She married John Winslow, brother of Governor Edward Winslow, had nine children before 1650 and died at Boston, New England, in 1679.

The 22nd household:

79. *Edward Fuller.*

80. *His wife*, whose name we do not know. Both were victims of the Spring epidemic at Plymouth in 1621.

81. *Samuel Fuller*, their son, a child who married in due time, and died at Barnstable, New England, 1683.

The 23rd household:

82. *John Turner.*

83. *A son, unnamed.*

84. *A second son*, also unnamed. All three of them died at Plymouth, New England during the Spring epidemic of 1621. The family was not entirely wiped out, as a daughter who had been left behind in England emigrated to Salem, New England, some years later and was living there, married, in 1650, though there is no later record of her life and death.

The 24th household:

85. *Francis Eaton*, who married for the second time and who, after that second wife died, married for the third time. He died at Plymouth in 1633.

86. *Sarah Eaton*, his first wife, who died in the epidemic of 1621.

87. *Samuel Eaton*, a son, a baby-in-arms who in course of time married. He died at Middlesborough, New England, in 1648.

The following were single men who died in the epidemics that caused so many deaths at Plymouth, New England, during the first long winter there, 1620/21.

88. *Moses Fletcher.*

89. *Thomas Williams.*

90. *John Goodman.*

91. *Edmund Margeson.*

92. *Richard Clarke.*

93. *Richard Britteridge*, who died aboard the *Mayflower*, as it lay in Plymouth harbour, New England, on 21st December 1620.

94. *Degory Priest*, who died on 1st January 1621, at Plymouth, New England. His wife and children subsequently arrived in New England; she was the sister of Isaac Allerton.

Only three of the single men survived that dreadful epidemic:

95. *Richard Gardiner*, who later became a seaman and died abroad.

96. *Gilbert Winslow*, another brother of Governor Edward Winslow who eventually returned to England and died there.

97. *Peter Browne*, who married twice in New England and had two children by each of his wives. He died at Plymouth, New England, in 1633.

There were also five hired men with the Pilgrims:

98. *John Alden*, who was engaged at Southampton as a cooper and who eventually elected to remain in New England. He married Priscilla, the daughter of William Mullins, and died at Duxbury, New England, in 1687.

99. *John Allerton*, who was hired in London as a sailor, although it is said that he was, in fact, one of the Pilgrims. He was to have returned to England to collect the second party of emigrants but he died in the Spring epidemic of 1621.

100. *Thomas English*, a sailor who was engaged as master of the shallop. He died in the epidemic of 1621.

101. *William Trevore*, a sailor.

102. *Ellis*, another sailor, whose christian name we do not know. Both of these were hired to stay a year in the colony; both returned to England when their contracts expired.

The foregoing list of passengers who crossed to New England in the *Mayflower* – the "First Comers" or the "Old Stock" as they were sometimes called – comprises the élite, historically, among the Pilgrim Fathers. Generally, those who can lay claim to the title "Pilgrim Father" include all the members of the Pilgrim Church at Leyden who voted for the migration to America, whether or not they were able to go, together with those from England who joined them later.

10 The Atlantic Crossing

No shipbuilders' plans for the *Mayflower* exist, but it seems that she was of weight about 120 tons and of length a mere 90 feet or so: a very small vessel to face the hazards of the Atlantic and to bear so many people.

On 6th September 1620 Captain Jones dropped down the companion-ladder to his private quarters, immediately below the poop deck and flush with the maindeck, and prepared to have a final conference with Christopher Martin, the Ship's Governor, his Assistants, and the senior Master's Mate, Robert Coppin.

The Master's Mate would report that the stores, including those transferred from the *Speedwell*, had been restowed and secured so that they would not shift in heavy seas, that the shallop had been taken apart and distributed in the holds to serve as partitions and tables until it was required again on the other side of the Atlantic, and that the hatches that opened up through each of the decks just forward of the main-mast had been battened down. He would inform the Master, too, that the running gear was all in working order and that the crew were aboard and ready to sail.

Ship's Governor Martin would then report that the 102 passengers were already crowded into the chill, dark and bleak spaces between decks to lay out their bedding wherever they could find room, and to devise the erection of partitions and furnishings to suit themselves, to create play-spaces for the children,

This artist's impression of a cross-section of the *Mayflower* indicates the appalling overcrowding the Pilgrim Fathers must have suffered.

messing arrangements for them all and to organize times for ablutions, toilets, meals – and even religious meetings.

Once he was satisfied that everything was in order and the ship ready to put to sea, Captain Jones returned to the poop, and ordered the shore-lines to be cast off. With a wisp of sail at the foremast, he eased the *Mayflower* clear of the Barbican steps . . . and the last link with England was cut.

As she headed out into the Channel, she met a light wind blowing from the east-north-east and the Captain hoisted sufficient sail to take advantage of it. He swung the ship to pass at a safe distance from the treacherous Eddystone Rocks before turning to the south-west.

Some hours later they sighted the Manacles, turned a few points onto a more westerly heading and began to pitch in the long, rolling swell of the Atlantic – and before she slipped by the Scilly Isles, leaving them on the starboard beam, the majority of the passengers were suffering from seasickness.

The emigrants received little sympathy from the crew. Apart from the fact that they lived in an age when common miseries were rarely shared beyond the ties of a family, the crew had seen far too much of the frequent bitter arguments, accusations, lack of leadership and disorganization that had been prevalent among the Pilgrims since the moment they had stepped aboard the *Mayflower* at Southampton six weeks earlier, and looked upon them as an ill

The *Mayflower* in high seas. For much of the voyage she was troubled by adverse weather – to the considerable misfortune of the overcrowded Pilgrims.

disciplined, bad-tempered and discontented mob.

Nor did they receive much consideration from the ship's Master. He had fully expected to sail from Southampton not later than the end of July and, with the summer weather covering the Atlantic, to make a quick passage with the prospect of reaching America not later than mid-September. But now six valuable weeks had slipped by. Although no threat of high seas showed as yet, Captain Jones knew that he could now expect to meet stormy seas and contrary winds long before he sighted the American coast, bringing with them the certainty of a great deal of discomfort aboard and some considerable danger to the heavily loaded vessel.

So little regard had he for them that despite a high reputation for being a kindly and considerate man he refused to interfere in any disputes between crew and passengers – so long as the Pilgrims made no attempt to disorganize the ship's management and navigation.

Captain Jones made no move even to control a particular foul-mouthed seaman who taunted the Pilgrims persistently and in the most obnoxious terms, who threatened to rob them of their possessions and to throw overboard any of them who got in his way. Protests, even from the Elders, met with no response from the Captain and merely drove the ugly-tempered seaman to fresh outbursts of bitingly cruel obscenities and threats of violence. But in the end, according to the Pilgrim Fathers, God intervened to put a stop to this persecution and to punish their persecutor – in an unexpectedly final manner.

Before the ship reached mid-Atlantic the seaman was suddenly taken ill with a disease that wracked his body with pain. Within days he knew that he would die and that there was no way of easing his passing. And die he did, in agony – and his body was thrown overboard.

The first days of the voyage passed with fair winds, gently rolling seas and under the warm skies that were to be expected in early September in those waters, but the Captain kept a wary and anxious eye on the heavy cloud banks that hovered over the northern horizon, threatening the onset of winter.

In those balmy days, not being weatherwise and having quickly recovered from their seasickness, the Pilgrims took advantage of the conditions and the fine warm breezes to wash their clothing and to dry them in the rigging, to ease their cramped bodies with exercise on the main deck unimpeded by a crew that could, for the time being, take things easy, and troubled only by the need to keep their children from mischief and from tumbling into the sea.

As the days passed, the black clouds to the north began to lumber heavily across the sky towards them, spreading out into great grey, rolling waves that gradually drew a pall between the *Mayflower* and the sunny skies above it. A drizzle of rain began to dampen the bulwarks and the deck, turning into a chill rainfall that drove all but the most hardy of the Pilgrims – and those who could not stomach the foul atmosphere below – to abandon the open deck.

As the days drew into weeks, the weather steadily deteriorated; gale force winds blew up and the sea rose until the *Mayflower* found herself in the middle of a series of fierce storms. Below decks the air grew stale, fetid and vitiated. Attempts to relieve the stench and to drive out the stale air by opening the scuttles and hatches were frustrated by the rush of seawater that soaked the bedding, the clothing and the bodies of the passengers. Seasickness broke out again and in the dank, stuffy stench in the passenger holds, conditions became almost intolerable.

In the middle of all this misery in a wildly tossing ship, the strain of the wind on the top-hamper began to test the seams below, to cause some leakage and more steaming dampness in the confined, over-crowded spaces between decks. But worse was to follow; one of the ship's main beams bowed and cracked under the pressure.

At first the Captain made no effort to warn his passengers of the danger, probably fearing panic among the women and children, but there was no disguising the seriousness of the situation for long. The ship lay hove-to in the trough of the waves; water was seeping in everywhere; there was the scared, over-anxiousness of the crew; all these gave their own warning of impending disaster. Then, prodded into action by the badly frightened Pilgrims, the Ship's Governor and his Assistants cornered the Captain and demanded to know what was happening.

Realizing that any further attempt at secrecy was more likely to create panic than to prevent it, the Captain called together the senior members of his crew and of the passengers to meet him in his quarters under the poop deck. Then he put the true position to them. One of the main beams that held the ship's hull firmly in position, had cracked and was in imminent danger of breaking in two. If this happened, he

One of the Bibles carried aboard the *Mayflower*.

explained, the ship would begin to break up. In the meantime he could do no more than ride out the storm by nursing the vessel gently into the wind.

Captain Jones had to admit too, that he was by now not at all sure of his position. The *Mayflower* had sailed, as near as the pilots could reckon in the stormy conditions, about halfway across the Atlantic.

Some of the officers were quick to point out that the prevailing winds and currents ran strongly in an easterly direction and that it would be wiser to try to return to England than to risk finding a safe haven anywhere else – or even to try holding their present position against the elements. They pointed out that in that direction they could hope to meet a friendly ship or finally find a safe haven where they could expect to be provided with food and shelter until the storm abated. In the other direction lay the unknown almost total isolation, no well charted harbours, no friendly welcome but possible starvation after being lost to the civilized world.

Other members of the crew were prepared to press on; their earnings from the voyage were urgently needed by wives and families at home, and there could be little for them if they failed to fulfil their contract.

The arguments were pressed from both sides; by those who preferred to risk their lives further in order to earn their wages, and those who thought the danger was too great – from those among the Pilgrims who had nothing left in England to return to but destitution, and those who dreaded to venture further into such a violent darkness.

Having heard all sides, Captain Jones made his own decision. Capable of assessing the situation expertly and of maintaining a ruthless discipline aboard his ship, he sent for the ship's carpenter and went into a huddle with him. Between them, they came to the conclusion that if they could strap the main beam with a metal collar to keep the split together, and from spreading and opening up, it might be possible to head up into the wind again and proceed on their proper course. But where were they to find such a piece of hardware, more than a thousand miles from the nearest land?

By the greatest of good fortune – attributed by the Pilgrims to the goodness of God – they unearthed the very thing they needed, a large and powerful iron screw that had been brought aboard with the stores for use in the new colony.

With what must have been a tremendous sigh of

The *Mayflower* in Cape Cod Bay.

relief from all aboard the distressed vessel, the Master and the carpenter superintended as the beam was strapped to a stout post set firmly against the lower deck and fastened under the collar to support the beam against further strain. Then they turned their attention to the leaks in the hull and were relieved to find that although they created a great deal of discomfort below deck, they were not a serious hazard. Jones kept the ship in the trough of the waves for a few days while they plugged the leaks as best they could and until the weather eased a little; then, cautiously, he brought the ship's head round to the west and headed for America.

Hardly had the *Mayflower* resumed its voyage before storms blanketed the seas around it once again. The ship pitched and rolled in the mountainous waves, and conditions in the passenger holds deteriorated appallingly. The wind shrieked frighteningly through the rigging, and spray whipped from the crest of the waves tumbled across the decks in a welter of grey-white spume that seeped below to add to the misery there. For days on end the galley fires remained washed out and hot meals were out of the question.

Time after time the storm struck the ship so violently that the Captain was compelled to take in every stitch of canvas and leave the vessel to drift helplessly like a piece of driftwood about the ocean, hammered by giant waves, rolled over to the gunwales, thrown high only to pitch forward again in a steep dive and generally to rattle the passengers about the holds like a load of rocks in a giant sieve.

The Pilgrims, in the depths of misery, must have been torn between the danger of being almost asphyxiated in the vitiated atmosphere below decks and risking the hazards of the open deck.

One who braved the latter at the height of the storm was John Howland, a young manservant in the employ of John Carver. He volunteered to check that none of the fittings were working loose and in danger of breaking adrift. He climbed up the gratings to get a good look at them when, suddenly, he was caught off-balance as the ship reared up. Before he could grab for a secure hand-hold he was pitched overboard. As he hit the water, Howland's hand was whipped by the topsail halliards which streamed overboard in the wind and sliced across the surface of the tempest-torn sea. By an incredible stroke of luck and a lightning-swift reaction to the touch, he succeeded in grabbing the thin rope. His weight carried him deep under the surface of the water as the halliárd ran out, but he held on grimly. The accident was seen from the deck and a rush made for the inboard stretch of the rope. Half a dozen men caught it and, careless of their own danger on the heaving sea-swept deck, they hauled young Howland to the surface. Then he was dragged close alongside with a boathook. As the roll of the ship brought him within reach, outstretched hands grabbed him by the hair and clothing and pulled him aboard.

And in the middle of all this misery and uncertainty, Elizabeth Hopkins gave birth to a son, whom she named Oceanus. And on 6th November 1620, three days before they first saw the coast of America, William Butten, a youthful manservant employed by Samuel Fuller, died and was buried at sea. An unknown sailor died also during those desperate days.

But even before these latter events the Pilgrims aboard the *Mayflower* had sunk into a mood that approached the depths of melancholy. Confined below decks in a dangerously vitiated atmosphere, thrown about so seriously and for so long that they no longer had the strength left to brace themselves to meet each roll of the ship, undernourished through the lack of opportunity to cook for themselves and often far too seasick to even look at the cold food that was offered them – all their hopes and enthusiasms had been crushed. It was strange indeed that, in their weakened condition and helplessness, no epidemic broke out on board.

And though the Captain and his pilots managed to keep the storm-tossed *Mayflower* headed towards the American continent, the vessel was driven further and further to the north and, despite all efforts to make a landfall near the Hudson River, it became increasingly certain as the days passed that their first sight of land would be as much as three hundred miles from their destination.

On 9th November "land ahoy" was called for the first time since the *Mayflower* had sailed out of Plymouth Sound, sixty-four days earlier – but it was some time before that land could be identified positively as Cape Cod.

11 Cape Cod

Over the years, there has been much controversy concerning the landfall made by the Pilgrim Fathers. It has been suggested that the true destination had been intended as the Hudson River, where the Pilgrims would have peace to live in their own way; as it happens, the patent granted to John Wincob on their behalf, did stipulate "northern Virginia" – the

boundaries of which were anyone's guess in those imprecise days. It was suggested, too, that the New Netherlands Company, having their eyes on the Hudson River as a prospective site for a settlement for some of their own colonists, bribed Jones to carry the Pilgrim Fathers to a more northerly destination.

Sir Dudley Carleton's report to the Privy Council on 5th February 1622 specifically denies any such plot and it would seem likely that, as England's Ambassador in the Hague, he was in a position to

New England, showing towards the bottom left (north is to the right of the map) Cape Cod and its bay.

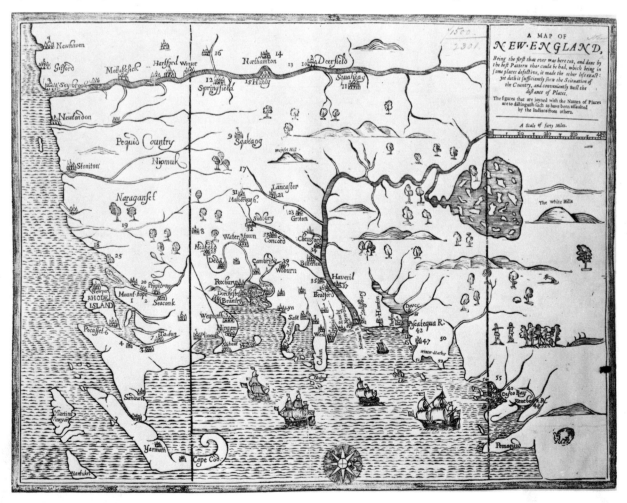

Some of the adventures recounted by Captain John Smith after his exploration of the eastern seaboard of the New World: one suspects that the artist's graphic imagination was allowed full rein. The map shows the region later colonized by the Pilgrims.

make the necessary enquiries. Besides, whatever accusations were levelled against the Captain in the years following his command of the *Mayflower*, it is evident that once the landfall had been made he was perfectly prepared to alter course to correct their position, if the passengers so wished.

It is doubtful whether the Pilgrims would have cared a snap of the fingers for any such plot if they had known of it or even suspected it. Their immediate reaction was to thank God that solid land was at hand. Despite the grey skies, the rain and the heavy breakers that pounded the beaches, and the total lack of anyone to greet them, the Pilgrims most assuredly looked upon the unmoving, unending vista of land as the answer to their prayers.

But, as the Captain tacked up and down the coast on the lookout for a good landing place, the utter isolation of the landscape and its absolute loneliness must have raised doubts in the minds of the Elders and made them hesitate to free the longboat ready for launching. It probably began to worry them, too, that being so far to the north of any known settlement there could be no help from outside if the need arose. If they had to fight against the natives, they would have to fight alone, and if they ran short of supplies there was nobody from whom they could borrow.

The snags of trying to create a settlement at Cape Cod began to fill their minds and to subdue their first enthusiasm at the sight of land. Would supplies be sent from England to support a settlement outside the bounds set by its patent? For that matter, would anybody ever know of this new site for their settlement? After their recent experience of the fury of the Atlantic Ocean, it seemed to the Pilgrims that there was a distinct possibility that the *Mayflower* would never safely reach England to give the news of their whereabouts – in which case they might well become lost to civilization for ever. With no fresh supplies arriving to support them, they would inevitably perish.

The Elders ignored the clamour to be put ashore and retired to the Captain's quarters to discuss the situation with him. They put the question to him: would it not be wiser to head south again in search of what is now called Nantucket Sound, and then to strike a westerly course towards their proper destination, known to their friends in England, the Hudson River.

Captain Jones warned the Elders that there could be considerable danger in rounding the promontory in the wintry conditions, although the gale had subsided for the moment and the skies were clear. He did, however, show that he appreciated the risk to the Pilgrims of their being stranded if they were landed at Cape Cod, and offered to attempt to complete the voyage in accordance with the original plan.

Agreeing that their best plan of action would be to try and find their way to the Hudson River, the Captain returned to the deck to check their present position more accurately. After some time spent in consideration of the land to the west, he came to the conclusion that they were off the most northerly tip of the peninsula, and brought his ship about and onto a southerly course. For half a day they ran down the coastline of the narrow neck of land that enclosed the Bay of Cape Cod, almost thirty miles wide, to the west, until they began to run into the dangerous shoal waters and roaring breakers which lie off the southern extremity of the Cape, near Point Care – now, Monomoy Point – and known as Tucker's Terror – today, Pollock Rip.

The sight of the tumbling waves and cross-currents alarmed both the Pilgrims and the crew, but before they could protest to the Captain the *Mayflower* was pitching wildly among the uncharted shoals and the short, steep waves that appeared to be coming from every direction at once.

Jones held on his course stoutly, and under his expert seamanship it seems likely that, if the wind had held for another hour or two, they would have cleared the dangerous waters and entered Nantucket Sound – from where, it is probable, they would have had a fair passage to the west under the lee of the land, into Long Island Sound to reach what is now New York, at the mouth of the Hudson River.

But the wind unexpectedly dropped while the ship was still in the grip of the Pollock Rip. It promptly lost steerage way and began to drift helplessly among the shoals.

The Elders had no need to carry their alarm to the Captain. The Master knew the danger only too well and, taking advantage of the first puff of wind, swung his ship about and headed for the open expanse of the Atlantic. Once he was free from the dangerous shoals, he turned his ship towards the north and in a wide curve headed for the northern tip of Cape Cod again and shelter within the Bay.

On 11th November 1620, the *Mayflower* rounded Cape Cod and entered the massive Bay; then, tacking close in round the point of the hook of Cape Cod, the Captain found a wide harbour opposite the place now known as Provincetown, and dropped anchor as close inshore as he could get.

At first sight it must have appeared a fair refuge to the dog-tired, sea-weary Pilgrim Fathers. The harbour consisted of a fine, wide bay, almost circular and about four miles across. They could see great oak trees, junipers, pines and other hardy trees, and roosting among them flocks of fowl. But it was a bleak, wintry scene nevertheless, of bare trees, grey sands, and no sign of habitation.

Arguments began to break out almost before they had absorbed the view and its implications. Some of the Pilgrims, having had more than enough of the stark misery aboard the *Mayflower*, were all for landing at once, despite the bitter cold and the unwelcoming prospect; others urged the wisdom of waiting for a few days until conditions made it possible to try again to round Monomoy Point and reach for the Hudson River where they hoped to find a kinder climate and the prospect of other settlements nearby.

For an hour or more it seemed that once again the Pilgrim community was to be split into a number of disgruntled groups, torn by dissensions and, through lack of firm leadership, incapable of making a decision. Then somebody – we do not know who – recalled the "large letter" written to them by their pastor, John Robinson, and read to them before they left England. Its production restored the good sense of the Pilgrims, particularly the 5th "spur of provocation": "Lastly, whereas you are to become a Body Politic using amongst yourselves Civil Government, and are not furnished with any persons

The first landing in the New World of the Pilgrims, at Cape Cod.

of special eminency above the rest to be chosen by you into Office of Government, let your wisdom and godliness appear, not only in choosing such persons as do entirely love, and will diligently promote, the common good; but also in yielding unto them all due honour and obedience in their lawful administrations . . ."

Tempers cooled as this purposeful point was put to the assembled Pilgrims. Finally, perhaps relieved at the opportunity to create a governing body and to be able to load it with all responsibility for the conduct of their affairs, they drew up the following "Association and Agreement": "In the name of GOD, Amen. We, whose names are underwritten, the loyal subjects of our dread Sovereign Lord King James; by the grace of GOD, of Great Britain, France, and Ireland King; Defender of the Faith; etc.

"Having undertaken for the glory of GOD, and advancement of the Christian faith, and honour of our King and country, a Voyage to plant the first Colony in the northern parts of Virginia; do, by these presents, solemnly and mutually, in the presence of GOD and one another, covenant and combine ourselves together into a Civil Body Politic, for our better ordering and preservation; and furtherance of the ends aforesaid: and by virtue hereof, to enact, constitute, and frame such just and equal laws,

ordinances, acts, constitutions, Offices, from time to time, as shall be thought most meet and convenient for the general good of the Colony; unto which, we promise all due submission and obedience.

"In witness whereof, we have hereunder subscribed our names. Cape Cod, 11th of November, in the year of the reign of our Sovereign Lord King James, of England France and Ireland 18; and of Scotland 54. Anno Domini 1620."

There followed the signatures of John Carver, John Turner, William Bradford, Francis Eaton, Edward Winslow, James Chilton, William Brewster, John Crackston, Isaac Allerton, John Billington, Miles Standish, Moses Fletcher, John Alden, John Goodman, Samuel Fuller, Degory Priest, Christopher Martin, Thomas Williams, William Mullins, Gilbert Winslow, William White, Edmund Margeson, Richard Warren, Peter Browne, John Howland, Richard Britteridge, Stephen Hopkins, George Sowle, Edward Tilley, Richard Clarke, John Tilley, Richard Gardiner, Francis Cooke, John Allerton, Thomas Rogers, Thomas English, Thomas Tinker, Edward Dotey, John Rigdale, Edward Leister, and Edward Fuller.

The signatures are chiefly those of the heads of the various households, representing themselves, their sons, daughters and wives: women in those days were

"They spotted more than one whale but had no tackle with which to catch them . . ."

presumed incapable of entering into any formal agreements. Of the eleven men who failed to sign the Association and Agreement, two were temporary sailors, Trevore and Ellis; as eight of the other nine died soon afterwards it is probable that they were ill at the time.

It is notable that the agreement expressed no desire or intention on the part of the signatories to withdraw their allegiance from the Crown, nor to sever their association with the Old Country – although they were aware that they were lying off territory for which they held no patent from the London Virginia Company on behalf of the Crown; nor, as it turned out, were they aware that the Plymouth Company had been superseded, on 3rd November 1620, while they were still at sea, by a Council for New England.

Having drawn up the Association and Agreement, the assembled Pilgrim Fathers then elected John Carver to be their first Governor, to hold office for one year.

Immediately afterwards, fifteen or sixteen of the men were sent ashore to procure wood and fresh water, to scout around to see what the prospects were generally and to find out if there were any other human beings in the vicinity.

The party had to wade through icy waters for almost three-quarters of a mile as, being unable to find a channel through the shallow waters of the harbour, the Captain had been compelled to anchor the *Mayflower* well clear of the land. But the party went ashore eagerly – the first to set foot on dry land since the Pilgrim Fathers had left England.

They found the ground sandy, even clear of the beach, but below the surface was good black soil – although at that time of the year it was hardening rapidly under the bitter winter winds. Among the trees they had seen from the ship the shore party now found and identified birch, holly vines, ash and walnut – most of the woods being free from entangling undergrowth. They again saw fowl – but no other animals. They spotted more than one whale but had no tackle with which to catch them; they were surprised and disappointed to see no sign of cod – although this was probably a matter of the season. Finding no trace of human life in the vicinity, the men set about filling the water casks and carrying them out to the *Mayflower*, the need being urgent. They also took aboard a load of juniper to replenish the exhausted stocks of firewood for the galley stoves – the sweet smell of which pervaded the vessel for days.

They made a second excursion ashore that day, intent on finding any sign of habitation that might assure them of help and advice, if needed, or threaten them with danger – but they found nothing to indicate that there had ever been another human being on Cape Cod.

On 13th November the shallop was got out of the ship and hauled ashore, but it had been taken very thoroughly apart to get it into the *Mayflower* and had received some rough treatment from both the gales and the passengers, who had used parts of it for bedboards, partitions, tables and forms; it was to take a full thirteen days of hard work on the part of the carpenter and a few of his assistants before the vessel was fit to be launched.

During those early days, so soon after that long and miserable voyage, every crewman and passenger who was fit enough waded ashore through the icy, uncertain currents and varying depths, drawn there by the urgent need to wash bodies and clothes in fresh water, to have space to build big, drying bonfires to take the dampness out of bedding, and to be able to do some real cooking on a steady platform for a change. But the long wade rapidly resulted in a widespread bout of coughs and colds.

It soon became evident that the harbour around Provincetown was not going to provide a safe haven for the *Mayflower* during the ravages of a northern winter, and Captain Jones made it clear that the Pilgrim Fathers must either go ashore at once or find a secure harbour within the next few days – or return to England.

The Pilgrims themselves had had more than enough of the cramped, dank, heaving 'tween decks of the ship, but at the moment they saw no practicable means of establishing a colony at Cape Cod – certainly not in the conditions they faced: a whole winter without adequate shelter and the ground too hard to clear and prepare for planting. Nor could they face with equanimity a return to England, where bitter persecution awaited them so long as they chose to maintain their nonconformity.

They did all they could to help the carpenter prepare the shallop as quickly as possible, as it was the best way of exploring the coastline for a more suitable tract of land on which to found a settlement, but the time needed to piece it together again tried the patience of all – nor could all of the passengers be employed in the task.

A number of the men decided that in the short term the sensible thing would be to explore along the coastline from the landward side. They talked to the Elders, who put the matter to Governor Carver, and as it was obviously going to be impossible for more

than a hundred passengers to remain aboard all winter, even if the Captain's refusal could be overruled, the Governor was very anxious that no time should be wasted in finding a suitable site for a winter camp ashore. The men's suggestion met with his instant approval.

Captain Miles Standish was given command of the little expedition; of the fifteen men who were to form the party, William Bradford, Stephen Hopkins and Edward Tilley were included as a sort of panel of advisers to the Commander. On 15th November they were helped ashore, each wearing a corslet and carrying a musket and a sword in case they should need to defend themselves against hostile natives. Enough provisions were landed, together with hatchets and cooking equipment, to last a week.

The members of the expedition turned to the south and stepped out in single file, eagerly and hopefully. But it was soon apparent to them that it was going to be hard work to make headway in the soft, shifting sands – especially tiring because of the long weeks of lack of exercise aboard the *Mayflower*. Nor dared they turn aside from the narrow strip of beach: thick woods left few open tracts of land and it was impracticable for the explorers to follow the coastline further inland without making long diversions – which meant some danger of becoming lost.

The little party had covered barely a mile when a cry went up from the leader and they saw five or six people and a dog coming towards them along the beach. But as soon as the newcomers heard the shout they fled into the woods, whistling a command to the less frightened dog to follow them. Initially Captain Standish and his men assumed that they had spotted Captain Jones with some of his sailors, whom they knew to be ashore, but then they guessed that they had sighted Indians.

Standish's men raced in pursuit of the natives in the hope of preventing them from warning others of their presence and setting an ambush, or gathering up a sufficient force to overwhelm the Englishmen. But the natives knew the territory, had no heavy loads strapped to their backs and had not gone "soft" in confinement as had the Pilgrims. Dodging between the trees, they quickly disappeared.

The explorers kept up the chase, however, worried since it now seemed likely that there was an Indian habitation somewhere nearby – but they found that wherever they went, even into the woods, the sand clogged their footsteps and slowed them down. On

An elderly Red Indian man dressed in winter garb; engraving by Theodore de Bry (1590) after a drawing by John White.

the other hand, the sand did show the footprints of the retreating Indians, and Standish and his men, although growing weary, followed the tracks for about ten miles, until sundown – when they saw the last of them leading up a hillside.

Standish realized that the Indians had a vantage point from the top of the hill and could overlook any move he and his men made; so, as night came down, he ordered a big bonfire to be lit on the beach and enough wood collected to keep the fire burning all night. Sentries were posted and the rest of the party slept uneasily, partly roasted by the blaze and partly frozen where the glow of the fire could not reach them. On the following morning, the 16th, he waited only until it was light enough to see the footprints in the sand again before he ordered a continuation of the pursuit.

The Pilgrims were still following the trail when they reached the head of a long creek – East Harbour Creek, as it is known today – where the tracks led into some woods. Still worried by the possibility of having to face a stronger force of Indians if he did not make some form of peace with those ahead of him, Standish kept his party following the tracks into the woods for another couple of hours, but as they moved further inland the layer of sand under their feet grew thinner – until the footprints finally disappeared.

The explorers fanned out and probed the area all around them, forcing a passage through bushes and scrub, marching through valleys and climbing over hills, until they were exhausted – but they saw no more of the Indians. Hungry and thirsty, they cast around for fresh water but were too weary to persist for long. They rested and made do with the only liquid refreshment they had with them, a small bottle of brandy; their food was limited to Holland cheese and some hard biscuits.

It was past midmorning, probably after ten o'clock, when the explorers moved off again. Within an hour they found themselves in a deep valley – where Truro now lies – which was full of brush and long grass through which ran little paths and tracks. They followed one of these at random and almost at once spotted a deer – which fled the moment it caught their wind – and, further along, a spring of fresh water. They rested again and then headed due south with the intention of reaching the beach where they could light a bonfire to be seen across the Bay by those on the *Mayflower*.

They found an ideal site for their signal-fire, lit it and, as soon as they were satisfied that their position had been noted by their friends on the deck of the distant ship, marched on again until they found a freshwater pond – known today as Pond Village, Truro. Around it were small vines and sassafras, and there were plenty of signs that both wild fowl and deer frequented the pond. Nearby they discovered almost fifty acres of land fit for the plough, and there were indications that Indians had, at one time, planted corn there.

This was a cheering sight, but they examined the ground warily, keeping a watch in all directions in case they were interrupted by hostile Indians. They noted the position as a possible site for a settlement but hoped to find another where there was less chance of it being disputed by some dispossessed Indians as native land, developed by them to produce crops for their own people.

Realizing that there must be an Indian village within easy reach, Standish decided to return to the beach where his future movements could be signalled to the *Mayflower* and, if necessary, where he could summon help if attacked. But once the expedition again found itself trudging through deep sand, the debilitating weeks aboard the vessel took their toll. Standish realized that he must turn aside from the shore if he were to make any progress, and, reluctantly and warily, he led his party into the woods again. He soon found a narrow, well trodden path where the going was easier and, though it turned inland, marched ahead along it. Within a mile or two the little expedition came across a number of earthmounds, partially silted over by sand – in the area now known as the village of Great Hollow.

One of the mounds in particular intrigued the party. It was covered with old, rotting grass mats and arched over with a crude wooden affair, crowned by an earthenware pot set into a little hole cut in one end of the cover. Puzzled, some of the men tried digging into the ground under this strange, sheltered mound of earth, and within a spade's depth they unearthed a bow and what appeared to be arrows, although they were so rotten with age that it was difficult to be certain. Then it dawned on them that they might be interfering with an old Indian graveyard; they promptly returned the bow and arrows and reset everything as they had found it.

Moving on, the explorers found a stubble of corn that had obviously been harvested that year, a large number of walnut trees full of nuts, and a number of both strawberry- and grapevines: the area had certainly been under recent although not extensive cultivation. Close by was another field where they found half a dozen wooden planks hanging together, suggesting that at one time there had been a shack there. Beside these remains was a large ship's kettle, rusty but obviously having come at some time or other from the far side of the Atlantic.

Again some of the explorers probed into a mound of earth, one that looked less like a grave than the one they had disturbed earlier. They dug up a small, old basket filled with maize. Cautiously, Standish set a circle of sentries about the site while the party examined the place more closely. Digging further, they found yet another basket of corn which was certainly of that year's growth. There were thirty-six ears; some yellow, some red and others tinged with blue, filling three or four baskets in all. It was a heartening sight and a promise that the land on which they stood was fruitful – even this amount of corn

A romantic view of the *Mayflower*, with the shallop in the foreground.

would be a valuable addition to their own slender stocks.

The little party decided it was too precious a hoard to be left behind. They promised themselves that if the owners ever did ask for its return they would gladly reimburse them as soon as their own first harvest was gathered in – a promise that was to be kept in full measure.

They filled the big kettle with maize and hooked it onto a pole to be carried between two of them. They filled their pockets with more. That had to be the limit of their load: they were already carrying a considerable weight of armour, muskets, swords and other supplies. The rest of the maize they buried to be collected by the shallop when it had been rebuilt.

Before moving on again the explorers took a further look around the locality and came across a crumbling palisade of stakes driven into the ground to form a fortress, its construction suggesting that it had been erected by Europeans rather than Indians – whom the party presumed to be savages and quite incapable of thinking along such lines. The fortress overlooked two arms of a river, the larger apparently capable of harbouring small ships. They took a closer look and were surprised to find two canoes beached on the opposite bank; but, as time was running out for them, the little party made no attempt to cross the river.

Burdened with the kettle of maize, on top of their own equipment, they made heavy going of it on the return journey, and, when they reached the freshwater pond again, they decided to camp down close to it for the night.

But there was a bitter winter wind blowing and they had to build a bonfire to keep themselves warm. They erected a barricade of logs and boughs to shelter them from the wind, and Standish gave the order that throughout the night sentries should stand on guard, to be relieved at regular intervals, and that their muskets should be primed and a slow-burning match kept alight until morning. He was well aware of the danger of being ambushed during the night and, while they had not seen a single native all day, the signs warned him of their silent presence, probably all around them, waiting for an opportunity to attack.

The sky was dark and louring as they cooked their

evening meal; before they could bed down for the night a cold rain had begun to fall. As the hours went slowly by, the rain increased to a downpour. It persisted until morning, soaking every one of them to the skin.

In the misery of that night the explorers slept only fitfully, and they were up and about before the grey, sunless dawn. They wrung as much water as they could from their clothing, cleared their muskets, knowing that their powder was wet, and sadly emptied their pockets of maize which the rain had turned into a sticky mess. Then, sinking the kettle into the pond where they could hope to find it again, they set out on the journey back to the ship through soaking grass, under streaming trees and over slippery rocks.

They tried to find a way around the woods rather than penetrate the dark interiors, and attempted to plough their way through dense, clinging, wet and treacherous undergrowth, but soon lost their sense of direction in the misty rain and had to cast around in search of a path – or some open ground or a convenient hill from which to sight the Bay and pick up their bearings again. Eventually they struck a vague track, probably made by animals, but they had advanced along it for only a few hundred yards before they found that a young tree had been drawn down tautly across the trail to form a trap. The leading file stopped to examine it. Hopkins suggested that it had been set by Indians in the hope of catching a deer.

William Bradford, bringing up the rear of the party, failed to hear the warning or to see the loop of the roughly woven rope that lay on the path – and tripped it. The loop promptly caught him round the leg as the tree whipped upwards and held him fast. He was released by his companions who, intrigued by the effectiveness of the trap, took it away with them as a souvenir to show their friends on the *Mayflower* – as a warning to them that the savages in those parts were cunning, if not actually aggressive.

The men found their way clear of the woods at last and discovered a creek where they were thrilled by the sight of three deer and put up three brace of partridges – which would have done something towards replenishing their dwindling food stocks aboard *Mayflower* had not their powder been so uselessly wet.

Later, flocks of wild geese and duck swept away as they approached, convincing the party that there was sufficient game in the district to ward off any possibility of starvation – news which would be received with great relief aboard the ship.

They ploughed on again through the woods until at last they found the beach. They took their bearings and then began the weary trudge through the deep, shifting sands, wading through the chill streams that crossed their path, and enduring the misery of the ever-increasing rain that soaked their clothing. But by evening they came opposite the ship, where they were eagerly welcomed and helped aboard.

The shallop sets forth from the *Mayflower* for the shore at what was to be christened Plymouth.

12 New Plymouth

While the shallop was being assembled, those Pilgrim Fathers not engaged in helping the ship's carpenter spent their time gathering wood for the fires ashore and the galley aboard the *Mayflower*, in sharpening their tools and in cutting timber with which to build a new shallop. But it all went very slowly and dishearteningly.

Only at high tide could the *Mayflower*'s longboat approach the beach; as the ship itself had to lie well out in deep water, a great deal of time and patience was lost in getting to and fro between ship and shore. And with the never-ending rain, the persistently cold winds, wet clothing and damp bedding, coughs and colds spread and became a serious hindrance.

However, by 26th November the shallop was at last ready to be put into the water.

By then everybody had become desperately anxious to be free of the comfortless confines of the *Mayflower* and to find some place ashore where they could spread themselves out and build shelters for their families before the anticipated January snows. Captain Jones was calling, equally urgently, for a harbour to be found where his ship could lie secure against the worst of the weather; and, no doubt tired of the fractious discord that persisted aboard the vessel, he was only too anxious to be rid of his passengers.

When the shallop was ready Jones, as a practical seaman, was appointed to lead the first seaborne expedition to search for a permanent settlement and a safe harbour. He took with him nine of his own men and twenty-four of the Pilgrims. Before going ashore

he assembled them and gave them his instructions. He proposed to wait until morning and then to send them out in two parties; one being put ashore in the longboat to patrol along the beach, while he with the rest of the party would run parallel to them in the shallop. He told them that he was particularly anxious to investigate the mouth of a river he had seen from the rigging of the *Mayflower* as a possible harbour.

When morning dawned it came with grey, overcast skies: the weather was anything but ideal for the start of the venture. The wind was blustery, and even in the thirty-mile-wide shelter of Cape Cod Bay there was a nasty swell on the water to make things difficult for the shallop. The shore party waded ashore and, despite the appalling weather and the heavy going in the loose sand, made their way along the beach for some six or seven miles before they had to give up and make camp for the night. By then the persistent rain had turned to snow. During the night it fell heavily and froze the clothing onto the bodies of the men.

By next morning, although the snow still fell incessantly, the drive had gone out of the wind and the temperature had lifted a little above freezing point. The shore party was too exhausted to take advantage of the improved conditions, but before midday the shallop, under a more favourable wind and a determined Captain, drew alongside and took them aboard.

Then they examined the river that Captain Jones had hoped would provide good harborage for the *Mayflower* – but it turned out to be quite unsuitable for anything except small boats. In the steadily improving conditions, the Captain led a party ashore to march along the beach while the shallop kept pace some two or three hundred yards off shore.

But again it was to prove heavy going for those on the sandy beach. The snow lay deep on top of it and they were forced by the terrain time and time again to divert inland, to clamber over steep hills and to slide down them again into the valleys. And all the time, to make any progress, they had to avoid the snow-laden sands where they sank as deep as their thighs at almost every step.

Captain Jones, probably never before having undertaken such an excursion on foot, tired before they had covered more than four or five miles and suggested that as night was not far off they should camp. Although some of them would have preferred to push on in the hope of finding a more sheltered spot, most were as weary as their leader. They decided to bed down under a clump of nearby pine trees.

Luck was with them, for they shot three fat geese and six ducks for their supper; and, although the snow continued to lie deep on the ground and the air was brittle with cold, the wind dropped and the skies cleared.

Next morning, Wednesday 29th November 1620, the party hesitated over their plan to explore up-river in search of fresh water. It seemed to them to be a risky business to attempt to climb the slippery slopes with the possibility of spraining ankles in unseen ruts, or even of breaking limbs through a fall into some snow-hidden pit. Instead, they turned towards the creek and the area where the previous expedition had found the Indian burial ground, the ruined shack and the cached Indian corn.

They reached the little river after a great deal of hard marching through the snow, and found there one of the abandoned canoes lying high and dry on the bank. One of the party shot two geese while the others examined the canoe and decided that it was a native-built craft. Surprisingly, when they launched it they found that it was quite sound and could not have lain there for more than a few weeks.

The explorers used the canoe to ferry themselves, seven or eight at a time, to the far bank of the river. Then they beached it safely and marched off towards the spot where the Indian corn had been left behind. They found it undisturbed and added it to their load. A few cast around the site to see what else they could find and one, despite the frozen ground, unearthed a bottle of oil. They found too about ten bushels of corn, a bag of beans and yet another store of wheat ears.

The Pilgrims appreciated the enormous luck that had come their way in the two expeditions – and, no doubt, thanked God for it. The first expedition, only a few days earlier, had found the hidden grain before the ground froze too hard to prise it loose until the Spring, and the second had been able to take advantage of the find. When the time came, it was to provide the Pilgrim Fathers with an invaluable stock of seed. They had none of their own; the reason for this is not known today, but it seems likely that they might well have starved had it not been for the corn they discovered at that point.

The find gave the Pilgrims a sense of security that they had so far lacked, and they decided that it would be well worth their while to explore the locality further. But Jones felt that, if the weather were to break, his place was on board the *Mayflower*. The party talked the matter over briefly and reached a compromise. Jones would return to the *Mayflower* in the shallop and would take with him the corn they had dug up as well as those who had found the struggle too hard and preferred to return to their families. Some were clearly showing signs of sickness, too; the heavy going in the appalling weather, following the weeks of close confinement on board ship, was probably beginning to take its toll on their strength. But of the thirty-four men who had set out on this second expedition eighteen stayed behind to carry on with the exploration. Jones promised to return for them on the following day, all being well, bringing with him more serviceable tools so that they could dig deeper into the frozen ground in search of further grain.

The shallop left that evening and the shore party made themselves as comfortable as they could for the night. In the morning they ventured along some of the tracks that led into the woods in all directions, hoping to find one that led to an Indian village. One cast led them along a path which suddenly widened to almost two feet and was obviously in frequent use. Feeling sure that they were approaching some well populated place, the Pilgrims loaded and primed their muskets and set their slow-burning matches smouldering against the possibility of a sudden attack. Then they moved forward, cautiously.

But the track petered out after they had followed it for some five or six miles and the party decided that it must be a drive where deer were hunted together. They turned back, but used another track so that their search would cover as much ground as possible, and as they came out of the woods into the open again they found a mound similar to the graves located by the earlier expedition, but very much larger. Shovelling the snow to one side, they were intrigued that the mound was covered by wooden boards. Prising these up, they dug down and gradually unearthed a succession of surprising items: a mat, then a bow in a fair state of preservation; then another mat covering a strangely carved and painted board, a little over two feet in length and with three prongs at the top to suggest a sort of crown; between other mats were trays, bowls, dishes and an assortment of trinkets. Deeper down was a larger mat and under it two bundles: the larger, on being opened up,

Red Indian tombs ranged from the simple affairs found by the Pilgrims to elaborate edifices such as this, the Tomb of the Kings of Virginia.

was found to contain a fine, red, sweet smelling powder – covering the body of a man. The powder appeared to be some sort of embalming agent, for the flesh still clung to the bones and there was plenty of yellow hair on the head. Besides the body, the bundle contained a knife, a packing needle and two or three unidentified pieces of iron, wrapped up in a sailor's blouse and a pair of cloth breeches. The smaller bundle also contained a body protected by red powder, this time that of a child: it was decorated with strings and bracelets of beads, and a bow, only about two feet in length, lay at its side.

A few of the men concluded that they had discovered the bodies of an Indian king and his little prince, although others preferred to believe that the larger figure was the prince's guard; but it was impossible to be certain: they knew that they would never know the answer to the mystery unless they came across a party of Indians, made friends with them, and spent some time learning their language. The Pilgrims selected a few of the more attractive items to take away with them and then, with all reverence, replaced the bodies in the grave and filled it in again.

After a further look around the area, the explorers discovered other less pretentious mounds; although they probed into them they found nothing of value or interest.

While the shore party continued its investigations, the shallop, which by now had returned from the Mayflower, put two of its sailors ashore to let them know where the boat was lying. By chance, the sailors stumbled on two strange dwellings that had obviously been occupied until a few moments earlier – the occupants probably having fled at their approach. The sailors loaded their muskets, advanced cautiously and peered into the dark interiors. Once they had satisfied themselves that no one had been left behind on guard, but still nervous of the unknown, the pair entered the first hut stealthily, grabbed up a few trifles and hurried off to report their discovery to the shore party.

The shore party followed the two sailors back to the Indian dwellings (in fact, they had already passed within bow-shot of them without knowing it); taking a close look at them they realized that these were wigwams. They were constructed from long, pliant saplings that had been bent until both ends could be stuck into the ground to form a large arbour. They had then been covered over with thick sturdy mats.

The doors consisted of single mats not more than a yard square, in the form of flaps that reached to the ground.

Taking a look inside, the explorers found that there was enough room to stand up; they saw that in the middle of the floor space stakes had been driven into the ground on which to hang cooking pots, and around the fireplace were spread mats to make beds for the inhabitants. More mats were hung around the framework inside the wigwams to form an inner skin, of finer and more decorative workmanship.

They found pots, wooden bowls and trays, dishes, baskets made from the shells of crabs laced tightly together, some tobacco and other seeds and, unexpectedly, a bucket (less its handle) that had certainly originated in Europe. There were all sorts of decorative items too, such as deer's feet, harts' horns and eagles' claws. A fresh deer's head, some pieces of fish, baskets of parched acorns and a piece of broiled herring confirmed the fact that the Indians who lived there had fled within the hour, almost certainly alarmed by the approach of the sailors. Scattered around outside the wigwams were sedge bullrushes and other materials required for the making of mats, and pieces of venison presumably intended for the dogs.

The Pilgrims took away a few souvenirs but left the wigwams undamaged in any way. Then, at the earnest request of the sailors to board the shallop before it had to sail because of the ebbing tide, the whole party hurried down to the beach. Before dark they were back aboard the Mayflower.

Once the story of their exploration had been told and the souvenirs admired, a full and protracted discussion broke out over what it could mean to them all. Should they take advantage of the situation and make that place their permanent settlement? Within a few leagues there was a river mouth that would serve as a harbour for small boats, although not for a ship the size of the Mayflower. There was ground already cleared and ready for planting in due season, which had shown itself to be capable of yielding a plentiful crop. Cape Cod promised some excellent fishing: they had seen plenty of whales in the surrounding waters that seemed to fear them so little that they could easily be shot and caught, once they had devised some heavy tackle; from that source they would get oil as well as flesh. (Two of the Pilgrims tried to prove how simple it was to catch a whale by selecting one that lay basking within half a musket's

An Indian village as seen in the late sixteenth century.

shot of the *Mayflower* – but the musket of the first to fire burst in his face and he was lucky indeed not to have had his head blown off.) The site was healthy and easily defensible. And, most urgently, winter was already on them and in consequence it would be risky to waste time sending out further expeditions, and dangerous for those engaged in any such explorations. Storms threatened to curtail the use of the shallop and the land parties could so easily lose themselves in the snow storms, or perish in the icy cold currents of the streams and rivers that they would have to ford. Besides, so many of them were suffering from the privations of the long voyage from Europe, were wracked with coughs and colds,

becoming neurotic because of the confinement and physically weak through the limited exercise available to them, that the sooner they were put ashore, the better. Moreover, food supplies were by now low and Jones had warned his passengers that, as soon as there was only enough left to take himself and his crew back to England, he would sail and leave the Pilgrims to their own devices.

But there were arguments against. There were much better harbours to the north on what could be described as the mainland at Anguum – near what is now Ipswich on the northern mainland of Massachusetts – and there was better fishing to be had there, and finer soil. It was likely that there would be a more suitable settlement area in that region, and it would be a sore trial to the Pilgrims if they settled on the promontory of Cape Cod, found it unsatisfactory and had to move again. And it seemed that the fresh water nearby came mainly from ponds which might well dry up in the summer.

The outcome of the discussions was that further investigations should be made within the limits of Cape Cod Bay, certainly not as far away as Anguum – the shoreline of the Bay had a circumference of about sixty miles and the majority felt that they had neither the time nor the resources to search further afield. The Pilgrims were undoubtedly influenced in making their decision by Robert Coppin, their pilot, who had sailed previously aboard a fishing vessel in the waters of the Bay and knew them perhaps better than anyone else there. He told them of a headland – now Manomet Bluff – on the opposite side of the Bay, no more than twenty-four miles west, where he had landed with a party from a fishing vessel some years earlier. He told them how an unexpected party of savages had stolen a harpoon from them while they were exploring. They had given chase until they came to a really fine harbour to the north of where they had gone ashore – although they had failed to catch the thieves. They had then named the spot "Thievish Harbour". (As it happened, the harbour had even earlier been given the name of Plymouth; it appeared as such on a map of New England prepared by Captain John Smith, dated 1614. It is possible that Robert Coppin had learned the fact on his return to England after that earlier voyage and now told the Pilgrim Fathers that the map showed it to be named "Plimouth"; it is equally possible that, having sailed from Plymouth, the Pilgrims gave the harbour that name to commemorate the fact but the *Mayflower* Pilgrims arrived in the New World under the banner of the London Virginia Company, not the Plymouth Virginia Company, which makes it unlikely that they would have given the place the name Plymouth.)

On Tuesday 5th December 1620 the decision was made to send the shallop out on the third exploration, this time under the personal command of the Governor, John Carver. With him were to go William Bradford, Edward Winslow, Miles Standish, John Howland, Richard Warren, Stephen Hopkins, Edward Tilley, John Tilley, John Allerton, Thomas English and Edward Dotey; Robert Coppin and John Clarke, the pilots; the Master Gunner; and

three ordinary seamen from the crew of the *Mayflower*.

While that decision was being taken by the men, other incidents among the women and children aboard the ship were enlivening the day. Young Francis Billington, probably bored by the absence of his father, got his hands on some gunpowder, loaded his father's piece with a charge of flints and scrap-iron in the cabin below decks and, careless of the fact that a half-full keg of explosive had been scattered around in the confined space, fired the weapon within four feet of the bunk. The makeshift cabin was peppered with flints and pieces of old iron, and the gunpowder caught fire – but, mercifully, the fire was quickly extinguished by the crew and the youth came to no harm. But the disturbance must have shaken Mrs Susannah White, who gave birth to a son, the second child to be born aboard the *Mayflower* and the first to see the light of day for the first time in New England. The boy was named Peregrine – and lived to the ripe old age of 84, dying on 20th July 1704.

Next morning the Governor took his party aboard the shallop (it seems that twenty men sailed in it instead of the eighteen chosen for the venture, but the names of the two extras are not known to us). Unaccountably, it took them almost all morning to get aboard the shallop and to pull clear of the parent vessel into a bitterly cold wind that blew from the northeast across the Bay. The intention was to make the direct crossing, but the blustery, chilling wind persuaded the explorers to bring the shallop close inshore and to circle the Bay, in the hope of at least gaining some shelter from the stormy conditions. But even in the first furlong of that voyage, while they rounded Long Point, both Edward Tilley and the gunner were overcome by cold and seasickness.

As soon as they drew clear of the long sandy spit of land, Long Point, which served to give some shelter to the area of Provincetown, they managed to get some sail onto the boat and edged in towards the lee shore where they found smoother water – although the air continued to be icily cold and the spray to freeze in ironclad fashion to their clothing.

They continued to sail close inshore and to the south for eighteen to twenty miles, but saw no creek nor any other possible harbour until they ran back again to a point about twelve miles south from their starting point (Billingsgate Point) where they spotted a fair-sized bay (Wellfleet Bay) reaching across to the mainland about three miles distant.

They veered to one side of the bay and headed towards the beach, intent on finding a resting place for the night and exploring the bay on the following morning. As they approached the shore they caught sight of ten or more Indians crowded about a black object. As soon as the natives spotted the approaching boat, they gathered up whatever it was they had been busy with and fled inland.

The explorers landed some five or six miles further down the coast, with the greatest of difficulty, amongst the stretches of sandy flats that offered neither shelter nor a safe footpath inland. Almost desperate with cold and fatigue they prepared to spend the night on the beach but, despite their weariness, they dared not relax until they could establish a safe camp against any possible attack. They built a stockade in which to shelter from both the wind and any hostile arrows; gathered firewood and built a smudgy, reluctant bonfire from the ice-coated brushwood; and set sentries on watch before bedding themselves down in whatever comfort they could find.

For much of the night the sentries could see the blaze from a fire that burned about five miles further up coast, and they guessed it had been set alight by the Indians whom they had seen earlier.

In the morning, following the regular prebreakfast supplication to the Almighty, the Governor divided his party into two sections, eight men returning aboard the shallop and twelve remaining ashore to investigate the possibilities of Wellfleet Harbour as a permanent settlement. The water-borne party satisfied themselves that there was sufficient depth for the *Mayflower*, but the shore party found things much less satisfactory: the soil in the immediate neighbourhood was much too sandy for cultivation and, although there were two fresh water brooks, they each measured little more than a yard across, suggesting they might well disappear in the summer. They found a dead grampus on the beach in the vicinity of where the Indians had been seen on the previous day. Two more were found in the bay, up to fifteen feet in length, fleshily fat and promising a fine yield of oil – if weather and time had not been against the explorers. They found the tracks of the Indians, who had obviously been cutting up the dead fish – the black object seen from the shallop – and followed them for some considerable distance along the beach and then into the woods to a pond known today as the Great Pond near Eastham.

Moving deeper into the woods, the shore party passed beyond sight of the boat and found a deserted wigwam and a graveyard partly enclosed by a palisade. Inside the palings, the graves lay close-packed together, some covered by small wigwams, suggesting that this was some special part of the burial ground where, perhaps, the more important of the Indians of the district had been interred. Beyond the palisade the graves were much less evident and apparently had never received any attention after they had been filled in. The wigwam nearby appeared to have been abandoned for some considerable time and, had it not been for the sight of the Indians on the beach the day before, the Pilgrims would have thought the region uninhabited.

They returned to their encampment on the beach, signalled to the shallop, which was at some considerable distance, to come near, and then set about the heavy task of collecting firewood and building a bonfire around which to spend the night. While they ate their supper they made up their minds that the place was not suitable for a permanent settlement, and decided to carry on towards Manomet Bluff next morning.

Wisely, sentries were posted before the men rolled themselves up in their blankets to sleep – for in the middle of the night two of the patrolling sentries began to cry out the warning "Arm! Arm!" A couple of musket shots were fired into the darkness; and there was a brisk crackling among the brittle undergrowth, as though someone were retreating hurriedly out of range through the woods.

Peace settled down again, but the Pilgrims spent some time anxiously discussing the incident, concluding finally – but somewhat doubtfully – that the threshing about in the brush had been made by wolves or foxes, scared off by the musket shots.

By five o'clock all were up and about again, stamping their feet to restore their circulation, firing their muskets to make sure that they had not frozen up, and carrying their equipment to a convenient place to stack it until the tide was high enough to permit the shallop to come close to. Sixteen of them, despite the warnings of the others, included their armour and weapons in the stack, and then returned to the camp for breakfast and to wait for high water.

The meal was suddenly interrupted by a wild scream coming from the nearby woods: one of the Pilgrims, who had been collecting wood, raced back crying out that the scream had come from a party of

Celebrating the Sabbath on Clarke's Island, so named for John Clarke, the first to step ashore there.

hostile Indians. Almost at the same moment a flock of arrows slashed down into the ground and the palings around them. Those who had their weapons handy grabbed them up, while the men who had piled theirs on the beach rushed out into the open and made a dash for them.

Miles Standish had a more modern weapon than any of the others, a musket that fired automatically by flint and steel when the trigger was pulled, and he took a snap shot into the woods in the general direction from where the sound seemed to have come. He fired a second time, giving Bradford and one of the others time to load and prime their pieces. An experienced soldier, he then ordered them to hold their fire and to stand ready to defend the entrance to the encampment. He was worried about the safety of the shallop but hoped that those who had run down to the beach to collect their arms would stay there to defend the little boat. They heard three or four shots being fired in that direction and Standish called out to them encouragingly. Then a cry went up for a light with which to set their slow-matches burning – and one of the four left in the camp snatched up a brand from the bonfire and raced off towards the beach.

The Indians shrieked fearsomely from the shelter of the trees, then quickly surrounded the beach party. By the noise and the scuffle they made it seemed probable that some twenty or thirty natives were in the attack – but in the early morning light it was impossible to be sure. Their leader moved forward quickly to take his place close up behind a tree within half a musket-shot range, and loosed three arrows at the Pilgrims, only one of which came near the target. Three musket shots were fired at him in reply: at the third he cried out as though wounded, turned and fled into the woods, followed by the others.

The Pilgrims took up the chase at once, leaving six men behind to guard the shallop. They followed the Indians for about a quarter of a mile but the natives were too fast and knew the terrain well enough to outdistance their pursuers. The Pilgrims fired a couple of parting shots after them as they finally disappeared from sight in the woods.

Returning, the Englishmen picked up no fewer than eighteen arrows that had been fired at them, some of them tipped with harts' horn, others with eagles' claws and yet others with brass.

Then the expedition boarded the shallop, with the exception of a small party who followed it along the beach to demonstrate to any watching Indians that they were not afraid of them – but, after about a quarter of a mile, having seen no sign of them, the shore party embarked too.

They held the shallop close inshore during the rest of the day and covered about forty-five miles as they circled the Bay to the west, but they saw no river or even a creek that suggested itself as a safe harbour for the *Mayflower*.

The weather did nothing to help the search. Within an hour of their sailing it had begun to snow and, as the day progressed, the wind increased to drive the snow into the faces of the Pilgrims with the force of a blizzard – even within the innermost reaches of Cape Cod Bay, twenty miles or so from the Atlantic, the sea became so rough that the rudder hinges of the shallop sheared through and snapped off, and the boat was left without any means of steering, at the mercy of the gathering gale.

Under the orders of the experienced Coppin, the crew fought desperately to get a pair of oars into the water to act as steering arms before the shallop could be driven high and dry onto the beach. Stout muscles and expert seamanship prevailed, and the men succeeded in getting the blades into the water to bring the shallop under some sort of control, just in time to back it away from the breakers along the shore.

The gale grew savagely as they rounded Manomet Bluff and approached the open Atlantic, but Coppin held the boat under the minimum of sail for the harbour he could see to the north of it, which he knew of old. The crew had to use their oars to hold the vessel to a steady course as it sped towards two narrow spits of land that served as the natural piers to protect the harbour. Then, as Coppin manoeuvred the boat by the fitful light of the stars to turn it from its northerly heading into the west, the mast snapped – breaking in three places and bringing down the sail it carried.

The sailors at the oars were husky men and they heaved hard to breast the steep, threatening waves while Coppin did his best to keep them to a course, only vaguely visible to him in the darkness through the curtain of snow – taking his direction principally from the eye of the wind.

Luck – or Divine Guidance – was with them and the boat ran into the harbour, all unknown to those on board until they suddenly found that the wind and sea had eased and they caught the gleam of white sand on a beach. Nor did they know until later that they had been driven blindly through the only gap in a circle of dangerous rocks and carried just out of reach of an island to make a safe landing at the only suitable place within miles.

In the calmer waters of the harbour some of the Pilgrims, wary of Indians, decided to spend the night aboard the shallop, but the majority could no longer tolerate the wet, cramped conditions and moved ashore at once. They posted sentries, gathered up what brushwood they could find within a few yards of their landing place, got a bonfire going with the greatest of difficulty, and steamed some of the water out of their clothing and the chill from their bodies.

In the morning, stiff, tired and no doubt hungry, they were met by another cheerless dawn. Rain and snow, grey, cold waters, a biting wind and a leaden sky had to be endured if they were to continue their explorations.

They soon discovered that they had landed on an island of no considerable size and that it was uninhabited. (As one of the sailors, Clarke, had been the first to step ashore there, the Pilgrims named it Clarke's Island.) It was well wooded, however, with oaks, pines, walnut, beech, sassafras, vines and a few species of trees strange to the Englishmen.

They spent the rest of the day baling out the shallop and drying out their clothing and bedding. As the following day, 10th December, was a Sunday, they kept it, as usual, for rest and prayer.

On the Monday morning the Pilgrims circled the harbour in the shallop and soon convinced themselves that here indeed was a safe haven for the *Mayflower*. In fact, the harbour was large enough to hold a substantial fleet of ships, in all weathers, with plenty of water under their keels and with as many beach landing places as they could need.

They stepped ashore at Plymouth and were delighted to find a number of cornfields and freshwater brooks. They trekked around the district in every direction, their hopes soaring as they discovered more and more land that gave promise of excellent crops, timber within easy reach and country that was sufficiently open to facilitate the building of a settlement. So attractive was the whole prospect that, almost without discussion, the explorers determined to found their new homes at some point along the coast of Plymouth Bay.

The day was Monday 11th December 1620.

13 Plague

Hurriedly, the Pilgrim Fathers and the ship's crew prepared the *Mayflower* for the 24-mile crossing, desperately eager to see the site chosen for the settlement. They used both the shallop and the longboat to pick up all they had taken ashore since their arrival in the New World, exactly thirty days earlier, and restowed everything into the ship.

On 15th December 1620 Captain Jones weighed anchor, and manoeuvred the crowded vessel out from the shallow harbour into the open waters of Cape Cod Bay – the shallop taking station ahead to lead the way. But, aggravatingly, the wind proved to be anything but favourable, blowing strongly from the northeast, and, although the *Mayflower* sailed across the bay without difficulty to approach to within six or seven miles of Plymouth harbour, it could not make the entrance in safety. Bitterly disappointed, they had to put the ship about and head for open water. Jones tacked skilfully in the neighbourhood all night and in the morning, with the wind more favourably placed, he turned for the harbour again and entered it without hazard. Strangely, the moment the vessel was safely between the narrow strips of land that sheltered the harbour the wind suddenly swung back into the northeast again, as though – as the Pilgrims were to assert afterwards – God had given them just sufficient time to find security, and to make it clear to them that here they were to remain and set up their new homes.

Jones edged his ship cautiously around in the enclosed waters of the bay, anxious to confirm that Plymouth harbour was, in fact, as secure as he had been led to believe. When he had satisfied himself that it was indeed an ideal place in which to winter the *Mayflower* he cast around for the best anchorage.

The impatient Pilgrims discussed their prospects eagerly, pointed out to one another the salient features of Clarke's Island, Town Brook and the Jones River – as they were to be named – Captain's Hill, and more than one possible site for their proposed settlement.

It was late in the afternoon, and too late to land that day, before Captain Jones chose his anchorage and secured the vessel – where it was to lie at anchor until the Spring. No attempt was made to go ashore on the 17th, a Sunday, but hopes were high and the prayers of the Pilgrims came from the heart as they gazed continuously at the apparently hospitable landscape around the well-protected harbour.

At first light on Monday the shallop was pulled close alongside the *Mayflower* in readiness to take the first party of Pilgrims ashore, but Governor Carver ordered a preliminary expedition to make sure that there were no hostile natives in the vicinity. Captain Jones took ashore three or four of his crew, together with a strong party of Pilgrims, in the shallop. They landed within the inner harbour, to the southwest of the bay, and marched along the coast in a north-westerly direction for eight or nine miles. They saw neither Indians nor wigwams, but by the number of abandoned cornfields they came across it was clear that the district had at one time been inhabited.

Satisfied that there was no immediate danger, the force checked the rivers but found that neither of them were navigable, although there was no shortage of freshwater streams around the bay. They tested the frozen earth with spades and found that the soil was a black mould that almost certainly assured them excellent crops in due season. There was plenty of woodland all around, and the sight of cherry trees and plum trees pleased them.

On Tuesday 19th, they examined the larger river, Jones River, on the banks of which Kingston stands today. They followed it upstream for about three miles, but at low water they realized that it would be too shallow even for the shallop. The area was heavily wooded, too, leaving little open ground for cultivation, and was too far from where the fish ran in shoals – and they rejected it as a suitable site for a settlement.

Others used the longboat to land on Clarke's Island, hoping that such a location would give them protection from marauding natives, but discovered

The landing of the first Pilgrims at Plymouth, with the *Mayflower* in the background.

that it was only about two miles in circumference and the little fresh water they saw was likely to fail in the dry season.

Both parties of explorers returned to the *Mayflower* for the night, but this time determined that on the following day a final choice of a site should be made. Winter was already too near to allow further delay: it would not be long before it would be almost impossible to work in the open to build shelters, or even to cut logs for the purpose – and, the longer they had to subsist on the food still on the vessel, the sooner it would be exhausted. The shortage of beer seems to have been a prime problem, although there was little they could do to remedy the deficiency in the immediate future. Besides, Christmas was almost on them and they wanted to celebrate it joyfully, rather than have to make the best of it in the overcrowded 'tween decks of the *Mayflower*.

Two possible sites were again investigated – and the die was cast. A vote was taken and the decision went in favour of Plymouth – long known to the Indians as Patuxet.

It was agreed that the settlement should be built on high ground overlooking the bay and where an extensive stretch of land, on the north bank of the Town Brook, had been cleared and planted with corn

no more than three or four years since. The brook ran down the hillside to a convenient safe place in which to harbour the shallop, and it provided fresh water and drained the site. To the south of the stream there were more cornfields, all ready for their use in due season; and to one side there was a large hillock – known today as Burial Hill, although in the seventeenth century it was called Fort Hill because it formed an excellent site for the planters' ordnance, commanding all sides of the settlement and its approaches. From the summit it was possible to see Cape Cod on the far promontory of the Bay.

It was strange indeed that the Pilgrims should find this site which had once been inhabited and was now deserted but left all ready for them; the land cleared for dwellings, ideally close to the brook, and the cornfields already cleansed by earlier crops. It is possible that, had it not been for this very lucky strike, the Pilgrim Fathers would never have cleared sufficient land in time to build shelters before the worst of the long winter came to take its toll – and without the "farmland" they would almost certainly have starved. If it was the Almighty who led the Pilgrim Fathers to Plymouth harbour, it remains inconceivable that he had planned that those who

The Pilgrims survey their new home, a stark and wintry scene.

had cultivated the ground should be dispossessed of it by means of a vicious plague, which had ravished the Pawkunnawkuts Indians in 1617, killing off almost the whole tribe and dispersing the few that survived. Yet it is strange, too, that the plague did not spread beyond the immediate locality. But the Pilgrims knew nothing about this visitation and were a little nervous about taking over where others had obviously done the ground-work.

For security purposes it was decided to leave about twenty Pilgrims ashore that night and to bring the main party of the men to the site on the following morning, with the object of making an immediate start on the building programme. It was almost certainly going to be a tremendous task to cut timber and to dig foundations in the icy conditions, but a start had to be made at once to erect some shelters ashore before the weather became too bad and the almost intolerable situation aboard the overcrowded *Mayflower* sapped the will and strength of the Pilgrims.

But, in their eagerness to see all there was to be seen in the neighbourhood, the party left ashore that night neglected to take proper precautions until it was too dark to see what they were doing. They failed to build even a light stockade, and there was no shelter for them when the rain began to fall. And fall it did, in torrents of water, lashed into their faces by a gale of wind that veered from point to point. Nor had they any provisions with them, expecting that food would be brought to them from the *Mayflower* at first light. But the gale was so severe that the shallop was unable to leave the ship before eleven o'clock – and when supplies had been off-loaded onto the beach it was found impracticable to beat back again to the *Mayflower*, which was, despite the almost landlocked harbour, having to ride out the storm with three anchors.

The gale persisted throughout the day and night and into Friday 22nd December without any sign of letting up. Mary Allerton gave birth to a child at the height of the gale, but it was still-born, probably because of the conditions aboard the restlessly pitching ship.

Saturday proved to be less violently stormy and every man who could be spared and who was fit enough to work was taken ashore in the shallop to start felling and cutting timber.

As usual that Sunday – 24th December, Christmas Eve in both the calendar of that era and the modern one – was passed in rest and prayer, regardless of the urgency of their need to build shelters ashore. But they were suddenly disturbed at their devotions by a series of wild shrieks from the shore that almost created a panic among the women and scared the men badly. Silence followed at once and, search as they would, the Pilgrims saw no sign of Indians or wild animals.

Christmas Day was not to be a holiday. Every available man returned to the task of felling trees, cutting and trimming logs, and hauling them to the site of the new township. Towards nightfall, tired and sore from the unaccustomed toil, and about ready to give up for the night, the men were again alarmed by a series of weird shrieks that suggested to them the war-cries from a party of hostile Indians. Muskets, after the previous day's scare, were all ready and were grabbed up on the instant. But again, although they searched the neighbourhood warily and carefully, the Pilgrims failed to find any sign of human life.

As night came down, most of the Pilgrims returned to their families aboard the *Mayflower*, leaving about twenty to guard the timber and to sharpen their tools ready for the morning. Unexpectedly, before they had even settled down, a high wind sprang up and contact between the shore party and the vessel was lost for the rest of the night.

Nevertheless, some effort was made to celebrate Christmas on board, although it was to prove something of a fiasco, for the men were too utterly tired and muscle-weary to enjoy it. Nor, at first, had they anything but water with which to encourage some good cheer amongst themselves – until Captain Jones, a good-hearted man, if determined where the conduct of his ship and his crew were concerned, ordered some of his private store of beer to be made available to them.

It was Wednesday before the weather let up sufficiently to allow the cutting of timber for the settlement to continue, and on that day plans were discussed for siting the buildings – including the design and location of a fort from which to defend the village. The hilltop offered an excellent field of fire, and would be difficult to surprise. Also the ground there seemed more easily workable, and it was decided to erect a platform for the cannon on the summit of the hill, and to build a street of houses on either side. The street is now Leyden Street.

Further days of careful planning went into the scheme while the main party continued with the job of cutting and preparing logs for the work of construction. The single men were encouraged to join

up with individual families to form units, so as to reduce the number of houses immediately required. Nineteen family units were organized in this manner. The street was measured out and lots were to be drawn for position. Then the size of each plot was fixed by the number in the family, at $2\frac{3}{4}$ by $16\frac{1}{2}$ yards per person – in the belief that the men were too weakened by the long Atlantic crossing and the dreadful weather to have the strength to build on a larger scale.

But, as a matter of urgency, it was decided to complete the Common House first, so that the Pilgrims could transfer their stores and tools ashore and so save themselves the often difficult passage to and from the *Mayflower* each morning and evening.

Edward Thompson, one of William White's menservants, had died aboard the *Mayflower* on 4th December, exhausted by his experiences; two days later Jasper More, a boy attached to Governor Carver's family, also had died while the ship lay in Cape Cod harbour. It was a time of tragedy for the Pilgrim Fathers – tragedy that was to deepen sadly as the days went by. Dorothy Bradford, wife of William Bradford, met her death while her husband was away with the second expedition sent out to explore the Cape: stepping down from the *Mayflower*'s ladder into the longboat, she was caught unawares by a sudden upheaval of the boat as it was struck by a particularly vicious wave; she was flung over the side before anybody could make a grab at her, and snatched away by the fast-running seas – never to be seen again. Richard Britteridge died aboard the *Mayflower* on 21st December – the first to die in Plymouth harbour – and Degory Priest followed him to the grave on 1st January 1621. Rose Standish died on 29th January; Solomon Prower, a manservant in the employ of Christopher Martin, died on Christmas Eve, to be followed by the second manservant in that family, John Langemore, before the end of 1620.

And so, exhausted, without proper rest, hot meals and adequate shelter, the Pilgrims began to slip away, one by one.

The weather continued wet, bitterly cold and with high winds to make the necessary task of tree-felling a dangerous one. And the travelling between ship and shore was a sore trial and sometimes a hazardous business.

Then, on 3rd January 1621, just as the workers had

returned wet and exhausted to the *Mayflower*, a cry almost of despair rose from among them as they saw a flame begin to flicker among the stubble of the cornfields. From the *Mayflower* there was nothing that the Pilgrims could do about it but watch in growing horror in the gathering darkness as the fire spread and raced through the fields. It had to have been set alight deliberately; the stubble was too wet to have caught fire from some accidentally dropped spark – but there was no sight of natives in the glare from the flames. The fire quickly died down again, although acrid clouds of smoke drifted across the harbour and the ship for the rest of the night.

Next morning, worried by the arson and the threat of attack by hostile Indians, Standish took four or five men ashore to see if he could locate the danger before the main party disembarked.

They searched the area where the fires had burned and found some wigwams, probably old and long since abandoned, but no sign of any Indians – nor were they able to discover the cause of the fire.

But at that time, sickness posed a far greater danger to the Pilgrims than any threat from unseen Indians. Christopher Martin, their somewhat arrogant and aggressive Treasurer, who had just lost both of his menservants through death, fell ill and lay helpless in his bunk aboard the *Mayflower*. Surgeon Fuller did what he could for him, but soon realized that his patient's constitution had been so undermined by the trials of the three months since they had sailed from England that there could be no hope for him – and sent for Governor Carver.

Quietly, Carver familiarized himself with the dying man's accounts, prayed with him and stayed at his bunkside until he lost consciousness, never to recover it again.

It started out to be an unusually fine day on 8th January 1621, the day Martin died. Jones sent the shallop out to sea in search of fish in the hope of relieving the shortage of food aboard the vessel, and although the boat ran into a short, sharp storm it returned that evening with three large seals and a sizeable cod. On the same day, Francis Billington, son of the notorious John Billington Senior, and one of the pilots went off to investigate a large tract of water that he had seen to the west, a few days earlier, from the masthead of the *Mayflower*. It proved to be only about three miles distant, consisting of two large lakes, the more extensive being about five or six miles in circumference. The lakes drained into Town Brook, which flowed past the new settlement and into Plymouth Bay. The pair found that the lakes appeared to be well stocked with fish and that there seemed to be plenty of fowl in the woods around them.

Later, Billington and his companion came across seven or eight wigwams; although these appeared to have been long abandoned they steered well clear, having only a single musket between them.

On 9th January the Common House, some twenty feet square, had reached the stage where it needed little more than roofing; it was decided that, when the thatching and mortaring were complete, each family would work better and faster if they were then freed to start on their own homes rather than continue building the village as a communal effort. Lots were then drawn for the sites along both sides of the street.

On the 11th, William Bradford was suddenly struck down in agony as his hip-bone seized up on him. His ankles began to ache and swell, and it was evening before the worst of the pain passed to leave him weak and only just able to sit up again.

Rain came down in such torrents after noon on the following day that all work was brought to a standstill. But four men had been sent out that morning to cut thatch for the roof of the Common House. About half a mile from the work site they cut enough to make two large bundles. Two of the men then left the others to bind the bundles, and went prospecting for more. When they returned, they found that the pair, Peter Browne and John Goodman, had gone. They took a look around and called after them, but gained no clue as to their whereabouts. Worried at last by the continued absence, they returned to the work site to warn the builders that two of their number were missing.

Carver, despite the appalling weather, took three or four men with him and made a search in the area where they had last been seen. Having no better luck they returned to organize a larger search party.

By nightfall the second party returned, soaked, exhausted – and empty-handed.

Seriously concerned by now at the possibility that Goodman and Browne had been captured by Indians, Carver had ten or twelve men fully armed and ready to continue the search at first light – but, despite the most rigorous search of the district all during the following day, no signs were seen of the missing men. But, just as darkness was falling and the

weary searchers were about to give up until the next morning, Goodman and Browne staggered back into the settlement, desperately tired, very hungry and almost frozen to death. Goodman needed to have his shoes cut from his feet, and it was to be a long time before he was able to stand again – longer still before he was fit to work.

Browne explained that, shortly after their companions had left them, they finished binding the bundles of thatching and decided to eat the meat they had brought with them: they wanted water to drink with the meal. Strangely, although we know that the Pilgrims brought their dogs with them to the New World, we have no knowledge of how many there were, nor even of the breeds they favoured; and this is one of the very few references to them that appears in any of the contemporary chronicles of the events surrounding their first arrival in the Americas. Browne told his friends that they had taken a mastiff bitch and a spaniel into the woods with them: when they went in search of water the beasts followed them to a nearby lake. There the dogs caught sight of a deer and gave chase. Goodman and Browne ran after them – and lost themselves completely.

A scene of industry not long after the first landing at Plymouth; from an illustration by Currier and Ives. Despite many hardships – including fire – the Pilgrims were able to construct the basics of the Plymouth colony with remarkable speed.

The two men wandered about in the pouring rain all afternoon in search of their bearings – as it had been fine when they started out that morning they had taken no raincapes, so that they were soon thoroughly soaked. So utterly miserable did they become that, despite having only sickles with which to defend themselves, they looked around for an Indian wigwam – anywhere, whatever the risk, where they could obtain shelter from the torrential rain and the biting wind.

By the time night had fallen they had still found no sign of a shelter and had been without food since midday. Too tired to tramp further, they had curled up on the wet ground, trembling with cold. They had heard wolves baying all night and at least one of the animals had sounded frighteningly close. Badly scared, the pair had decided that their only hope, if wolves were around, was to climb into a tree – although they feared they might freeze to death in the wind. Browne and Goodman – and one of the dogs, it seems – had spent the night standing terrified under a tall tree; by the time daylight had come to relieve the horrors of the darkness, they were both on the verge of collapse.

Again they had set out to find their way back to the settlement, stumbling past a lake, wading through icy streams and skirting forests without being able to recognize any of them. Fortunately, they still had enough sense to seek some high ground and, by late afternoon, had reached a hilltop from where they could see the Bay. They had then been able to plot their position accurately. Even so, it had taken them until sunset before they stumbled, completely exhausted, back into the settlement.

Sunday 14th January, as seemed to happen so often on that day of the week, was not to be a day of peace, devoted entirely to rest and prayer as the Pilgrims so earnestly hoped. By now the larger proportion of the men were camped ashore, or had found shelter in the Common House. The new building was crammed with beds, and among the sleepers lay Governor Carver and William Bradford, ill and exhausted.

It had been intended that the very first service to be held ashore should be on this day, and everybody was to be brought from the *Mayflower* for the event. But at 6 am, before it was even daylight, those aboard the ship were shocked to see a fire break out somewhere in the settlement and, fanned by a strong wind, blaze up fiercely. Unable to see much in the darkness of the early hours of the morning, the terrified women almost convinced themselves that the village had been attacked and set alight by Indians, and that everybody in it had been murdered.

Nor were the shore party in any state to set their minds at rest immediately; they were much too busy, fetching and carrying water from the brook to put the fire out, to spare men to man the longboat or the shallop to carry the news, and it was too dark as yet to signal. Besides, there was some panic in the Common House where the fire had occurred, because the Pilgrims had stacked their muskets inside, together with the gunpowder needed to charge them.

But the fire died as quickly as it had blazed up and it was discovered that some chance spark had got into the thatching over the roof to set it alight. Fortunately, although the thatching had flared up spectacularly, the roof timbers had hardly been scorched.

And so the days went by, a few like 15th January, when the rain had come down so heavily and the water in the harbour had lashed about so treacherously that those aboard the *Mayflower* had been unable to get ashore, and those already in the settlement had been unable to do any work – while other days had been brighter and even occasional spells of sunshine had helped the strong and healthy to make some real progress in the erection of their houses.

On the 20th, using both the shallop and the longboat, the Pilgrims began to ferry ashore the food stocks and the general stores to be stacked in the now finished Common House. By the following day Captain Jones was glad to know that his holds had been cleared of all but a few of the men and the women and children. During those busy days occasional distant parties of Indians were seen, but they never attempted to approach the settlement or the Planters.

Sunday 4th February brought its usual Sabbath spate of troubles. The day started with rain and the weather quickly deteriorated until a full-scale gale was raging – the worst the Pilgrims had yet known. The *Mayflower*, despite its well protected anchorage, received such a buffeting that, being light in the water since the removal of the stores and most of its passengers, it was for a time in some danger of capsizing. Ashore, the Pilgrims fought hard to strengthen their buildings, although few other than the Common House had been completed.

The monument commemorating the Pilgrims' landing.

On that day the first of the smaller houses to be completed was commandeered on the orders of the Governor to provide shelter for the growing number of sick – but on the 9th it caught fire through a spark that got into the thatching of the roof, as had happened to the Common House nearly a month before; just as fortunately, the fire did no more than destroy the thatching.

Jones, although he had no concern in the building of the settlement, proved himself helpful in many little ways. On the evening of the fire, for instance, he shot five geese which he handed over for the benefit of the sick – but kept for himself and his crew a deer that he had found freshly killed and with its horns removed, no doubt by Indians who had quietly disappeared at his approach.

But insidiously, and despite the care of Surgeon Fuller and those detailed to assist him, sickness continued to spread among the Pilgrims and the crew of the *Mayflower*, both ashore and afloat, until at one time it reached such proportions that only seven out of the whole company were left fit enough to care for

The Pilgrims celebrate their success at having found a new home.

the others. The appalling conditions, the heavy labour for men and women alike, the not always noble (though in many ways understandable) behaviour of some of the Pilgrims in adversity, the lack of hot meals at regular intervals and the unbalanced diet went far towards sapping the strength and stamina of them all – until slowly but surely the toll of death among them rose from a trickle to a disastrous flood.

During the Spring of 1621 Roger Wilder, a manservant employed by Governor Carver, died; the second of the More boys attached to the family of William Brewster died; Elizabeth Winslow died on 24th March; Elias Story, a manservant of Edward Winslow, died; Ellen More, the young sister of the three More boys, died soon after two of her brothers; Mary Allerton died on 25th February (her daughter was to survive until 1699 to be the last survivor of those who sailed to the New World in the *Mayflower*); John Hooke, a servant boy in the Allerton family, died; John Crackston Senior died; Rose Standish, the wife of Miles Standish, died on

29th January; Christopher Martin, the Treasurer of the Pilgrim Fathers, died on 8th January and his wife died soon after him; William Mullins died and his wife died shortly afterwards; Joseph Mullins, their son, and Robert Carter, their servant, died almost at the same time; William White died on 21st February; William Holbeck was the second of the menservants in the employ of the White family to die; Oceanus Hopkins, the infant son of Stephen and Elizabeth Hopkins, who had been born at sea aboard the *Mayflower*, failed to survive the epidemic; Edward Tilley died that Spring, followed by Ann Tilley, his wife; John Tilley was also followed to the grave by his wife; Thomas Rogers succumbed, as did Thomas Tinker and his wife, and their son – the whole of the Tinker family; John Rigdale and his wife Alice died, which ended that family; the widow of James Chilton died; Edward Fuller was followed to the grave by his wife; John Turner died, as did his sons; Sarah Eaton died; Moses Fletcher, Thomas Williams, John Goodman, he of the frozen foot, Edmund Margeson, and Richard Clarke, all died during the epidemic that

The view in the nineteenth century from Burial Hill, known to the
Pilgrims as Fort Hill.

year; Degory Priest died on 1st January; and John Allerton, one of the sailors hired by the Pilgrim Fathers, died, as did his colleague, Thomas English.

Before them, during the last days of 1620, had died Jasper More, his brother, William Butten, Solomon Prower, John Langemore, Edward Thompson, James Chilton, Richard Britteridge and Dorothy Bradford, who had been accidentally drowned – to make a total of fifty-two deaths. Except for little Oceanus Hopkins, who had been born at sea, they were all members of the Pilgrim Church and their entourage of servants and hired hands – exactly half of the original 102 who had sailed from Plymouth, Devon, in the *Mayflower*.

One of the tragic features of the epidemic was that, although thirteen of the twenty-four husbands died, no fewer than fourteen of the eighteen wives were lost. Of the twenty-four families, four had been wiped out and sixteen had suffered loss. Surprisingly, the survivors resolved to remain.

And, in April, almost the last to fall to the epidemic was Governor Carver, who collapsed while planting in a field and died within a matter of hours – only a few days after the *Mayflower* had left Plymouth for its return journey to England. Carver was a severe loss to the tiny community. An excellent farm organizer, a leader that all found pleasure in following, he was so respected that he had been re-elected to the office of Governor on 23rd March, only thirteen days before the departure of the *Mayflower*.

To end this sorry chapter, Catherine Carver, the Governor's widow, followed her husband to the graveyard within a month.

An early meeting in the New World.

14 Contact with the Indians

During all the dreadful days of the sickness the fact that Indians, possibly hostile, surrounded the slowly growing and still wholly unprepared settlement hung like a black cloud of worry over the heads of the Pilgrim Fathers: to hide their losses from the natives, graves were flattened and planted with corn. And the Indians were more in evidence from the early days of February 1621, although they perpetrated no real warlike act.

On one occasion, a settler while out fowling caught sight of twelve Indians marching towards the plantation and, by the noise coming from the nearby woods, estimated that there were many more of them in hiding there. He lay in some undergrowth until the natives passed him, then quietly raced around them to reach the settlement ahead of them and to give the alarm.

The Pilgrims assembled quickly, fully armed, to defend themselves, but the Indians failed to arrive – although when darkness came their fires could be seen at some distance from the plantation.

Subsequently, Standish and Francis Cooke, while felling trees in the woods, left their tools behind them when they returned to the settlement for a meal. When they went back, the tools were gone. From then on the Pilgrims considered it wiser to keep their

tools and equipment, especially their weapons, close at hand at all times.

At a meeting of the Pilgrim Fathers on 13th February it was decided that the time had come to establish some form of military preparedness – and Miles Standish was elected "Captain". And out of the blue, while the meeting was in progress, two Indians appeared on the top of Cantaugcanteest Hill – Strawberry Hill, now called Watson's Hill – less than a quarter of a mile away on the opposite side of Town Brook, and began to signal. It took a few minutes before the Pilgrims realized that the Indians were actually signalling them – and longer before they understood that they were asking them to move forward to meet them.

The Pilgrims armed themselves quickly and, despite their numbers, held back and made signs that the Indians should come to them. The natives, probably wary of the overwhelming strength of the Pilgrims, made no attempt to accept the invitation.

After a few minutes spent in fruitless gesticula-tions, Standish, feeling that it was safe enough and being very anxious to make contact with the natives, took Hopkins with him, waded across Town Brook and strode up the hill towards them. As they approached, the two Englishmen saw that the Indians had only a single musket between them and that it lay, pacifically, at their feet.

The two parties were still some distance apart when there came a sudden hullabaloo from the surrounding woods, warning Standish that there must be a large number of natives hidden there – and, unexpectedly, the two on the hilltop suddenly ran off.

With this evidence that there were large numbers of Indians in the region, and unable to contact their leaders to agree peace terms with them, Standish decided that it was time to bring ashore the heaviest weapons the Pilgrims possessed and to site them on top of The Mount – afterwards called Fort Hill, and

One of the Plymouth houses in the process of construction; detail of a model by M. J. Jane.

now Burial Hill – where they could command the ground all around.

The buildings were going up slowly, chiefly because of the sickness that was prevalent in the settlement, but partly also because of the need to keep back a few of the fit men to act as guards against any sudden attack. Nor was it considered wise to send out hunting parties except in sufficient numbers to be able to defend themselves; when the Governor went inland to investigate the prospects of fish in Billington Sea he had to take five others with him for security – a very high proportion of the few fit men. Happily, the lake gave promise of good fishing and there were innumerable signs of the presence of deer.

On that day, 7th March, some garden seeds were sown – the first planting by the Pilgrim Fathers in New England.

On the 16th Standish called another meeting to finalize his military preparations; strangely, for the second time the meeting was interrupted by the appearance of an Indian. Surprisingly, the Indian marched boldly forward between the skeleton houses towards the gathering, until he stood before them. He saluted in English fashion and greeted them with the word "Welcome!"

Eagerly the Pilgrims began to question him, but his English was limited to only a few broken phrases that were difficult to understand; it became evident that he had learned them on the island of Monchiggan –

Monhegan – off the coast of what is now Maine, some 150 miles to the north, from the captains and crews of fishing vessels that had ventured across the Atlantic in search of the rich shoals that inhabited those waters. He told the Pilgrim Fathers that he was called Samoset and that he was the Sagamore – the Paramount Chief – of the Morattigan Indians, who flourished in Pemmaquid – now Bristol, Maine. He explained that the previous July he had gone aboard Captain Dermer's ship at Monhegan and had been carried in it to Cape Cod. Samoset had found plenty of friends in those parts and had stayed there for a time.

So glad of his presence and his apparently wide knowledge of the coast for hundreds of miles to the north were the Pilgrims that they presented him with a horseman's coat to keep out the bitterly cold wind – in the hope that he would stay with them. He asked for beer but was given some brandy, a biscuit and other oddments to eat.

Over the makeshift meal Samoset told them that the place where their growing village now stood had once been occupied by the Patuxet Indians. He told them, too, of the plague that had depopulated the region four years earlier.

He spent the night in the house of Stephen Hopkins but next day said that he intended to return to the Massasoits, not far away, where he had been staying. But before he left he warned the settlers against a tribe that lived to the north-east of them – the Nausets,

The visit to the colony by Samoset, Sagamore of the Morattigan Indians.

Early North American colonists trading with the Indians for furs.

whose village was near the site of the present Eastham. Samoset explained that they mustered about one hundred fighting braves and had good reason to detest the English. He went on to tell, as best he could, how a Captain Thomas Hunt had persuaded a mixed party of Indians to approach him and his crew, on the pretext of wanting to barter trinkets and beads for animal skins. As soon as the natives came within reach of the Englishmen, twenty of the Patuxet tribe and seven of the Nausets had been seized and made captive. They had been taken aboard the English ship and transported to Spain to be sold as slaves – where they had fetched £20 a head. Subsequently, in about July of the previous year, the Nausets had captured five of Sir Ferdinando Gorges' men and killed three of them in reprisal for the kidnapping of their fellow tribesmen by Hunt – the other two had escaped to Monhegan with the news.

Samoset was then presented with a knife, a bracelet and a ring and urged to return with some of the Massasoit Indians to trade trinkets for beaver skins – although he was told to warn them that they must leave their bows and arrows at least a quarter of a mile from the settlement.

Next morning, a Sunday, was again to be disturbed as Samoset appeared with five Massasoits – as tall as himself, sturdy, and reminiscent of English gypsies. They were clothed in deer skins with leather leggings and aprons. Some had painted a broad black stripe

from their foreheads to their chins – and the leader carried what appeared to be a cat's skin over his arm. And in accordance with the warning given to Samoset, they had left their weapons some distance from the settlement. The natives had brought three or four pelts with them but, as it was Sunday, the Pilgrims refused to trade, although they did urge the Indians to return another day and to bring more skins then.

The Indians left in great good humour, having been given some few trinkets as an earnest of the Pilgrims' readiness to trade, but Samoset was not to be got rid of quite so easily. He pleaded sickness and stayed in the settlement until the Pilgrims sent him away on the Wednesday, disappointed that the Massasoits had not returned with skins for barter.

For the third time Standish convened a meeting to consider military affairs – and for the third time the session was interrupted by the arrival of Indians. Two or three of them suddenly appeared on the top of Cantaugcanteest Hill opposite and began to act in a provocative manner, making pretence of whetting their arrow-heads and stretching their bows threateningly. But when Captain Standish and the two Master's Mates – the pilots of the *Mayflower* – strode in their direction they ran off.

On the same day, 21st March 1621, the shallop was used to bring ashore the last of the Pilgrims and everything else aboard the ship that belonged to them

– and so, finally, the Pilgrim Fathers left the *Mayflower*.

Next day Samoset returned yet again, this time bringing with him Tisquantum – to become known as Squanto – who claimed to be the only surviving Patuxet from the site where the settlement was being built. His story was indeed a strange one. He had been one of the twenty-seven Indians kidnapped by Captain Hunt to be sold as slaves in Spain. But he had managed to escape while the slave-ship was in English waters and had found employment with a London merchant named John Slany, living with him in Cornhill. He had learnt some English during his stay there but had eventually been taken back to America by a Frenchman, Captain Dermer, to act as a guide – and had again escaped.

Squanto arrived at the settlement with three companions. They had brought some pelts and dried red herrings with them to trade, but it soon appeared that they had more serious business to transact. They told the Pilgrims that hidden not far away was Sagamore – Paramount Chief – Massasoit, the Chief's brother, Quadequina, and a large party of braves.

After a great deal of talk and shouting that lasted for about an hour, the Massasoits and their Chief came out onto the summit of Watson's Hill, opposite – but the Indians were as unwilling to send their Chief across to the English colony as the Pilgrims were to risk their Governor at the hands of the Indians.

It has to be remembered that by then the Pilgrims had been badly ravaged by disease. Only thirty men and youths remained alive, many of whom were sick, while Massasoit's party on the hilltop opposite mustered about sixty fit men.

Squanto acted as go-between, and eventually Edward Winslow climbed Watson's Hill as Governor Carver's representative. Presents were exchanged and Winslow made a speech conveying the good wishes of King James for peace and goodwill, and informed them that Governor Carver was ready to barter with them.

How well Squanto translated the speech can only be guessed at now, but at best it must have had little relation to the sentiments expressed. We can be fairly sure, in any event, that few if any of the Massasoit Indians had ever heard of King James, but in the end it persuaded Sagamore Massasoit to accept Winslow as a hostage and to leave him in the custody of his brother Quadequina while he and about twenty tribesmen laid down their bows and arrows and crossed the Town Brook, to be met by Standish, Isaac Allerton and six musketeers.

Six or seven Indians were held as hostages for the safe return of Winslow, and then the Sagamore was conducted to a partly built house that had been hurriedly decorated with a green rug and a few cushions.

Carver appeared, accompanied by a drummer, a trumpeter and a small escort of musketeers. The two leaders sat down to negotiate a peace treaty. First, the Indian Chief was offered meat and drank an enormous beaker of brandy that caused him to sweat during the whole of the meeting, while Massasoit provided the tobacco as his share in the hospitality.

A seven-point treaty was drawn up and agreed – although how accurately it was translated for the benefit of the Indian Chief we shall never know. It read:

1. That neither he, nor any of his, should injure, or do hurt, to any of our people.

2. And if any of his did hurt to any of ours; he should send the offender, that we might punish him.

3. That if any of our tools were taken away, when our people were at work; he should cause them to be restored: and if ours did any harm to any of his, we would do the like to them.

4. If any did unjustly war against him; we would aid him. If any did war against us, he should aid us.

5. He should send to his neighbour confederates, to certify them of this, that they might not wrong us; but might be likewise comprised in the Conditions of Peace.

6. That when their men came to us, they should leave their bows and arrows behind them; as we should do our pieces, when we came to them.

7. Lastly, that doing thus, *King James* would esteem of him as his friend and ally.

The Governor and the Sagamore parted at the brook, although Standish held onto his hostages until Winslow should be released. However, Quadequina then arrived with a company of Indians expecting to be entertained in their turn.

The Sagamore's brother apparently enjoyed the entertainment that was quickly provided for him; a

A sample of Edward Winslow's handwriting. He was the first colonist to import cattle from England
and this agreement records the sale of six shares in the "Red Cow" to Captain Standish.

Governor Carver and Massasoit negotiate the seven-point peace treaty. The Pilgrims
provided meat and brandy for the meeting; the Indians brought tobacco.

modest, quietly cheerful man who withdrew in good order in due time – whereas some of his followers seemed more than prepared to make a night of it, had the Pilgrims given them the slightest encouragement.

Winslow was freed as soon as Quadequina returned to his tribe. Samoset and Squanto then spent the night in the settlement while the Massasoit Indians, with all their womenfolk, camped down in the woods not a mile away.

The Indians were excitedly noisy and Standish kept his weak force alert all night; but, except for a great deal of friendly coming-and-going between the Englishmen and the Indians during the next few days, no threat was apparent in the Indian attitude towards the Planters.

At last Standish was able to conduct an effective and uninterrupted meeting to regularize military matters, and during it John Carver was re-elected to the office of Governor, to serve as such during the following year (in the 17th century the year commenced on 25th March, and the election therefore took place on New Year's Day 1621).

Samoset and Squanto were to spend much of their days thereafter with the Pilgrim Fathers: Squanto was to be of immense help to the settlers as he was able to teach them how to prepare the land for sowing Indian corn, how to plant it and how to manure it with fish from the brook – an enormously valuable asset to the Pilgrims when their own seed failed. Without the Indian corn in due season, it is probable that the Pilgrim Fathers would have starved.

15 The Paramount Chief

In April 1621, as we have seen, Carver died; in his place William Bradford was elected to occupy the office, despite his having far from recovered from his illness. Perhaps for that reason, Isaac Allerton was chosen to be his assistant.

The *Mayflower*, which had delayed its sailing from Plymouth because of the epidemic which had carried off half its crew – besides half its passengers – and the difficulties of handling an undermanned vessel in the Atlantic before the last of the winter gales blew themselves out, finally put to sea on 5th April 1621.

As far as we know, the voyage passed without any notable incident – but, as it reached London on either 5th or 6th May, the *Mayflower* must have made an unusually swift passage. Thereafter it had a refit and made a round trip to la Rochelle, France, discharging its cargo of Bay Salt in London Docks on 11th October.

Captain Jones, its Master, died the following summer, and by 1624 the vessel lay at Rotherhithe so near dereliction that she was valued, together with "one suit of worn sails" and her fittings, at £138–8–0. Although it is possible that she was again refitted and used to carry further batches of emigrants to New England, the *Mayflower* and her Master disappear from our story at this point.

The fact that the patent granted by the London Virginia Company to the Pilgrims who sailed on the *Mayflower* did not cover the territory so far north of their intended destination posed a problem for the London Company. The decision, too, to supersede

The departure of the *Mayflower*, bound for England, on 5th April 1621. This was to be the Pilgrims' last sight of the vessel which had brought them across the Atlantic.

The *Mayflower* lies in the harbour of Plymouth, Devon,
preparatory to her voyage to the New World; model by E. J. Jane
built as part of the celebrations commemorating the 350th
anniversary of the Pilgrim Fathers' epic voyage.

the second of the two Virginia Companies with a "Council of New England" on 3rd November 1620 complicated matters further.

It became necessary for the London Company of Adventurers to apply to the Council for a new patent in order to legalize the standing of the Pilgrim Fathers in New Plymouth.

Such a patent was granted on 1st June 1621 to "John Peirce and his Associates" on behalf of the original Adventurers and Planters. This patent gave to each of the settlers one hundred acres of land, and the power to make their own laws and govern themselves as they saw fit.

With all his old courage apparently restored, Robert Cushman prepared to sail with the second party of Pilgrims to join the "Old Comers". He chartered a small vessel (about fifty-five tons), the *Fortune*, for a voyage due to leave England at the beginning of July.

He gathered together thirty-five Pilgrims, some from Leyden, some from England; but entirely without foresight he gave no attention to the problem of the colony's requirements for food and provisions – tools, clothing, rope and cord, nails and knives, canvas and oil and, of course, seed. In fact, when the *Fortune* finally cleared England and stood out into the Atlantic, after persistent westerly gales had delayed the departure for six long and frustrating weeks, there was little aboard the vessel other than the emigrants, the crew and sufficient supplies to see them to New England and for the crew's return journey – assuming a minimum delay at New Plymouth.

The Pilgrim Fathers in New England knew nothing of all this, of course: there could be no news from the Old Country until the *Mayflower* had passed the information to their friends of their whereabouts and a second ship was chartered to sail to their assistance with supplies and reinforcements for their diminished numbers.

Suffering no doubt from homesickness, from the heartbreak of losing so many of their relatives and friends during the epidemic, bone-weary from the toil of building the settlement during that dreadfully cold, stormy winter, and fearful of running short of food before help arrived – it was perhaps as well that, during the late spring and the early summer of 1621, the settlers should have been diverted by having to give so much of their attention to the problem of dealing with the natives.

Statue by Cyrus Dalin of Massasoit, the Indian Sagamore who proved to be the Pilgrims' most important ally in their dealings with the natives surrounding their colony. Without his friendship it is unlikely that the colony would have survived.

(*opposite*) The *Mayflower* in high seas; a nineteenth-century illustration, by Marshall Johnson, which appeared in *Munsey's Magazine*.

Since the meeting with Sagamore Massasoit the settlement had been inundated by parties of visiting Indians. As they came to understand that the Englishmen were entirely friendly, they had begun to arrive in ever greater numbers, bringing their wives and children with them to enjoy the food and hospitality provided by the Pilgrims as an assurance of goodwill. But so many took to wandering through the half-completed buildings and strolling into the settlers' homes to satisfy their curiosity that they soon became an embarrassment to the Pilgrim Fathers.

Work was being held up on every building project and the laying-out of gardens and fields, the manufacture of furnishings and the essential need to repair and replace worn-out tools were being badly delayed by the invasion. And, even more worrisomely, the need to feed the Indians was causing a severe run on the slender stocks of corn the Pilgrims needed.

At the end of June 1621 Bradford decided to send representatives to Massasoit with a message of goodwill, to perform the delicate task of protesting about the flood of visitors to the settlement and to explain, as gently as possible, that the run on their food stocks was so great that if it continued the Pilgrims would be in danger of starvation. The Governor chose Edward Winslow and Stephen Hopkins for the task, and detailed Squanto to go along as interpreter.

The trio left Plymouth on Monday 2nd July, taking a fine red horseman's coat and a few trinkets as presents, intent on reaching Namaschet (now Middlesborough) on the Namaschet River, some fifteen miles inland, as the first resting place on their journey to Massasoit's "capital" at Sowans – around what is now Massasoit's Spring.

It was from Namaschet that much of the nuisance came. It had a sizeable population of Wampanoag Indians and, being near enough to Plymouth, acted as a magnet.

As they trekked inland towards the Indian village Winslow and Hopkins were met by ten or twelve Wampanoag Indians and could not get rid of them. The natives pestered the Englishmen for food, despite all that Squanto could do to discourage them. For hour after hour they ran alongside the trio, begging ceaselessly. Not until three o'clock, when the three entered Namaschet, did the Indians abandon their unwelcome pursuit – just as the population of the village turned out to greet the Englishmen. The

visitors were offered a meal of Indian bread and shads (fish rather like herrings). This must have embarrassed them considerably, their being on an errand designed to bring to an end the practice of entertaining the villagers in the English settlement.

The Indians thoroughly enjoyed the company of the two Englishmen, and managed to persuade one of them to fire his musket at a crow to scare away the masses of birds that did so much to damage their crops. But Squanto urged Winslow and Hopkins to press on further towards Packonokik.

The Pilgrims took their leave as courteously as they could and headed for Sowans; but after a march of about eight miles they came across a large party of Indians fishing at a weir who greeted them as cheerfully as had the natives of Namaschet, giving the Planters all the fish they could use. In return, because they now believed that they were to be given food wherever they went, Winslow and Hopkins readily handed over part of the food they had brought with them for the journey.

In the morning the trio strode off on their mission, but six of the Indians tagged on to them. After about six miles they came to a ford across a river – the River Taunton – and waded through it, to be challenged on the far bank by two elderly Indians, apparently quite undeterred by the six natives that accompanied the Englishmen; they soon became friendly when they realized that no attempt was to be made to attack or rob them – and again the Pilgrims parted with food in exchange for that offered them by the Indians.

The day was very hot but there was no shortage of fresh water, although Winslow and Hopkins were quick to note that the Indians would not drink except from springs. As they tramped along, the Pilgrims decided that the countryside was very much like that of faraway England. There was a lot of excellent timber – oaks, walnuts, firs and beech trees – but the woods were never so dense as to prevent easy passage. Although the terrain was gently hilly, cut about by streams and rivers and in places rocky, there was much cultivable land – although it was now a mass of weeds, sometimes standing head-high, a great deal of it had at one time or another been cleared.

As the two Pilgrims and Squanto progressed they kept meeting small parties of Indians, the women often carrying crabs, oysters and other dried shellfish which they offered to the Englishmen generously. It was late in the afternoon before they reached Sowans, about forty miles from Plymouth.

But Sagamore Massasoit was not there.

The willing villagers promptly sent runners off to find him and to bring him back. While the trio waited Squanto, understanding and appreciating the full status of a Sagamore, urged the two Pilgrims to greet Massasoit, when he arrived, with musket shots as a sort of Royal Salute, but Winslow and Hopkins, who had already scared away some of the women and children through the mere act of loading their weapons, were reluctant to risk giving the impression of bearing arms against the Chief. However, they were persuaded to make some gesture when the Sagamore arrived. As soon as he appeared, accompanied by a large party of braves, he was given a two-gun salute – which, to the relief of the Planters, was received with delight.

With Squanto to interpret for them, the Englishmen gave Bradford's message of goodwill and conveyed his assurance of the settlers' wish to live in peace and friendship with everybody. As a token of that friendship they presented Massasoit with the horseman's red coat and a chain to hang around his neck. The messengers then went on to explain to the Sagamore how the Pilgrims were being seriously hindered by the large number of Indians who persisted in coming into the settlement in the expectation of being entertained – and, more importantly, were rapidly reducing food stocks until, if the Pilgrim Fathers' crop failed, a famine in the settlement might result. They told him of Bradford's friendly wish that the visits be stopped until the result of the harvest was known, but added that the Sagamore, or any friend of his that he should send, would always be welcome.

The Englishmen handed over a copper chain which they suggested should be worn by any authorized visitor so that he could be identified as such and properly received.

Lastly, they told the Indian Chief that Governor Bradford would be glad at any time to barter for skins to be made up into clothing and bedding, and would be pleased to trade English seed for Indian corn to find out which produced the best crop from the local soil. It was explained that, when they first arrived at Cape Cod, the Pilgrims had found some substantial stocks of buried corn; they wanted to assure the Indians that, if the store belonged to any of them, the Planters would gladly recompense them, in due season, if they made their claims known.

Massasoit's reply was all the Pilgrims could

Winslow's visit to Massasoit forged important trade links and allowed the Pilgrims to protest about the large numbers of Indians inundating the colony.

possibly have hoped for. He reciprocated Bradford's good wishes and promised to put a stop to the constant pestering of the settlement by members of his tribe and, further, he promised to provide the corn needed for seed.

The Sagamore's speech to the Pilgrims and the surrounding Indians was evidently a cheerful affair. He encouraged his own people to trade skins with the settlers and talked at length to the Englishmen about England and the King's Majesty – deploring the fact that since the death of the Queen, Anne of Denmark, in 1619 he had had to live without a wife. Massasoit also solemnly warned the Pilgrims to have nothing to do with the French and to refuse to let them stay on what is today King James's Land – altogether a most unexpectedly knowledgeable speech from an "ignorant savage"!

But, unexpectedly, Massasoit had no food to offer his visitors. He had arrived in a hurry and had brought nothing with him. And Winslow and Hopkins had been too free with their own supplies in the expectation of further gifts of food from the Indians – not understanding the natives' careless improvidence. They had to go to bed hungry – and discovered that they were expected to share some planks laid close to the ground with the Sagamore and his wife and two of the Chief's men, all huddled tightly together and covered with only a mat or two. Nor were they prepared for the strange and noisy habit the Indians had of singing themselves to sleep, while they shared their bed with lice and fleas that infested the wigwam and almost drove the visitors out into the night.

They had no sleep at all that night and, when morning came, there was no breakfast for them either – but the settlers from Plymouth were quickly surrounded by a number of Sachems (Village Chiefs, inferior to the Sagamore) ready to trade skins for knives and ornaments.

Shortly after midday Massasoit returned with two fishes. They had the appearance of being bream but were three times as big and, when it came to the test, better meat. But more than forty people were to share the food and, after two nights and a day without a good meal, Winslow and Hopkins were almost as hungry after the fish as they were before it.

Massasoit tried hard to persuade his visitors to stay for a few days, but the Pilgrims were anxious to spend the Sabbath at home – and it was already the afternoon of Thursday. Equally, they were in no mood to tolerate again the uncomfortable and embarrassing conditions of the previous night. But by the time everything had been settled it was too late to leave Sowans that night.

By Friday morning Winslow and Hopkins were at their wits' end because of lack of sleep and food, and it took a great deal of patience on their part to listen to Massasoit's long-winded apologies. The Indian Chief retained Squanto to send him from village to village to organize the procurement of pelts and corn, but provided one of his tribe, Tokamahamon, to take his place as interpreter for the settlers – a man who was to prove himself both useful and loyal.

After a little fish and a handful of parched corn, the Englishmen set out on the return journey to Plymouth accompanied by Tokamahamon and about six other tribesmen. After they had covered about five miles the Indians led the Pilgrims out of their way to a wigwam in the hope of obtaining food – but there was nobody at home when they arrived and there was nothing edible in the wigwam. The hungry travellers had to trudge all the way back to the track that they had been following – and at the weir, where they felt certain that they would be as well received and entertained as they had been on the outward leg of their journey, they were disappointed to find that the place was now deserted.

One of the Indians succeeded in shooting a shad in the water, and a small squirrel from a tree which he shared with them; but so hungry had the Pilgrims become that they wrote a note to the Governor at Plymouth asking him to send food to meet them at Namaschet; they sent Tokamahamon running ahead with this message.

Fortunately for the famished Englishmen, soon after the runner had trotted off with the message two of the Indians caught sight of some fish and managed to catch enough for a good meal for them all before they lay down to rest for the night, Winslow and Hopkins being desperately tired after the discomfort and sleeplessness of the two previous nights.

But they were not to rest in peace for long. At about 2 am a sudden, violent storm of wind whipped around them, followed instantly by torrential rain, thunder and lightning. The rain came down so heavily that almost at once it doused their fire and, without shelter, they were soaked to the skin.

It was still pouring with rain as Winslow and Hopkins continued their way towards Namaschet next morning, where they were received with all the

Billington Sea, by the Plymouth Colony, provided an important source of fish; moreover, the surrounding area was well populated by game.

welcome and food they could possibly want. In view of the rain, the Indians offered the Englishmen accommodation for the night in one of their wigwams – but, because the next day was Sunday, the two were anxious to complete their journey to Plymouth.

Before they left Namaschet, they presented the villagers with a few trivial gifts in exchange for the kindness they had been shown – and for the second time the Pilgrims must have felt an acute sense of embarrassment because of the prohibition they had asked Massasoit to place on visits to Plymouth.

Having covered two more miles, Winslow and Hopkins were relieved and cheered by the sudden cessation of the rain and, within another hour, just as night was falling, they reached the settlement – wet, weary and footsore.

At the end of July young John Billington lost himself in the woods south of the settlement. After he had been gone five days the Governor ordered a search to be made in that direction. Bradford was uneasily aware that the Narragansett Indians lay in that direction and were unfriendly towards the settlers – if the experience of being attacked by them during the very first expedition ashore from the *Mayflower* was anything to go by. Besides the danger to the boy, there would be the risk of an attack on his rescuers

which might necessitate the sending of a sufficiently powerful force to be able to defend itself; and only thirty-two adult men were left in the colony.

The Governor had little sympathy for any of the Billington family – they were troublemakers of the worst kind – but to abandon young John was unthinkable. Some attempt to find and if necessary to rescue the youth had to be made. Bradford detailed ten of his men for the venture and instructed them to arm themselves and to take with them both Squanto and Tokamahamon to act as interpreters. They were to search along the coastline from the shallop, the quickest way of covering the region and the best means of defence if they were attacked.

The searchers sailed in fine weather, but hardly had they left the shore than they suddenly found themselves at the centre of a squall of wind and rain, thunder and lightning – and to their amazement they saw, for the first time in their lives, a waterspout form and rise nearby. Fortunately it twisted away from the boat, but the Pilgrims were more than glad to put into the harbour of Cummaquid – the most southerly point inside Cape Cod Bay, and near the present day Barnstable. But rather than risk being overwhelmed in the darkness ashore the rescue party remained aboard the shallop – only to find that, when the tide ran out, they were hard aground.

Statue by Cyrus Dalin of Governor Bradford.

In the morning they saw Indians searching for lobsters, and the two interpreters were sent through the shallows to question them. Their luck was in; they knew all about the Billington youth and told Squanto that he was safe at Nauset – Eastham today – the site of the earliest of the explorations of the Pilgrim Fathers and close to the spot where they had been attacked by hostile Indians.

The Cummaquid Indians invited the expedition ashore for a meal and, as soon as the shallop was refloated on the rising tide, six Pilgrims went ashore while five of the Indians were taken aboard as hostages.

The Sachem of the Cummaquid Indians, Iyanough – a handsome warrior in his mid-twenties – received them with a friendly cheerfulness but, unhappily, the Planters found themselves confronted by an aged woman who broke down in a storm of tears at the sight of them. They learned then that the woman had had three of her sons taken by Captain Thomas Hunt, who had carried them off to Spain and sold them there into slavery. Squanto, who had been captured with them but had escaped, did what he could to comfort the Indian woman while the Englishmen did their best to apologize for the behaviour of one of their countrymen, and gave her a few trifling gifts as some token of their sincerity. But they were seriously worried now that they knew that young Billington was in the custody of the tribe that had suffered at the hands of Hunt and had already murdered three Englishmen in reprisal. After the meal – and having no cause to trust the Indians after that revelation – the Pilgrims quickly re-embarked in the shallop and, with two of Sachem Iyanough's men aboard as guides, they sailed round the coast to Nauset.

The day was well advanced before they got there; they remained on board their craft, sending Squanto and Tokamahamon ashore with the Cummaquid guides in search of news of the missing youth. Hardly had they left than a party of Nauset Indians suddenly crowded down onto the beach and into the sea to surround the boat. They clamoured for the boat to be beached but the Planters held off, knowing that they were in a better defensive position offshore in the boat than they would be if they became scattered on the open beach.

Again the shallop was caught by the tide and the Planters found themselves aground. The Indians crowded around menacingly but the Englishmen steadfastly allowed only two of the Indians to board – they had, apparently, taken the corn of one of them on their first visit to that district in the previous November. The Planters readily promised to recompense the Indian for his loss if he would come to Patuxet to collect it. He agreed quite cheerfully to do so – and in the meantime offered to barter a few skins for ornaments.

The sun had set before Aspinet, the Sachem of the Nauset Indians, came down to the beach, followed by a company of Indians – on the shoulder of one was John Billington.

There were at least a hundred braves; and the Pilgrims noted, warily, that they appeared to be unusually well disciplined. Half the company kept their distance, their bows and arrows all ready for action, while the other half laid down their weapons and with their Sachem carried the young Billington down to the shallop and put him aboard. The vastly relieved rescue party presented Aspinet with a knife and made a similar gift to the Indian who had found the boy suffering from exposure and weak with hunger.

Then the Nauset Indians silently withdrew.

Squanto and Tokamahamon returned later with the news that the Narragansett Indians, of whom both the Nausets and the Cummaquids were part, had attacked Massasoit and taken Billington from him. Shocked by this totally unexpected piece of news, and frightened that Massasoit might have reacted to the attack by turning against the Pilgrims, the rescue party was in a hurry to return to the settlement, which they knew to be weakly held with only twenty-two fighting men. At first light they hoisted sail on the shallop, but because of the contrary winds they had to tack right around the coast line of the Bay until, short of water and still more than forty miles from home, they put in at Cummaquid again.

Sachem Iyanough received them welcomingly as before, and sent a party of his men to fill an eighteen-gallon cask with fresh water – while the Indian women sang and danced for their pleasure. They got away at last, only to find that the water given to them was too brackish to drink. As darkness came down they were compelled to lie miserably just off the beach again.

Next morning Sachem Iyanough again sent a party for water and again the Planters were entertained by the women on the beach. When the cask had been brought aboard the Pilgrims, on edge with frustration and anxiety, tested the water and, satisfied that this time it was genuinely fresh, sailed for Plymouth.

Certainly their preoccupation with the Indians, friendly and otherwise, took up a great deal of the settlers' time, just when they were fully employed in completing their homes, tending their crops, hunting, fishing, cutting logs and laying up great stores of kindling wood for their winter fires – while the few women who had survived the epidemic earlier that year were hard pressed to make and repair the men's clothing and to make warm bedding from the skins they had procured by hunting or through barter with the natives.

But when it was learned that the Narragansetts had attacked the Massasoits and that a Sachem, Corbitant, was attempting to divert the loyalty of the Paramount Chief's followers to the Narragansetts, the Pilgrims began to prepare for battle. Then they learned with dismay that Sagamore Massasoit had disappeared under suspicious circumstances. Finally, when Bradford was told by Hobomok, one of the Indians who lived and worked on the settlers' plantation, that he had only just escaped with his life from Corbitant and that he feared that Squanto had been murdered at Namaschet, he decided that it was time to make it clear to the Indians that he would not tolerate attack on any of the Planters or their friends.

Tokamahamon volunteered to make his way to Namaschet to discover the actual fate of Squanto and to get what news he could of Massasoit – but he did not return.

On Tuesday 14th August 1621, ten armed Pilgrims, with Standish in command, and with Hobomok for their guide, stepped out in a rainstorm for Namaschet to avenge the supposed death of Squanto and to discover the whereabouts of Massasoit. They approached to within three or four miles of the Indian village and then settled down to wait until midnight, when Standish proposed to make the attack. At midnight they moved forward – but Hobomok lost his bearings and they wandered around in the rain and the darkness until they were utterly weary and disheartened. At last the village was sighted under the faint glow from the night sky, but Standish decided to rest his men before he ordered the attack.

The little force sat on the wet ground, getting as much shelter as they could from the rain under the

A large Indian village in Carolina around the time of the Pilgrim Fathers.

trees, and made the best of a cold meal. Then, an hour or two before dawn, Standish ordered them to stockpile their knapsacks – and they moved quietly forward.

Slowly and stealthily they entered the village, found the largest wigwam and entered it, to find that it was full of sleeping Indians. Suddenly, at a word from the Captain, they started waking the Indians and the interpreters demanded of each of them in turn to know where Corbitant was lying – promising that nobody would be hurt if they told the truth.

But in the darkness some of the Indians managed

The Allyn House, the last surviving example of the houses the
Pilgrim Fathers built at Plymouth, was demolished in 1826.

to escape through the rear of the wigwam, though not
without suffering some cuts and bruises from the
swords of the Pilgrims, a few having been wounded
by musket balls. The women were terrified, but
knowing Hobomok they did their best to assure him
that everybody was friendly and that both Squanto
and Tokamahamon were safe and well in the village –
and that Corbitant had gone off with his supporters.

While the Pilgrims searched the wigwam
Hobomok climbed up onto the roof and called out
for Squanto and Tokamahamon, both of whom
appeared almost at once, accompanied by a few
excited Indians who were promptly disarmed. Then
the large wigwam was turned into a temporary
fortress for the rest of the night.

Next morning, after breakfast, Standish assembled
the Indian villagers and told them, through his
interpreters, that although Corbitant had escaped for
the moment he would be captured sooner or later and
would then be punished. He promised them, too, that

if Massasoit were not set free by the Narragansett
Indians the whole tribe would be made to suffer.

Standish expressed his regret that some of them
had been injured by musket balls, but pointed out
that they had only themselves to blame for resisting
those whom they knew to be their friends – and
offered to take back to Plymouth with him any that
would like to go there for skilled medical care.

Having done all that he could for the time being,
Standish withdrew his men, taking back with him a
man and a woman who had been wounded for the
attention of surgeon Samuel Fuller. A large party of
Indians came along, cheerfully carrying the equipment, the haversacks and, had they been permitted,
the muskets and swords of the little force.

Massasoit reappeared. In due time, Corbitant,
ostracized by the rest of the Sachems in the region,
sued for peace through Massasoit – but many months
were to pass before he dared show his face in the
presence of the Pilgrim Fathers again.

16 The Coming of the *Fortune*

Having established good relations with the Indians all around Cape Cod Bay, Bradford turned his attention to the constant rumours of threats from the Massachusets Indians around Boston Bay, to the north. He was unwilling to give much credit to the many stories that came to his ears, but did feel that it would be wise to try to establish contact with them and come to some sort of peace terms with their leaders.

Again the Governor sent Standish, the military leader; this time in charge of nine settlers, Squanto and two other Indians, in the shallop to find the Chiefs of the tribe. They sailed just before midnight on Tuesday 18th September 1621 in the hope of reaching Boston Bay by morning. But Standish had not realized that he had to cover about forty-five miles against contrary winds, and it was late in the following day before the little expedition felt its way around the spit of land now known as Allerton Point (probably named after Isaac Allerton, who was at that time assistant to the Governor) and dropped anchor without having seen anyone on any point of the surrounding landscape.

The Pilgrims spent the night in the shallop for safety against any sudden attack, but in the morning raised the anchor again and edged the boat inshore until they found a suitable place to beach it.

As they stepped ashore, the Pilgrims came across a pile of lobsters that had obviously been freshly gathered in by the natives; but, as there was nobody in sight, they built a fire, cooked some of the shellfish and made a good breakfast of them.

Standish then set a guard over the shallop and, taking an Indian guide and four of his men with him, moved inland in search of some habitation. They met an Indian woman on her way down to the beach to collect the lobsters and told her where to find them. She seemed not at all nervous and pointed out the way to her own village.

Squanto went forward alone – so that the party would not present the appearance of an invasion –

and had instructions to invite the local Chieftain down to the beach for talks.

In this way Sachem Obbatinewat was contacted, and he came down to the shore to meet the Pilgrims readily enough. He told Standish, through Squanto, that he and his tribe were subjects of Massasoit, although they were some considerable distance from him. But he warned the Pilgrims that they were in very real danger from the Tarrantine Indians who inhabited the banks of the Penobscot River (Maine) far to the north, and from the Squaw Sachem – the Queen – of the Massachusets Indians, their habitation being much nearer on the northern side of Boston Bay.

Captain Standish decided that his best plan would be to see the Squaw Sachem as the quickest means of establishing peace in the region; Obbatinewat was persuaded to point out the best way of doing so. The Pilgrims then re-embarked in the shallop and navigated their way through the many tiny islands of the Bay from what is now Quincy to Charlestown on the northern shore. Again they were met by a deserted beach. Standish landed his three Indians and sent them to reconnoitre the immediate neighbourhood – but they returned by sunset having seen no sign of an Indian.

In the morning Standish left two men behind to guard the boat and led the rest of his party inland to see what they could find.

Three miles from the Bay they came to a large open space from which corn had recently been harvested and, close by, a wigwam that had obviously been pulled down just as recently – and abandoned. A mile further on, at a place now known as Medford, the settlers were checked by a totally unexpected sight; at the top of a hill (now Rock Hill) a shack had been built on stilts, about six feet above the ground, and at the foot of the hill there was a fort surrounded by a whole thicket of poles, anything up to forty feet in length, enclosing an area of some forty to fifty feet in all directions. The timber walls were protected by a

Standish leading an expeditionary party, with Squanto as guide. Standish's "Long March" was perhaps the most important of the Pilgrims' trading expeditions.

breast-high ditch all around, with only a single bridge across it to give access to the fort. In the middle of the fort they found a lone wigwam, and under some mats on the ground they discovered the grave of an Indian.

The Pilgrims were told later that the body was that of the dead "King" Nanepashemet – one-time Sagamore of the Boston Bay Indians – who had lived in the house on the top of the hill and who had built the stout fortress in which he had lain since his death two years earlier.

Standish decided to make his base nearby, and from there despatched his Indians to make contact with the nearest tribe.

A mile away they found the women of the tribe beside a heap of corn. They learned that the whole tribe had hurriedly gathered up their stocks of corn and everything else they possessed and made off the moment they had heard of the shallop's arrival. But it had been too much to carry at speed, so the men of the tribe had left the women to guard the corn.

Squanto brought up Captain Standish and some of his men. They then advanced to where the terrified women indicated their village lay. The Pilgrims were appalled to find that the wigwams had all been hurriedly pulled down and that further stocks of corn lay protected only by nets that had been thrown over them before the natives had fled. There was not a single man of the tribe to be seen anywhere.

The Pilgrims dealt gently with the women until they regained some of their courage. Then, as they became less fearful, the women began to prepare a meal of boiled cod. Squanto sent one of the women to seek out their menfolk and urge them to come forward; but there was a great deal of coming and going among the women before a single, trembling warrior could be persuaded to show his face.

Standish enquired about the Squaw Sachem and her whereabouts, but the Indians knew little other than that she was far away.

Disgusted with the whole proceedings, Squanto urged the Pilgrims to strip the women of their animal skins and to take anything else from them that might be of use, insisting that the whole tribe was bad. But Standish refused to do anything of the kind, although he left a warning with the women that it would go ill with any of their menfolk who attempted to molest them.

Happier by now, the women flocked down to the beach as the Pilgrims returned to their shallop – and there they suddenly removed their furs and offered to barter them with the Pilgrims for ornaments: although they were obviously embarrassed by their own nakedness they were eager to impress the Englishmen with their readiness to please by trading with them, and promised to have many more heavier skins available the next time they returned to the region.

The Pilgrim Fathers trading with local Indians.

Food supplies aboard the shallop were running short and Sunday was not far off, so, with a fair wind and a full moon in a clear sky, the little expedition guided the tiny vessel around Allerton Point that evening, stood out into the vastness of the Bay of Massachusetts and swung towards the south-east. By noon next day, Saturday 22nd September 1621, they re-entered Plymouth harbour.

The summer had done much to improve the health and courage of the Pilgrim families at Plymouth and, with the lessening worry of Indian interference – or actual hostility – the settlement began to take shape and prosper. The harvest gave them renewed heart and their growing expertise at hunting and fishing was supplying them with all the food they needed to give them the strength to build improvements to their original homes in the village. But, as the need for day and night toil became less urgent, it was natural that the full effect of their losses during the previous Spring should begin to make itself felt – perhaps even more deeply than at the time they had buried the many unhappy victims of the epidemic. Until now, they had never had time to sit down and ponder over the dreadful events of that season and the great gaps

that had been cut into their families – and, as they relaxed for a while, homesickness struck. They had had no news of family and friends in over a year.

And then, quite unexpectedly, the *Fortune* dropped anchor in Plymouth harbour.

So suddenly did it appear that, fearing that it might be French, Bradford ordered the warning cannon to be fired to call the settlers to arms, and the whole male population promptly grabbed up their weapons and rushed down to the beach – in time to welcome Robert Cushman and thirty-five Pilgrims who had come to join them in the New World. And, not least, the letters from friends and relations in Leyden and London.

But the *Fortune* had not found its destination without some difficulty. The first landfall had been at Cape Cod on 9th November and, strangely ill-informed, they had searched along the coastline for the settlement. Finding nobody and nothing to suggest that the Forefathers were close at hand, the Captain and crew, and the newcomers, began to fear that all those who had sailed aboard the *Mayflower* had either died of some dreadful disease (as had seemed possible from Captain Jones' report in London) or had starved to death – or been slaughtered by the Indians.

Anxiety had reached such a pitch aboard the ship that some of the seamen had been unwilling to go ashore in case the Master should sail away without them and leave them marooned in an impossible land. Even the newcomers became alarmed and, having brought so little with them in the way of supplies, they joined with the seamen who threatened to make no further search for the settlement unless they took the ship's sails with them as a safeguard against being left stranded.

The Master, Captain Thomas Barton, pacified them all with some difficulty, assuring them that he had in his possession sufficient reserves of food to continue the search briefly and then, if it failed, to carry them all on to Virginia. But it must have dawned on him, or others aboard his vessel, that Captain Jones of the *Mayflower* had described the place where he had left the Pilgrims as being on the other side of the much larger Cape Cod Bay, for by 11th November the *Fortune* sailed into Plymouth harbour and dropped anchor there – to be received with heartfelt gladness by the original settlers. With the *Fortune* came the second Peirce Patent, which in effect confirmed the *Mayflower* Compact.

And, during the very first night ashore, the widow Foord gave birth to a son.

But Cushman had no intention of remaining in New England to experience all its hardships, isolation and dangers – although, while the *Fortune* lay in Plymouth harbour, he proved very ready to exhort those who had already settled there and those who had come to join them.

It is unlikely that he was received with open arms; the Pilgrims who had endured that storm-wracked voyage aboard the *Mayflower* and survived that first dreadful winter cannot have forgotten the squabbles that had centred around him before they sailed from England, or the bitter accusations he had levelled at the now dead Christopher Martin and John Carver. Nor could they have felt anything but a cold politeness for the man who had left the *Mayflower* and its Pilgrims before it sailed for the New World – and had now come to lecture them and to depart again. And, almost certainly, the Forefathers must have been very bitter to discover that Cushman had failed to bring with him the urgently needed supplies that had been promised – had failed even to see to it that the newcomers had brought sufficient food or equipment to maintain themselves. Despite Captain Barton's earlier assurance, he had not even enough

A procession of Pilgrims on their way to Church. It is interesting that, throughout their adventures and whatever the circumstances, they obeyed if possible the dictum that no work should be done on the Sabbath day.

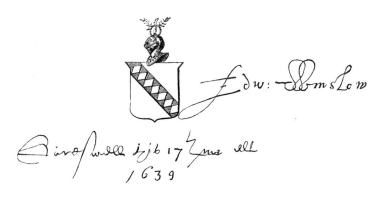

Edward Winslow's coat of arms and autograph.

food on board to provide for himself and his crew during the return journey.

Yet, on 11th December, Cushman delivered a discourse to the Pilgrims assembled in the Common House. He spoke of the sins and dangers of self-love – which they could accept – but more to the point he did his best to force upon them his own conviction of the need for a communist society with no private property whatsoever – despite the fact that the Pilgrim Fathers had refused to accept any such ideology, even before they had left the Old World. He passed on the threat that the Adventurers would send no further help to New Plymouth until the long-outstanding agreement had been signed by them – still incorporating the clauses that required that the Pilgrims' very homes should be included in the eventual dividend and that no time should be allowed them in which to forward their own affairs.

This was alarming. Although the harvest that year had been good it had not been sufficient to support the suddenly increased population for a full year, and in the emergency the settlers had no option but to agree to the terms and sign the agreement without any further argument. They were not to know that the failure of Cushman to bring supplies with him in the *Fortune* was destined to bring every one of them to the verge of starvation before their stocks of corn were to be replenished.

Despite the bitter struggle for survival that the Forefathers had endured, they had accumulated some trade goods for the profit of the Adventurers in England; clapboard – or rough-sawn timber – three hogsheads of beaver skins and some sassafras – laurel that contained a powerful stimulant – were loaded aboard the *Fortune*, before she sailed, on 11th December 1621. And with it Cushman carried home reports of the progress and activities of the Pilgrim Fathers in New Plymouth, from Governor Bradford to the Company of Adventurers and to the parent church in Leyden.

Edward Winslow wrote to an unknown friend in England through the same channel; his letter has been preserved to give us some valuable insight into the progress made in the settlement of New Plymouth by the Pilgrim Fathers.

Winslow wrote of how seven dwelling houses had been completed in the twelve months since the first landing – four for the communal use of the settlers until the village should be finally completed, and three as private homes. And a start had been made on two more.

During that dreadful Spring, when so many had perished, they had still managed to sow some six acres of barley and peas, and twenty of Indian corn. The peas crop had failed, the barley was barely successful; but the Indian corn had done well – their own maize had not been worth even the planting.

He tells of the three days of immensely successful celebration that followed that first harvest – the first "Thanksgiving Day" in New England. Four men had been sent out by the Governor on a fowling expedition and had brought back enough to last the community for a whole week. The happy Planters had entertained themselves with ground sports and a little musket drill, and then, with the arrival of Massasoit and about ninety of his braves, who brought five deer with them, they held a joint feast.

Of the Indians, Winslow wrote of them that they became very friendly with but little persuasion, that they had no knowledge of God, but were quite trustworthy, quick-witted yet nervously inclined. The climate he described as "English", "though some

A painting by Jennie Brownscombe of the first Thanksgiving. Since 1863
Thanksgiving has been celebrated in the USA as a national holiday on the
fourth Thursday of November, in Canada on the second Monday of October.

A general view of the Plymouth Colony in 1622, showing the harbour in the
background.

think it hotter in summer and colder in winter". He regretted the lack of cattle, horses and sheep – fish and shellfish being plentiful, as were great flocks of fowl. All that New England required, according to Winslow, was industrious men to cultivate the land.

He advised those who planned to follow the early settlers to "Be carefuly to have a very good Bread-room, to put your biscuits in. Let your caske for beer and water be ironbound; for the first tyre, if not more. Let not your meat be dry and salted. None can better do it than the sailors. Let your meal be so hard trod in your cask that you shall need an adze or hatchet to work it out with. Trust not too much on us for corn at this time: for, by reason of this last company that came, depending wholly upon us, we shall have little enough till harvest. Be careful to come by some of your meal, to spend by the way. It will refresh you. Build your cabins as open as you can; and bring good store of clothes and bedding with you. Bring every man a musket, or fowling piece. Let your piece be long in the barrel; and fear not the weight of it, for most of our shooting is from the stands. Bring juice of lemons; and take it fasting. It is of good use. For hot [distilled] waters, Anniseed Water is the best; but use it sparingly. If you bring anything for comfort in the country; butter, or salted oil or both, are very good. Our Indian corn, even the coarsest, maketh us pleasant meat as Rice: therefore spare that, unless to spend by the way. Bring paper and linseed oil for your windows; with cotton yarn for your lamps. Let your shot be most for big fowls;

and bring store of powder and shot . . ."

But the *Fortune* was not to have an uneventful voyage back to England. As she entered the Channel she was overhauled by a French warship and ordered to heave-to. She was escorted as a prize to the Isle d'Yeu, off the Biscay coast of Brittany, and handed over to the Governor of the Isle, the Marquis de Cera.

The English Captain complained bitterly that, as there was no war between England and France, and as they were obviously not pirates, the French had no right to interfere with them, but the unscrupulous Governor imprisoned Captain Barton in his castle and placed his crew – and Cushman – under guard.

The guard robbed the Englishmen of everything they possessed of value while the Governor looted the *Fortune* of about £400 worth of cargo, the chain-cable and anchor, the cannon, muskets, powder and shot, and the ship's instruments. The Marquis opened and delayed the delivery of the letters brought from the New World, including the despatches from Governor Bradford.

But on the 1st February, without either explanation or apology, the *Fortune* and its crew were suddenly released. They were provided with sufficient food to see them to England but were compelled to sign a statement to the effect that the Governor, the Marquis de Cera, had taken only two hogsheads of skins from the ship's cargo.

The *Fortune* arrived in London on 14th February 1622.

(*opposite above*) A lithograph by Currier and Ives showing the Pilgrim fathers landing in their new home.
(*opposite below*) The fort of the Plimoth Plantation, a painstaking twentieth-century reconstruction of the Pilgrim fathers' original settlement.

The *Mayflower II*, a reconstruction of the original vessel which
sailed from Plymouth, Devon, to Cape Cod in Spring 1957 lies at
anchor at Plymouth, Massachusetts.

17 Squanto's Treachery

The *Fortune* was barely hull-down over the eastern horizon when the Narragansett Indians began to mutter threateningly against the English settlers. But the first real sign of their hostility came when Tokamahamon brought a runner to the settlement, from Sagamore Canonicus of the Narragansetts, with a message for Squanto.

As it happened, Squanto was not at home at the time – which seemed to please the Indian runner. Instead of waiting, he left a bundle of arrows wrapped in the skin of a rattlesnake. But he was not to get away so easily after leaving such a cryptic message.

Bradford was immediately suspicious when Tokamahamon told him of the gift; he was well aware of the strength of the Narragansetts, who occupied almost the whole of what is now Rhode Island. He knew that they were at loggerheads with the friendly Wampanoag Indians led by Massasoit, and were also constantly at war with the Massachusets Indians and the Packonokiks on their borders – and he wanted to know what message the gift was intended to convey.

The Governor ordered the runner to be held in custody until Squanto returned to translate the message for him, or one of the other Indians in the settlement told him what it meant. The Indian captive was handed over by Standish to Edward Winslow and Stephen Hopkins that night. At first the messenger was so scared that he could not speak, but he slowly relaxed as he came to understand that he was not being threatened with death. He reminded his custodians that some time earlier they had received a representative of the Narragansett Indians sent to them to agree peace terms. He told Winslow and Hopkins that the messenger had returned to Sagamore Canonicus bearing no news of peace but a threat of war – probably because he had not been given a sufficiently worthwhile present.

The prisoner then offered to agree peace terms with the Pilgrim Fathers on behalf of his Sagamore, but

The site of a Narragansett fort at Fort Neck.

after a conference between Governor Bradford, his assistant Isaac Allerton and Captain Miles Standish, it was decided that the man had not the authority to make any binding promises and was probably lying – as had his predecessor, in hope of a reward. The trio decided that, although it was purposeless to negotiate peace terms with the messenger, it might be as well to feed him and then send him off with a blunt message to Canonicus warning him of the reprisals that would follow any attempt on his part to put any of his threats into force.

Squanto returned to the settlement shortly afterwards and the parcel of arrows was handed over to him with a request for an interpretation of its significance. The Indian proclaimed it to be a sign of enmity and a challenge.

Bradford then took the rattlesnake skin, stuffed it with powder and shot, and sent it back to Canonicus.

The Indian Chief was so shocked by this sight of the symbolic threat that he would neither touch it nor allow it to be brought into his wigwam – nor even permit it to remain within his territories. The messenger, by then equally terrified, refused to carry it further, and for weeks it shuttled from hand to reluctant hand until it finally found its way back to Plymouth, still unopened.

Bradford was not fully satisfied with the outcome of his threatening gesture. Canonicus made no offers of peace and the rumours of an attack on the settlement persisted. The Narragansetts were said to number many thousands; estimates ranged as high as 30,000, of whom 5,000 were warriors – while the Planters, despite their reinforcements from the *Fortune*, had still fewer than fifty men with which to defend the settlement.

William Bradford

William Bradford's autograph.

Warily Bradford, with the support of his Council, ordered that the settlement should be turned into a fortress: in six desperately busy weeks a stout barricade of heavy timber palings was dug into the ground to surround the township and Burial Hill, with its cannon, above it. Four bastions were built beyond the palisade to command all sides of the town, and in three of them were constructed the only gates into the settlement – to be locked at night and guarded by day.

Having built the fortifications, Standish, as the military authority, then divided the available force into four companies, appointing a leader to each. Every man was told of the place at which he must muster in the event of an alarm, and each of the leaders was given the task of planning the defence of his own sector.

By March 1622 the arrangements for the defence of New Plymouth were complete.

Standish was well aware of the danger of fire-arrows among the wooden buildings, and detailed one of the companies to deal with any such emergency as their exclusive responsibility.

In that same month, March 1622, Hobomok, who lived in the settlement and who had acted as a guide when Standish had taken a small force in an attempt to capture Corbitant in the previous August, brought news that the Massachusets Indians around Boston Bay had made a compact with the Narragansetts to cut off Standish and his men next time they made an excursion from Plymouth; and, while they were separated from the main force, the Narragansetts would attack the depleted garrison in the settlement. Hobomok also asserted that it was Squanto's intention to join in the conspiracy and to draw off any occupants of the shallop into the Indian wigwams, on some excuse or other, to split the defenders even further.

Hobomok's story was disbelieved, particularly as Squanto had long been a trusted friend and a valuable aid – and the accusation was ascribed to sheer jealousy. But the Governor called together the Elders of the community to discuss the matter.

Stoutheartedly they decided that there was little point in confining themselves within the stockade around the town unless they were actually attacked. Their storehouse was almost empty after the long winter and it was absolutely necessary for hunting parties to be constantly on the move if they were not to suffer real hunger. Besides, they believed that a brave show might well deter enemies. It was decided, too, to continue sending out expeditions in search of trade and in the hope of picking up information while they were among the natives. One such expedition was organized to trade directly with the Massachusets Indians, in accordance with a promise made some time previously, and at the same time to check Hobomok's statement concerning them.

Standish, with ten of the settlers plus Squanto and

Some striking examples of Red Indian dress, weapons and ornaments. While these objects date from the nineteenth century, they cannot be too dissimilar to those owned by the Indians with whom the Pilgrims were trading.

Hobomok, boarded the shallop and made for the open sea on the first leg of a journey to Boston Bay. But almost as soon as they had rounded the northern arm that enclosed Plymouth Bay – known even then as Gurnet's Nose, and now as Gurnet Point – the wind dropped and within minutes had died away completely, leaving the shallop becalmed.

As they were about to unship the oars to row, a relative of Squanto came running down to the beach calling to them to return at once, claiming that he had been attacked and wounded in the face at Namaschet, some fifteen miles away, by Narragansett and Wampanoag Indians under Corbitant, for trying to dissuade them from taking advantage of the absence of Standish and his men to attack the settlement.

Standish immediately beached the shallop, jumped ashore, and took a look at the injured Indian. There certainly was blood on his face, as he had claimed, and the Captain took him aboard and ordered his men to row back to Plymouth. As they entered the harbour they could see that the settlement had already received the warning and had stood to arms.

Hobomok objected strenuously to the statement that Massasoit's men had joined forces with the Narragansetts. He swore that the Sagamore and the Wampanoags were loyal to their peaceful promises – although the Massachusets and the Narragansetts were not. He swore that Squanto, through his relations and friends, was doing his best to stir up disaffection between the tribes.

Perplexed, the Governor accepted Hobomok's offer to send his wife secretly to the home of Massasoit to find out the truth of the matter – at least as far as the Wampanoags were concerned. When she arrived at Sowans she found everything as quietly peaceful as usual; and she told Massasoit the reason for her visit and of the precautions that were being taken at Plymouth.

The Sagamore was deeply incensed by Squanto's accusations, and sent the squaw back with a message to Bradford assuring him of his peaceable intentions and that he knew of no such incident as that said to have culminated in the wounding of one of Squanto's relatives. He promised that if any such attack was ever initiated in his territory and it came to his ears he would send a warning at once to the settlement.

After some protracted and careful enquiries, it became evident to the Governor that Squanto had become swollen-headed and was striving to make

himself appear important in the eyes of the Pilgrim Fathers, while, at the same time, he was intriguing with various Indian factions to make it seem that war or peace could be obtained only at his behest. On occasion he had convinced certain Indian communities that the settlers intended to kill them – and received substantial presents from them to use his influence to avert the danger and to procure peace.

By the time the true extent of his intrigues was made plain he had become the wielder of so much sway among the surrounding tribesmen that he often had more authority than the Sachems themselves – so much so that many of them were beginning to look to Squanto for protection instead of to their Sagamore.

The discovery of Squanto's underhand scheming was a sad blow to Bradford, as it was through him that so much reliable information had been gleaned in the past concerning the intentions and activities of the natives, and he had always acted as a thoroughly reliable messenger and negotiator. Regretfully the Governor sent a message to the Sagamore and the local Sachems assuring them of the peaceful intentions of the settlers and to warn them to ignore and to treat as lies any statements or promises that came from Squanto.

Some of the Sachems responded by demanding that Squanto either be put to death or turned out of the settlement so that they could deal with him as he deserved. The Governor refused both requests. Squanto was still much too useful to be discarded. Instead, he gave the Indian a thorough tongue-lashing and warned him of the consequences of any similar treachery.

Having settled that issue, he sent Standish off again in the shallop, the main object being to trade for skins, but with instructions to keep his eyes and ears open to the attitudes of the natives towards themselves – and between tribes.

The first stage of his journey was to Massasoit's "capital", but the Sagamore was away when Standish and his men arrived there. Nevertheless, they were well received and continued to be made welcome wherever they went. Word of the little party's progress preceded it and, in almost every village the settlers visited, they found that a collection of pelts had been gathered up and made ready for their inspection and barter.

But when Standish and his men returned to the settlement with a goodly cargo of skins, they found

Negotiating with Indians on the Charles River.

that the matter of Squanto and his intrigues had not been disposed of as satisfactorily as the Governor had hoped. Massasoit was there, in person, demanding that Squanto should be properly punished. They saw, too, that the Governor was having the greatest difficulty in trying to persuade the angry Chief to leave the matter in his hands – and Massasoit withdrew from the settlement only after a great deal of bitter argument. When he left it was obvious that he had not been mollified – within a few days, a messenger arrived from Massasoit demanding the death of Squanto.

Bradford sent the messenger back with as pacific a reply as he could devise. He agreed that Squanto deserved death but assured the Sagamore that he must spare him because he was so valuable to the Pilgrim Fathers in their negotiations with the surrounding tribes. Massasoit received the messenger in friendly enough fashion, but sent him back again to Plymouth, accompanied by a supporting party of Wampanoag Indians, to remind the Governor that Squanto was one of his tribe and subject to his authority. And, devastatingly, he quoted the peace

terms agreed during the previous March – clause 2 of which read: "And if any of us did hurt to any of ours; he should send the offender that we might punish him." The message went on to assure Bradford that Massasoit had no wish to offend him and offered to compensate him for the loss of Squanto's services with beaver skins. He sent, too, a knife so that the Governor could carry out the execution himself, saying he would be satisfied at the sight of the severed head and hands, if they were sent to him.

Bradford must have consulted earnestly and anxiously with his Military Captain, his Assistant and the Elders of the community. Troubled less by the physical threat than by the loss of esteem that must follow from the failure to keep a promise, they finally decided that they must honour the terms of the peace treaty and allow Squanto to be taken away to Sowans to be dealt with by his own Sagamore.

Squanto made no attempt to escape but did do all he could to shift the responsibility for his actions onto the shoulders of Hobomok. Nevertheless, Governor

Bradford, understanding that Squanto was doing no more than aggravate his treachery to his own kind, was not to be diverted from his decision and sent word of it to Massasoit.

A boatload of Indians arrived a few days later to take Squanto back as a prisoner to face the Sagamore, but Bradford was wary of their identity. It seemed strange to him that the Indians had not entered the harbour but had held off on the other side of the southern arm and demanded that Squanto should be handed over to them there. There had been many rumours, often factual, of French incursions into the region and he wanted to be quite sure that these Indians were not friends of theirs and so his enemies – in fact, if not in law.

He sent a message to the beach demanding some proof that the Indians had been sent by Massasoit, but the natives, angry and impatient over the delay, and what they probably assumed to be intransigence on the part of the settlers, simply dug their oars into the water and headed for the open sea.

Some time was to pass before the possible reason for the failure of the Indians to come near to the settlement – and for their making off again in a hurry before the transfer of Squanto could be satisfactorily settled – came to light. It seems that Squanto's intrigues included the stirring up of fear of the settlers among the tribes by warning them that the English-men had a plague buried under their storehouse – which could be released at will to destroy their enemies. An almost believable story in that the settlement had been built on a site that had already, and quite recently, been depopulated by the plague – and, because it had not troubled the Englishmen, seemed to suggest that they had it under their "control".

The slanderous story reached the ears of Hobomok eventually and, with unexpected temerity, he quietly dug down into the ground inside the storehouse – and discovered a number of barrels. In a panic, he ran for the Governor and dragged him to the spot – and demanded to know if the barrels did, in fact, hold a plague. The Governor had the barrels opened up so that the frightened Indian could see that they contained nothing else but gunpowder.

But, unfortunately, one of the Pilgrims, without any malice in mind, told Hobomok that the God of the English did keep a store of plague which he could send down to destroy his enemies if the need arose.

Despite this latest discovery of Squanto's treacherous intrigues, Bradford made no effort to send him as a prisoner to Massasoit; nor, it seems, did Massasoit take any further steps to claim and punish the condemned man – possibly because the fear of plague being used by the settlers persisted after the tactless explanation given by one of the Englishmen.

18 Disruptive Elements from England

By the beginning of May 1622 the settlers found it necessary to impose a strict rationing on corn and all other cultivated food stocks – and to place more reliance on hunting and fishing. Unfortunately, the fish, although apparently plentiful, were not easily caught, as would have seemed likely; the lack of seine netting and other tackle having defeated the Pilgrims – strangely, one of the few essentials that they had failed to improvise for themselves. At this time of the year, too, fowl and deer seemed to have hidden themselves quite effectually.

The Pilgrims must have been feeling some bitterness towards the Company of Adventurers in London by then. They had sent home some considerable store of traded goods with the *Fortune* when it sailed from New Plymouth in the previous December; and, knowing nothing of the capture and looting of the vessel by the French, they must have anticipated that an equivalent amount of food and other supplies should have reached them in return before then. Nor had they any more reserves of ornaments, beads and trinkets to barter with the Indians for food; they had already expended all they had on some substantial purchases of pelts – which were of little use to them until they could be transported to England and sold there.

By the end of May the stock of corn had been reduced to danger level and the Pilgrims faced hunger, famine and starvation. And, to deepen their intense worry, a lone shallop sailed into the harbour and put ashore seven Englishmen and some letters, sent out from England by Thomas Weston. They landed without having brought so much as a single sack or barrel of supplies – not even sufficient food for their own needs.

Bradford took them to the Common House, summoned some of his advisers to join them there and then asked the new arrivals for an explanation.

He learned then that Weston and a partner of his had sent a fishing vessel, the *Sparrow*, to the fishing grounds off the coast of Maine, some 120 miles to the north of New Plymouth, and had taken the opportunity to send out with it the seven Planters to be landed in Plymouth harbour *via* the shallop from the *Sparrow*.

Bradford then gave his attention to the letter sent to him aboard that vessel from Thomas Weston, but it proved to be of little help. It merely informed the Governor that Weston had severed his connection with the Company of Adventurers and that the Company had refused to send out the rest of the Pilgrims still awaiting transportation at Leyden, because their religious preachings were causing a great deal of controversy in England, and – more certainly – because the Pilgrims were mostly so poverty stricken that they could neither contribute towards the shares of the Company nor provide themselves with the necessary minimum supplies needed for the voyage.

The letter, dated 10th April 1622, told the Governor that Weston was starting up a colony of his own in America, from which, obviously, he hoped to derive some considerable profit.

Besides Weston's letter, John Hudston, the Captain of a fishing vessel that had been in contact with the *Sparrow*, sent a letter with it to the settlers at Plymouth giving the news of a massacre that had taken place in Virginia, where no fewer than 350 colonists had been murdered by the Indians on 22nd March.

Bradford must have felt grim indeed as he considered the circumstances. There was the real danger that the success of the Indian attack on the James River settlers might well give courage to the less friendly Massachusets and Narragansetts in the region around Plymouth to attempt the same sort of thing on the very much weaker and smaller settlement there. Certainly they had been more openly hostile than previously, and even Massasoit was showing some signs of unfriendliness. And there was the more immediate problem of the shortage of food in the settlement.

"... no fewer than 350 colonists had been murdered by the Indians ..."

After some urgent consultations with the members of his Council, the Governor ordered that a stout fort be built within the already fortified town, and sent Edward Winslow in the shallop to find the *Sparrow* and to obtain whatever stocks of food the Captain was willing to let him have.

Winslow located a whole fleet of about thirty ships fishing in the waters around Monhegan, and was received by their captains with courtesy. But supplies were not easily obtained from them. The ships had been victualled to provide only for their own crews for the round trip from and to Europe and, carrying no passengers, there had been no reason to take on more than a reserve against the delays that might come about through bad weather – which might be required even now before they reached England again. The ships' masters refused to accept Bills of Exchange on London. They did give some token supplies – but very little in comparison with what was needed.

Although Winslow was away for only a few days on his almost abortive expedition he returned to Plymouth to find that the settlers were almost without bread, and deprived of their staple diet and often having to make do with nothing better than shellfish, their strength was giving out – although they continued to struggle urgently to complete the new fort.

At the end of June 1622 disaster struck the Pilgrim Fathers. Two ships, the *Charity* and the *Swan*, put into Plymouth harbour and from them between fifty and sixty men bustled ashore. They proclaimed, noisily, brashly and even impertinently, that they had been sent out by Thomas Weston and intended to stay at New Plymouth until the coasters they were sending out found a suitable place for them to establish a settlement of their own in the Boston Bay area.

The *Charity* sailed again immediately, still having aboard a substantial number of passengers bound for Virginia.

A letter from Weston gave no good account of the newcomers, and another from Cushman stated bluntly: "They are no men of us, and I fear they will hardly deal so well with the savages as they should. I pray you therefore signify to Squanto that they are a distinct body from us, and we have nothing to do with them, nor must be blamed for their faults, much less can warrant their fidelity."

Yet a third letter, from John Peirce, in whose name

Standish and his party grimly regard scenes of revelry.

the patent authorizing the Company of Adventurers to occupy the site of New Plymouth was issued, stated: "As for Mr Weston's company they are so base in condition for the most part, as in all appearance not fit for an honest man's company. I wish they prove otherwise."

Nevertheless the newcomers were made as welcome as possible by an impoverished community. There was little food to spare yet what there was of it was shared and room was made, where possible, in the homes of the Pilgrim Fathers for them to place their beds.

Despite the kindliness of their reception, the newcomers soon showed the justification of the reputation given to them in the letters from England. They did little or nothing to ease the burden on the already hungry and physically weakened Pilgrims and, having no permanent interest in Plymouth, gave no assistance in the building of the inner fort. They were an ungodly lot. They were quick to pilfer from the meagre stocks of food, and quicker still with sharp words and physical violence when challenged.

They treated the Pilgrims with contempt, harried their womenfolk and looted their homes almost at will. Yet the original settlers did their best to establish some sort of trust and friendship, to warn the newcomers of the hazards of creating a new settlement and to give them some insight into the ways and customs of the natives.

Word came at last that a site had been found at Wessagusset – now Weymouth, on the southern shores of Boston Bay – for the newcomers, who packed up in a hurry (not being too particular about whose property they included in their baggage) before they embarked in the *Swan*. They abandoned their own sick and lame until such time, so they said, as they had built houses to receive them.

The sick did well under the care of Surgeon Samuel Fuller and in time every one of them followed their companions to Wessagusset – although it is unlikely that they found that any homes had been built for them.

The exodus from New Plymouth occurred just as the Pilgrims had reached the stage of being destitute.

Within a matter of days, news of the Boston Bay settlers began to trickle back to New Plymouth, *via* the Indians resident among the Pilgrim Fathers. They learned that the newcomers had quickly created a real feeling of enmity between themselves and the natives around them, stealing the Indians' corn, beating them and occasionally using them for forced labour.

But there was little that so small a community as the Pilgrim Fathers, so far from Boston Bay and by now desperately weak and hungry, could do to help

A view of part of Boston or Massachusetts Bay. Boston, lying at the mouth of the Charles River, was settled by Puritans and soon became the capital of the Boston Bay Colony.

bring about peace in the region. Fearful of the repercussions from the vastly superior number of Indians, with the example of the James River massacre to goad them on, they pressed on with all their remaining strength to complete their fort, certain that without it they would inevitably be engulfed in any sudden uprising.

At the end of August a sixty-ton ship, the

162

Discovery, under the command of Captain Thomas Jones dropped anchor in Plymouth Bay. She was returning from Virginia *en route* to England, and rendezvoused there with the *Sparrow*, which returned almost at the same time from its fishing expedition to the north with full holds.

Before the two vessels sailed out again the settlers at New Plymouth were able to obtain some trade goods from the *Discovery*, although at some considerable cost – the exchange rate finally agreed being 3/– per lb of beaver skins, the market price of which was to reach 20/– per lb within a year or two. But at any price the trade goods were to engender a wild upsurge of hope among the Pilgrims for, at last, they felt in a position to barter with the Indians for corn.

The Pilgrim Fathers were not to know, however, that the *Discovery* had been trading with the Indians all along the coast and, in doing so, Thomas Jones had so cheated the natives (and had indeed attempted to kidnap some) that he had added another strand to the growing hatred of the Indian population for the settlers in the New World.

In September 1622, the *Charity* returned to Boston Bay from Virginia and off-loaded some considerable supplies for Thomas Weston's settlers at Wessagusset. Then, leaving the smaller *Swan* and its shallop behind for the use of the Boston Bay colonists, it departed for England.

But, left on their own, the joint Governors – Richard Greene, a brother-in-law of Weston's, and John Sanders – failed to exercise sufficient control over their people to ensure that proper steps were taken to establish the settlement on a sound footing, to safeguard their supplies, to plan their building programme, their defences and to enforce any sort of discipline. The men stole from one another, robbed the food stores, roistered endlessly, fought amongst themselves and, in general, created so much discord and chaos that within a very short time they had almost exhausted their provisions. And being thoroughly hated by the natives, with no harvest or prospects of one to fall back on, and with the winter not far ahead of them, the possibility of replenishing their food stocks seemed remote.

Richard Greene was the first to understand how desperate their plight might be, and he made contact with the Plymouth settlers to discuss with them the problem of supplies. Neither community had suffi-

cient corn or other foodstuffs to lend the other, and the Boston settlers had no trade goods to barter for food with the Indians – if they could persuade them to trade. But they did have the *Swan*.

It was arranged that the Plymouth Pilgrims should loan trade goods to the Boston settlers, and in return, that the *Swan* should be put at the disposal of a joint expedition to go in search of supplies. They decided, too, that using Squanto's local knowledge the expedition, under Richard Greene, should explore the southern coast of Cape Cod and the islands thereabouts in the hope of finding a short and safe route through the shoals of Pollock Rip to the James River settlements in Virginia, where they could expect to receive some help. They hoped, too, to find Indians along that coast who were still friendlily disposed towards them and willing to trade.

At the same time it was arranged that John Sanders should be given some trade goods to take with a small expedition among the tribes of the Massachusets Indians, in the hope of being able to deal with them. The collection made by both expeditions was to be shared equally between the two English settlements.

Unfortunately, before the expedition in the *Swan* could depart from Plymouth, Richard Greene died in the settlement, and a few more days went by before it was agreed that the expedition should continue under the command of Miles Standish.

But the weather was already deteriorating as the *Swan* put to sea – and twice it was driven back into Plymouth harbour by squally, contrary winds. On the second occasion Standish had developed such a fever that he was compelled to withdraw from the expedition. The urgency of the mission was so great that Bradford immediately took personal charge, but it was already late in November before the third attempt could be made to cross the wide Bay and to sail down the open, stormy Atlantic coast of Cape Cod.

Squanto assured everybody of his ability to pilot the vessel through the shoals of Pollock Rip, having sailed those waters before in both English and French ships, but his claims no longer carried the respect and weight they had done in the past, and the Captain of the *Swan* refused to risk navigating his ship through the unknown shallows and cross-currents in the stormy conditions that prevailed. He did, however, more through the lack of an alternative than from choice, allow Squanto to guide him close in towards the harbour of Manamoick – Chatham, today – and then, using the shallop to feel a way through the twisting, narrow channel between dangerously hidden rocks and fierce rip-currents, they entered the calmer waters of the little harbour.

From the safety of Manamoick the explorers could see the unexpected set of the tides, the tremendous strength of the currents as the water raged through the gaps between the tiny islets and the long spit of Monomoy Point that barred a safe passage, so close to the mainland, to the west.

That night the Governor took a small party ashore, including Squanto as interpreter, but at first the local Indians kept out of sight, possibly because that particular stretch of coast had never previously been visited by Europeans. But Squanto persevered. He disappeared into the woods, made contact with the natives of the district and did his best to assure them that the little party had come to them in all friendliness and in the hope of trading with them – nothing more.

Eventually he persuaded some of them to come out of hiding and very soon, seeing that there was no danger, they were joined by others and produced food to entertain their visitors. But they remained unwilling to say where their village was. When Bradford explained that he and his party intended to spend the night ashore in readiness to trade with them in the morning, most of the Indians ran off. Later, after some obvious delaying tactics, the remaining Indians conducted the settlers to their village, but they disappeared suddenly, just as the Englishmen paused to look around them – and the village was left totally deserted. A quick exasperated check through some of the wigwams and the settlers realized that the delay on the beach had been engineered to give the villagers time to gather up everything they possessed and to escape, in the obvious fear of being robbed.

A search in the immediate neighbourhood gave the settlers occasional glimpses of the Indians, but each time they disappeared again with their possessions.

Next morning Squanto succeeded, after a great deal of difficulty, in persuading the Indians to return to their village. And again they gradually recovered their courage and began to examine the trade goods offered for barter. Bradford was glad to be able to buy from them eight hogsheads of corn and beans.

Encouraged by this success and the growing friendliness of the Indians, Squanto made some enquiries among them and, being assured that a passage through the shoals to the west was possible,

and that it was even probable that further stocks of food could be obtained in that direction, urged the Governor to make a second attempt to negotiate Pollock Rip.

But with shocking suddenness, Squanto was overcome by a heavy fever, and died that same day. In accordance with his last wish, the Pilgrim Fathers prayed that his soul should be received by the Englishmen's God – perhaps the first American to die a Christian.

It was December now and the weather, already stormy, was becoming tempestuous. The Captain of the *Swan* voiced his concern for their safety if they persisted in attempting to find a passage to the south and west, and Bradford, lacking a guide now that Squanto had been buried, decided that they should abandon the expedition and head north for Boston Bay, to share out what they had procured and to see what success had favoured Sanders' attempt to trade with the natives around the Bay – and to learn what progress the Indians had made in planting corn for them for the following year as they had promised earlier.

Despite the winter weather the *Swan* made a quick passage to the settlement at Wessagusset, but the Governor and his party were concerned to find that the Indians around the settlement were being plagued by a virulent sickness. The Indians complained bitterly, too, about their treatment at the hands of Weston's settlers, particularly of their stupid habit of tramping over the cornfields – in reprisal the Indians had now refused further trade and even to tend the crops that they had already planted.

The Governor was equally bitter to discover that, even before relations had been broken off between Sanders' undisciplined men and the Indians, the English had bartered away all the trade goods supplied by the Pilgrim Fathers, with no regard for economy or even commonsense. They had given as much for a quart of corn as the Pilgrims had been in the habit of exchanging for a beaver's skin – so that there was little to show for their enterprise.

Bradford could do no more than point out exasperatedly to Sanders the damage his people were doing and the danger of starvation they faced if they continued to remain on bad terms with the Indians; and he reminded him sharply of the slaughter that had taken place on the James River in Virginia. The lecture had its designed effect. Sanders decided that the *Swan* should be left under the control of Bradford

The house of Governor William Bradford; detail of a model by E. J. Jane.

when he returned, as he intended, to the Cape Cod area in search of supplies.

Bradford headed for Nauset – Eastham – where he was by now well known and, as he expected, he was received in style by Sachem Aspinet, from whom he was able to obtain eight or ten hogsheads of corn.

But the winter storms had now become so severe and unpredictable that communication between ship and shore was becoming dangerous – and sometimes impossible. The *Swan* was compelled to ride out each gale five or six miles offshore and the shallop had to be used between the vessel and the beach – until it was suddenly picked up by a tremendous wave and cast away.

The ship's longboat was leaky and, as they had no carpenter with them to effect repairs, it seemed for a time that they would have to abandon all they had procured from Aspinet. But the Governor, determined to safeguard the precious supplies, had the corn heaped into a stack and covered with mats and cut sedge. Then the Sachem sent some of his warriors out to see if they could find the wreckage of the shallop. They did find it, at high water, almost totally buried in the sand. It was by no means the total wreck that the Englishmen had expected, but considerable repairs would be necessary to make it seaworthy again.

Bradford left both the shallop and the corn in the charge of the Sachem, promising to send for them as soon as it was possible. He also promised a goodly reward if, when they returned, they found that the shallop had not been broken up or despoiled in any way and that the corn had not been pilfered or vermin permitted to get into it. If Aspinet failed, Bradford threatened, he would not only make him and his tribe smart for their dishonesty, but he would take their corn and everything else they possessed in retaliation.

From Nauset the *Swan* sailed down the coast and into Cummaquid – Barnstable – harbour where Bradford was fortunate enough to accumulate another eight or ten hogsheads of corn, again having to stack it and leave it in the care of the Sachem.

The storms persisted and the *Swan* became weather-bound in the harbour, but Bradford, rather than remain aboard idle until the weather improved, took his men ashore again; ordering the Captain of the vessel to follow him to Plymouth as soon as the weather eased, he found an Indian guide and, despite torrential rain and high winds, he and his little party covered the fifty miles back to the settlement on foot.

Three days later the *Swan* arrived in Plymouth harbour and the corn in its holds was divided between the representatives of the two settlements. She then sailed to Boston with the corn belonging to the Wessagusset settlers. She returned to Plymouth at the beginning of January 1623 – no doubt hastened on her way by the hopelessly improvident settlers at Boston Bay, who were already in urgent need of the corn stacked around Cape Cod Bay – with a carpenter so that the shallop lying at Nauset could be repaired and the stacks of corn there and at Cummaquid could be recovered. Captain Standish took command of this latest expedition and, taking with him another shallop, sailed across the Bay in the *Swan* – despite the bitterly cold winds and the incessant rain and snow storms.

Happily, Sachem Aspinet and his tribesmen had guarded both the corn and the stranded shallop with care and, while the carpenter and a few helpers set about repairing the boat, the others transported the corn to the *Swan* in the second boat.

During these operations, the movement of the second shallop between the ship and the shore was constantly interrupted by the gales; on one such occasion the crew had to draw the boat up into a creek for safety, and prepared to spend the night ashore in whatever shelter they could find. They withdrew to the meagre cover of some trees. Standish posted a sentry with orders to patrol around the little encampment and as far as the beach where the shallop lay. Almost immediately after dark a routine check was made on the shallop by the sentry and he discovered that some of the trade goods aboard it had been stolen: knives, scissors, beads and ornaments. The theft was reported to Standish at once and he promptly took an armed party with him to confront the Sachem. He warned Aspinet that he must see to it that the goods were returned to the shallop before morning and have the culprits punished, or he would take reprisals on the whole village and appropriate enough of their possessions to compensate the settlers for their loss. Refusing to discuss the matter

or to accept any form of entertainment, he led his men back to their camp.

In the morning Aspinet, accompanied by a large party of his tribesmen, marched down to the beach and the settlers' encampment. He saluted the Captain in the manner taught him by Squanto – by putting out his tongue at him so that the root could be seen, licking his hand from wrist to finger-tips and bowing, English fashion. His braves repeated the salute with such emphasis that the Englishmen were torn between a desire to retaliate with a few more forceful gestures and laughing helplessly.

The stolen items were returned to the Captain and the Sachem swore that the thief had been thoroughly beaten. He had also made the women bake them a supply of Indian bread in token of his regret at the incident.

No sooner had the first shallop been repaired and both of them moored to the stern of the *Swan* than a short but violent gale snapped the moorings and both boats set adrift: fortunately they were not badly damaged, but there was some further delay before the expedition could recover the corn which was stacked at Cummaquid.

Back in Plymouth harbour, the corn was again divided between the two settlements. The *Swan* left for Boston Bay as soon as the weather permitted.

Bradford, after his experience of the previous year's food shortage and of all the privations that it had brought in its wake, was not yet satisfied. They had barely accumulated a minimum to keep them fed until the next harvest – and there was no assurance that the yield from the harvest would be as plentiful as they hoped, nor could they be certain that there would be no further encroachments on their hospitality by unexpected arrivals in the New World. So, as soon as the ship left for the north, he led an expedition to Nameschet – Middlesborough – and to Manomet – Sandwich – and at both places successfully negotiated further purchases of corn.

He left the Manomet corn in the charge of the local Sachem, but he organized the porterage of the Namaschet purchase to Plymouth on the backs and heads of the Indian women who, unlike their menfolk, could carry very heavy burdens for long distances without showing fatigue. Unfortunately, sickness broke out among the women during the trek and the settlers had to finish the task themselves – with nothing like the efficiency or speed of the Indian women.

19 Resentment Amongst the Indians

It was Standish's turn to make the next sortie in search of corn. He headed south aboard one of the shallops with a few of the Plymouth settlers, keeping within the sheltered waters of Cape Cod Bay.

The blizzards of winter were wreaking their annual vengeance on even those enclosed waters as they sailed towards the shelter of Cummaquid harbour, in the southernmost reaches of the Bay. But the Pilgrim Fathers had long learned that there would be little let-up in conditions until the winter had run its course, and in the meantime the need for corn overrode all other considerations.

The little expedition made Cummaquid harbour safely after a gale-tossed voyage down the coast; almost before they stepped ashore the shallop was frozen in. They were met there by a number of Cummaquid Indians who were willing enough to barter a fair measure of corn for the trinkets Standish offered – but the Captain was uneasily aware that there were a number of strange natives in the woods around. They kept peering out from between the trees and hiding themselves quickly again the moment they realized that the settlers were watching them, making no attempt to come forward to join in the trading.

It grew even colder as night came down and, with the shallop frozen in, the settlers were compelled to accept shelter in the wigwams offered to them by Sachem Iyanough. But Captain Standish was still suspicious of the mysterious strangers, and fearing some sort of a plot he arranged for six of his men to take it in turn to remain on watch around the wigwams during the night, leaving two to guard the shallop.

The sentries were not as efficient as they might have been, for within an hour it was discovered that some beads had disappeared from their store of trade goods. Standish promptly withdrew the guard from the shallop and with his whole party surrounded the Sachem's large wigwam. Then the Pilgrims suddenly burst in with their muskets at the ready – to find most of the tribe crowded around the Chief. The unexpected arrival of the Englishmen, armed and ready for action, dismayed the startled Indians and they offered no resistance.

Standish warned Iyanough that he would take compensation from the possessions of the tribesmen, by force if necessary, unless the stolen goods were returned at once and the thief punished. Iyanough conferred worriedly with some of his braves – and one slipped away from the back of the crowd in the wigwam. The Sachem continued to protest the complete innocence of himself and his tribesmen – until he caught sight of the man who had slipped out earlier. Then he begged Standish to check the shallop where he would find proof that nothing had been stolen.

The missing articles were there, of course, but the Captain left the Sachem in no doubt that he suspected him of trickery.

Scared by the way the theft had been discovered almost as soon as it had taken place, and by the prompt threat of force with which it had been met, Iyanough did what he could to soothe the ruffled feelings of the Englishmen by offering to barter further stocks of corn for trinkets.

In March Standish sailed again from Plymouth, this time to Manomet to collect the store of corn left there by Bradford. He was at some considerable distance from the shallop when he realized that his reception was not all he had anticipated – and he had with him only two or three of his men, with only a similar number left aboard the boat.

While he was in Sachem Cawnacome's wigwam trying to negotiate a further purchase of corn, two Massachusets Indians from the Boston Bay region suddenly entered – one of them, Wituwamat, an Indian well known to the settlers for his insulting manner and his persistent boast of having dipped his hands in both English and French blood. Wituwamat took a dagger which had been strung about his neck and presented it to Sachem Cawnacome. He started a

Modern Wampanoag Indians.

long speech in a dialect that passed right over the head of even Standish, who was by far the best linguist among the Pilgrim Fathers.

Later it was discovered that the Massachusets were determined to massacre the Weston settlement at Wessagusset – not altogether surprisingly. They had forty braves available for the enterprise, which they considered enough to overrun the settlement while the inhabitants slept, but they feared reprisals from the much more alert and efficient Plymouth Planters if they were not crushed at the same time. Wituwamat, a Pines (Councillor) of the Boston Bay Indians, regretted that it should be necessary to attack the Plymouth settlement as they bore no ill will towards the Pilgrims, but he reminded Cawnacome that no such friendship could outlast the massacre of their fellow Englishmen in the north – however much they might despise them.

The word he brought with him from the Massachusets Indians was that the Nauset, Pamet, Succonet, Mattachiest, Agawaywam and Capawack

Indians had already decided to cooperate, and they were now anxious that Cawnacome should join in.

It was in the very presence of Standish, although in a dialect unknown to him, that Wituwamat proposed that this was an ideal opportunity to kill Standish and his company and so reduce the effective strength of the Plymouth garrison even before it came under attack.

While Standish was quite unable to understand what was being said, he had heard all the rumours of the hooliganism and vandalism of Weston's settlers. Heedlessly, they had once again eaten all the corn that had been delivered to them and had started to batten on the Massachusets Indians afresh. The natives had brought the water and wood demanded of them, but had not been paid for their services. They had been robbed of their reserves of winter corn and, although Governor Sanders had had more than one of his men publicly flogged for the offence, it had done little to put an end to the wholesale thefts. By February 1623, so stupid had the Wessagusset settlers become that they had even squandered their stocks of seed, leaving them without the possibility of a harvest in due time.

It was so obvious to Standish that the two Massachusets Indians were being entertained in a much more lively manner than he and his men that his suspicions concerning the intentions of Cawnacome ran deep, but he could not bring up the three men he had left in the shallop to increase his bodyguard – they were needed there to safeguard the stocks of corn that the women were even then carrying down to it.

Also present was a Pamet Indian from Cape Cod who was well known to Captain Standish and who had always been very friendly towards him; but even he began to act suspiciously, by over-insisting on their friendship and by offering a large kettle to the Captain, refusing to accept anything in exchange for it. He offered, too, to help with the carrying of the corn, although it was much beneath his dignity to do so. And then he pointed out that in such a wind he would need to lodge in Standish's encampment for the night.

By then Standish was in no doubt that the Pamet planned to kill him during the night, but he dared not accuse him openly in case the tiny force were immediately overwhelmed. However, he strove to keep himself awake and alert by remaining on his feet and walking up and down, despite the bitingly cold wind in the open – and the Indian, seeing that the Captain was suspicious, had to abandon his treacherous plot.

Standish must have been mightily relieved next morning to find that the ice had broken and that the wind was fair, but he was certainly astonished to learn that the Pamet was anxious to sail with him, promising over-earnestly to find plenty of corn for the Englishmen if they carried him directly to Cape Cod. But, distrusting the Indian completely by now, yet unwilling to close the door altogether on the possibility of trading for food wherever it was available, Standish found some excuse to refuse to take the Pamet with him.

In the Boston Bay district matters were fast coming to a head between the Massachusets Indians and the Wessagusset settlers. By the end of February the Indians were flatly refusing to sell food of any sort to the Planters, many of whom were urging their Governor to strengthen the palings around the town so that they could make sorties against the Indians to capture their food stocks, and then have a secure base to retreat to afterwards. Others – either more honest or just wiser – advised Sanders to write to Plymouth for advice.

Sanders did write to Bradford, explaining his difficulties. He said that his men were on the verge of starvation and that sickness through malnutrition was widespread. He himself had intended to make his way with a small party to Monhegan to the north, where it was known that Sir Ferdinando Gorges kept a plantation and where fishing fleets were in the habit of putting in for fresh water, in the hope of being able to buy bread from the ships' Masters and corn from the plantation, but he feared for the colony in his absence, so far gone were they with hunger. He then asserted that he saw no alternative, since the Indians had refused to deal in any way with them, but to mount an attack against them to capture their hidden stocks of corn. However, he would hold his hand, pending the return of the messenger with Bradford's advice – if it were not too long in coming.

Bradford was well aware of the manner in which the Indians had been treated by Weston's settlers, and when he asked the messenger what stocks of corn the Indians were likely to have he was not surprised to learn that there was little that had not already been bought, stolen or otherwise taken – except their seed reserves which they had, understandably, hidden.

Whatever the situation, Bradford was not prepared to advise anyone to use force against the natives, or to do anything else that might precipitate a war. He wrote back pointing out that even in Plymouth supplies were short and that they themselves were forced to supplement their diet with groundnuts, clams and mussels. Oysters were still to be had in plenty in the entries to all the creeks and rivers in New England, he added, good and fatter than those known in England, and it was up to Weston's settlers to use their woodsmanship to fill their needs, as was being done by those at Plymouth.

Bradford offered the Wessagusset settlers neither sympathy nor help. He stated quite bluntly that no assistance would be given them in any attack on, or theft from, the natives – and reminded that one day the king would undoubtedly send out officers from England to report on his possessions in the New World, and would certainly take legal proceedings against those who flouted his laws. He followed up this letter with a private note for the Governor, couched in more kindly terms, but warning him that in the event of any legal investigation Sanders personally would be held responsible for the settlers' antics in Wessagusset.

So desperate was the situation in the northern colony that Sanders journeyed to Plymouth to make a personal appeal to Bradford, but he found the head of the Pilgrims adamantly unsympathetic because of the way his men had stirred up the Indians against the English. Bradford refused to victual the *Swan* for another combined expedition in search of food, but he did promise, reluctantly, to provide sufficient from the Plymouth settlement's slender resources to sustain Sanders and a few men in the shallop for a journey to Monhegan.

With that, Sanders had to be satisfied.

While Standish was in danger of being murdered at Manomet, news was received at Plymouth that Sagamore Massasoit was very ill and likely to die. At the same time word reached the settlement that a Dutch ship had been driven aground in heavy weather, at Sowans in Pokanoket – Warren today, in Bristol, Rhode Island – the main residence of Massasoit, and that it was unlikely to be refloated until the tides increased.

It was the practice among the Indian tribes to visit seriously ill persons, particularly those with the status of a Chief. Where it was impracticable to do so, it was

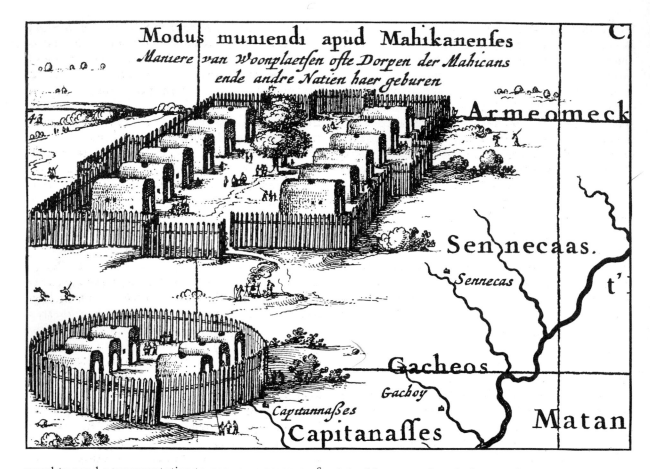

A detail from a map from the first part of the seventeenth century showing a typical wooden village of the east coast (in this case, of the Iroquois).

usual to send a representative to convey messages of good wishes and friendship. Sagamore Massasoit was the Paramount Chief in all the territories that surrounded Plymouth – his word was law over an area greater than that of England – and he had always been a close and sincere friend, and a great help to the settlers there. Bradford, therefore, on hearing the news considered it only right that one of the Pilgrims should make the journey to Sowans as his representative to assure the Sagamore of his hope that he would soon recover from his sickness. At the same time it would provide an excellent opportunity to contact the Dutch, even if only for news of the outside world, but perhaps to obtain from them some much needed food supplies.

Edward Winslow had made the journey with Bradford at the beginning of the previous July, so he was chosen as the Governor's representative; he was provided with some of Surgeon Fuller's medicines as a token of the regard of the whole community. With him went Hobomok and a certain John Hamden, a gentleman from London who was spending the

winter at Plymouth – for what reason we do not know, although it seems likely that he arrived aboard the *Charity* with Weston's settlers in the previous year. (It is improbable, however, as has been freely supposed, that he was the famous parliamentarian of those days, whose movements would have been recorded in letters and documents in both New England and at home.) He was anxious to see something of the country and asked permission to accompany Winslow, although it is probable that his real wish was to escape the narrow, primitive confines of Plymouth for a spell.

The trio spent the first night of their overland journey at Namaschet, where they were well received, but on the following day at about 1 o'clock, when they were about to cross the Taunton River – at what is now known as Slade's Ferry, Swansea – they were given the news that Massasoit was dead and had been buried that morning. They were told, too, that the Dutch ship had already been refloated and would almost certainly have sailed before they reached Sowans.

Edward Winslow hesitated to carry on towards the dead man's "capital". According to Indian intelligence it seemed very probable that Sachem Corbitant would be the new Sagamore and, as he had long been an enemy of the settlers, his accession as Paramount Chief of the Wampanoag tribes might well spell disaster. Winslow was seriously concerned over the possibility that Corbitant might link up with Sagamore Canonicus of the Narragansetts, who had made it clear that he needed only an excuse and – despite the fact that his men ran into thousands – some assurance of success to attack the settlers. Hobomok, too, was nervously anxious, and wished to return at once to the comparative safety of the fort at Plymouth, having real fear of the change of Indian leadership, having only in the previous August escaped with his life from Corbitant.

But Winslow, as courageous as most of the Pilgrims and knowing that Corbitant lived at Mattapoiset – now Gardner's Neck, in Swansea – only about three miles away, determined to make a bid to gain his friendship, or at least some undertaking of non-interference with the settlers. He asked the others if they would support him in such an attempt. Hamden was willing enough, and Hobomok trailed along with them, although a much worried man – in fact, so deeply did the fear of the Sachem bite into his spirits that he began pleading, wildly, with Winslow and extolling the praises of the Indian Chief. "Neen womasee Sagimus" – "My loving Sachem" – he cried time and again. He insisted that Corbitant was neither a liar nor so cruel as other Indians, easily turned from his anger and quickly reconciled with his enemies. He assured Winslow that he ruled better with a few strokes than most did with many, that he was always ready to listen to advice – and argued that it was only due to the Sachem's kindness that the Indians had been held back from attacking Plymouth. What Hobomok hoped to achieve by this *volte face*, especially in the absence of Corbitant himself, it is difficult to understand. Winslow – probably as puzzled as we are! – simply ignored his interpreter and led the way to Mattapoiset.

Corbitant was away from home when they arrived, having gone to Sowans to pay his respects to the dead Sagamore – and, in all probability, to make sure that his claim to the succession was thoroughly understood by all the other Sachems, especially those of them who might have ideas of their own. But the Squaw Sachem received the trio in friendly fashion and, while she fed them, explained that there was no certainty whatever about the news of the Sagamore's death – although she believed it to be true.

Winslow promptly hired an Indian to run to Sowans to let Corbitant know that he was in his village and to bring back confirmation of the news concerning Massasoit. The runner returned, half an hour before sunset, to report that Sagamore Massasoit was not yet dead but would be before the Englishmen could reach his deathbed.

Feeling it to be his duty to convey Bradford's message of good wishes to Massasoit so long as the Sagamore was alive to receive it – and perhaps because he saw some advantage in being on the spot among the mourning Sachems at the critical moment – Winslow wasted not a moment of time and, despite gathering darkness, led his two companions from the village and marched quickly in the direction of Sowans.

As they approached the "capital" they learned from some passing Indians that the Dutch vessel had indeed been refloated by the tide and had gone.

When they reached Massasoit's wigwam – a very much larger structure than the usual run of Indian homes – Winslow and his two companions were shocked to see that it was so packed with people that they had to force a passage to get inside. The crowd about the Sagamore's bed was making a raucous noise, led by the Powows (medicine men) with loud and monotonous incantations, while six or eight women knelt around the dying man chafing his arms and legs and thighs, in the hope of keeping the blood circulating throughout his body.

The noise died down and the women ceased their ministrations as Edward Winslow stepped to the bedside. For a moment or two everybody was too surprised by the intrusion even to greet him, and then one of the women quietly told the Sagamore of his latest visitor.

Massasoit's sight had gone but his mind was still functioning. He spoke to Winslow in a weak voice, and asked him: "Keen Winslow?" – "Are you Winslow?"

Winslow gave the Indian the affirmative: "Ahhe."

Then Massasoit said, and repeated the sentence:

"Matta neen wonckanet namen, Winslow." – "I shall never see you again, Winslow."

Winslow called Hobomok to his side and told him to inform the Sagamore that Governor Bradford had learned, with deep sorrow, of his illness and had sent him with English medicine in the hope that it would ease him. We do not know what the medicine was, but we assume that it was in the form of a paste as it was offered to the Chief on the point of a knife. Massasoit took it, although Winslow had difficulty in forcing it past his teeth. The Sagamore held it in his mouth until it dissolved, and then managed to swallow it.

The throng of Indians about the sick man's bed chattered excitedly and hopefully, declaring that the dying man had swallowed nothing in two days. Winslow examined Massasoit's tongue with some difficulty and found it badly furred and so swollen that it would be impossible for the sick man to swallow anything solid. He scraped the corruption from the tongue and washed out the Chief's mouth –

A typical east-coast Indian shaman, or medicine man; engraving by Theodore de Bry (1590) after a drawing by John White.

and then gave him another dose of medicine. Winslow was relieved to see that it was swallowed more readily than the initial dose.

Massasoit asked for water and Winslow dissolved some of the medicine in it. The Chief drank thirstily – and within half an hour seemed to regain some of his strength and a little of his sight. Winslow made some searching enquiries into Massasoit's physical condition: he wanted to know how much sleep the Sagamore had had and how clear his bowels were. He learned that Massasoit had not slept for two days and had not cleared his system in five.

Winslow then dissolved in water more of the mixture he had brought with him, and persuaded the sick man to drink it. He told him that a phial of an important medicine had been broken during the journey from Plymouth and suggested that some fast

A nineteenth-century engraving of Edward Winslow based on a
seventeenth-century portrait.

runners be sent there for a replacement and for a few chickens with which to make a heartening and strengthening broth. The Sagamore was only too ready to agree and by two o'clock in the morning runners were on their way to Plymouth, carrying a letter from Winslow to Surgeon Fuller.

Before morning Massasoit complained of hunger and he begged Winslow to use his musket to shoot some geese or ducks for him, but the Planter decided that, before he attempted to digest anything so strong, it would be better for him to eat some bruised corn with the flour extracted from it.

At dawn the two Englishmen made a search for some healing herbs, as far as they could recognize them, in the surrounding woods, but as it was still only March they found nothing but some strawberry leaves. They dug up a sassafras root, took a slice from it and added it to some broth to give it taste. Winslow boiled it up and then strained the brew through his handkerchief and managed to induce the Indian Chief to drink about a pint of the concoction. His efforts proved effective: the sick man cleared his system and his sight improved. He began to take an interest in all that was going on around him again,

and, at a whim, asked Winslow to tour the village and to wash out the mouths of all who were found to be sick and to give each of them a dose of the home-brewed medicine. Winslow, uneasily aware that he was not a surgeon, set the women busy brewing up a strawberry-leaf broth in large earthenware pots and then made the rounds of the sick, dosing each of them.

After the midday meal Winslow returned to Massasoit to find his patient progressing far better than he had ever believed possible; when the Sagamore again asked for a goose or a duck to be shot and cooked for him, he gladly agreed. He took an Indian with him so that he should not get lost and very soon spotted a brace of ducks at a range of about 120 yards. He fired at them, killing one – much to the astonishment of his Indian guide. The women quickly plucked the bird and cooked it, and the broth from it was fed to the Chief. He swallowed it gratefully and with a good deal of pleasure.

So rapidly did he recover that, when he asked for the flesh of the bird, Winslow gave him a little after cutting away the fat. But Massasoit enjoyed fat and, although the Englishman warned him of the danger,

A reconstruction of the interior of one of the Pilgrim houses at Plymouth – Hurlow House in the Plimoth Plantation.

insisted on making a full meal of it. As was to be expected, within an hour Massasoit was very, very sick. His nose began to bleed as the tiny capillary blood vessels burst under the pressure of the paroxysms. The spell lasted for four desperate hours.

The crowd of onlookers grew afresh as the Indians decided, for the second time, that their Chief was dying, and even Massasoit was convinced that his end was near. He slept at last, exhausted, for about six hours, but when he did waken he was obviously very much better, and by the time his runners returned from Plymouth with chickens and medicine he was so far recovered that he was easily persuaded of the dangers of overeating – and ordered the birds to be kept for breeding purposes.

Visiting Sachems continued to arrive to pay their respects to their Paramount Chief and learned how effective had been Winslow's skilled attention: his fame was spread among them and did much to check the rising tide of ill-will against the settlers.

When Massasoit found himself capable of sitting up and the trio from Plymouth were on the point of departure, he called Hobomok to him. In the presence of only a few of his most trusted Pineses he told the interpreter of a plot by the Massachusets Indians against the English colony at Wessagusset, to be supported by an attack on Plymouth, by the tribes from Nauset, Pamet, Succonet, Mattachiest, Agowaywam and from the Isle of Capawack (now called Eastham, Cape Cod, Falmouth, Barnstable, Wareham and Martha's Vineyard). Massasoit informed Hobomok that proposals had been made to him to join in the attack on the settlement and to kill everybody in it – but he had refused and had put a stop to any of his own people taking part in it.

Hobomok carried the warning to Winslow. Although the Pilgrim Fathers had long been aware that something was in the wind, this was the first direct warning they had received. With the detail so clearly set out, Winslow was in a hurry to return to Plymouth with the news.

But as he, Hamden and Hobomok made their departure from Sowans, Corbitant, who had remained to see the outcome of Massasoit's illness, begged that they spend the first night with him in his own village of Mattapoiset, so that they could have a talk. Winslow was ready enough to agree, although he was well aware of Corbitant's treacherous nature: despite their previous encounter, he hoped to be able to consolidate the wave of friendship engendered by his ministrations to the Paramount Chief.

Corbitant proved to be a witty and sarcastic man who was farsighted enough to realize that, so long as Massasoit remained alive, he could have no hope of being more than the leader of a minority faction. But his thoughts at that moment were concerned for his welfare rather than his aggrandizement – and he sought to arrange for "expert" medical attention, should ever the need arise. He wanted some assurance that Bradford would send medicine and Winslow to administer it to him if ever he should become ill. Winslow assured him that he would. And, unexpectedly, the Sachem asked Winslow to call down God's blessing on their meal, wondering at the same time why the Englishmen should keep such a custom.

Winslow's explanation must have turned the discussion towards the Ten Commandments and he learned, for the first time, that the Indians basically believed much the same things, and that the same powers as were held by the English God were ascribed to the Indians' Kietitan. How much of this was genuine and how much soft soap with which to convince Winslow of Corbitant's friendship cannot now be assessed, but we can understand that the settlers, although they were not prepared to relax their suspicions, were glad enough to accept the proffered hand.

The trio hurried on to Namaschet next morning. On the way they met a couple of Pamet Indians who told Winslow that Standish had left that morning in the shallop to visit the Massachusets Indians on a trading expedition. Badly worried that Standish and his party would fall foul of the Massachusets plot to massacre the settlers at Wessagusset, Winslow marched straight through Namaschet and on to Plymouth without pause. But contrary winds had so slowed down the shallop that Standish had put back into Plymouth harbour to await a more favourable opportunity.

Winslow told Bradford of the Indian plot, and Hobomok joined in with an urgent plea that the Englishmen should kill off the Massachusets Indians before the attack could be mounted – although he failed to suggest how some thirty thousand Indians could be dealt with by fewer than a hundred settlers. He added that, although the Wessagusset Planters deserved whatever came to them, if the Plymouth settlers waited for the attack they would find that immediately afterwards the Massachusets Indians would be free – and encouraged by success – to turn on them.

As it happened, Bradford had been given some intelligence and advice along the same lines by Sachem Wassapinewat, the brother of Sachem Obtakiest of the Massachusets Indians, in an attempt to ingratiate himself with the Englishmen – probably hoping to unseat his brother in that manner and to take over the tribe. But he felt that in any case he had no authority to involve the settlement in a war without the consent of the Pilgrim Fathers, so he decided to put the matter to them in open Public Court.

20 Confrontation at Wessagusset

On 23rd March 1623 – two days before New Year's Day, and the day established by the Pilgrim Fathers as the Yearly Court Day – Governor Bradford explained to the meeting the details of the Indian plot, as he knew it, against the settlers at Wessagusset and the danger that it posed to the safety of Plymouth.

The discussion was sombre: to take up arms to destroy the Indians seemed to them to be a dreadful thing to do – they had done the settlers of Plymouth no harm, and had often been of considerable service to them; and Weston's settlers richly deserved a very sharp lesson. Besides, more than one speaker reminded the meeting, however successful a pre-emptive attack on the Indians might be, so overwhelming were their numbers that inevitably there must follow a murderous war that would last for years and might well see the total destruction of every settlement in America and the death, through battle or starvation, of every settler from the Old World. On the other hand, to stand by while even so small, ill conceived and provocative a settlement as that at Wessagusset was massacred without going to their aid must, in all conscience, bring down on their heads the wrath of the government in England and the deadly enmity of every settler in the New World.

So delicate was the problem that it soon became apparent that it could not be resolved in public debate – there were too many options, points of view, scruples and fears to be considered. Wisely, therefore, the meeting laid the discussion in the laps of its three elder statesmen, Bradford, Allerton and Standish.

The committee quickly formed a plan. Standish was to take eight men with him and proceed to Wessagusset as fast as he could. There he was to satisfy himself beyond doubt that the settlement was to come under attack. If the threat were evident he was to warn the settlers there of his military intentions. These were to be based on the premise that, however many Englishmen they could mobilize, the force would be unlikely to exceed fifty – if

Plymouth were not to be abandoned – to fight against probably 5,000 Indian warriors. Muskets could be devastating in a single fusilade, but while the musketeers were going through the complicated and time-consuming task of reloading and priming their pieces the Indian arrows would shower down on them without a moment's pause.

Guile was required, and Standish planned to take only eight men out of the town so as to offer no apparent threat to the Indians, and then to trap them in small parties with the prime object of killing Wituwamat – the Pines of the Boston Bay Indians whom Standish had already met at Manomet and whom he knew to be the spearhead of the drive against the settlers. If possible, Standish and his tiny force would kill and behead the Indian, using the severed head as a bloody warning to the rest.

Next morning, before Standish's men were ready to board the shallop, a settler from Wessagusset arrived, having had a hair-raising journey through Indian territory, with a desperate tale of the conditions now prevailing in the northern settlement. This man, Phineas Pratt, told a quickly summoned gathering of the Plymouth Elders that most of the Wessagusset settlers had now abandoned their town: they had been driven from it by parties of marauding Indians who had continually raided the settlement, robbing every hut and even grabbing food from the cooking pots – and then disappearing again before any action could be taken.

Phineas Pratt explained how, in the absence of John Sanders on an expedition to Monhegan in search of supplies, they had tried to establish some sort of internal discipline – and, in an attempt to demonstrate that they were anxious to be on good terms with the Indians, had hanged one of their number who had been accused of theft. But even that salutary sentence had failed to convince the natives either of their regret for past misdeeds or of their good faith for the future – and the settlers had been forced to evacuate the town. Starving, the settlers had sold the clothes from their backs to the Indians for meagre rations of corn and were now dying in the woods from cold and hunger. Without powder and shot they had blundered off in three separate companies and it seemed that they might well never be seen or heard of again. Pratt himself had taken a chance on reaching Plymouth, rather than join in the fights and struggles that went on between the settlers as they stole from one another, completely unchecked. He knew that he had been followed by an Indian but, fortunately, had been able to throw him off the scent.

Almost at the same time some friendly Indians warned the Plymouth settlers that Pratt had indeed been followed but, probably believing that the Englishman had been taken by wolves or a bear, the tracker had merely trotted on past the settlement towards Manomet.

Standish sailed out of Plymouth harbour with his tiny force and, with a stiff breeze coming fair, he swung to the northwest and headed for Boston Bay. At the same time Bradford put in hand hasty preparations to strengthen the still unfinished fort, to service the cannon and to lay them in the direction from which he believed any attack likely to come; then he ordered the defences to be manned and lookouts posted on the towers.

As had been anticipated, the Indian who had trailed Phineas Pratt returned to Plymouth, where he stopped and too obviously sought to discover the strength of the garrison and what preparations, if any, had been made for its defence. He was arrested on the Governor's orders to be held prisoner pending Standish's return. The guard took no chances of having him escape to carry a warning of the Captain's whereabouts to his tribe: they chained him to a post in the guardroom – the first occasion anyone was ever held there.

Captain Standish saw the *Swan* first, lying in the harbour at Wessagusset, and boarded her – but there was not a soul aboard. He fired a musket to attract attention, and the Master of the ship and a few of the local settlers showed themselves on the shore.

Standish waded through the water to them and demanded to know what they were doing. They admitted that they were searching for groundnuts – or food of any kind. They were so destitute that they had already parted with everything they possessed, even their weapons, for food. Now they were living

A
RELATION OR
Iournall of the beginning and proceedings
of the English Plantation setled at *Plimoth* in NEW ENGLAND, by certaine English Aduenturers both Merchants and others.

With their difficult passage, their safe ariuall, their ioyful building of, and comfortable planting themselues in the now well defended Towne of NEW PLIMOTH.

AS ALSO A RELATION OF FOVRE
seuerall discoueries since made by some of the same English Planters there resident.

I. In a iourney to PVCKANOKICK *the habitation of the Indians greatest King* Massasoyt: *as also their message, the answer and entertainment they had of him.*
II. In a voyage made by ten of them to the Kingdome of Nawset, *to seeke a boy that had lost himselfe in the woods: with such accidents as befell them in that voyage.*
III. In their iourney to the Kingdome of Namaschet, *in defence of their greatest King* Massasoyt, *against the* Narrohigonsets, *and to reuenge the supposed death of their Interpreter* Tisquantum.
IIII. Their voyage to the Massachusets, *and their entertainment there.*

With an answer to all such obiections as are any way made against the lawfulnesse of English plantations in those parts.

LONDON,
Printed for *Iohn Bellamie,* and are to be sold at his shop at the two Greyhounds in Cornhill neere the Royall Exchange. 1622.

Title page of Mourt's *A Relation or Journal of the beginning and proceedings of the English Plantation settled at Plymouth ...* , first published in 1622. Little is known of "Mourt's" connection with the colony – it seems likely he did not exist and that the *Relation* was a collaboration between Bradford and Winslow. The introduction to the book is thought to be by Robert Cushman ("R.G." being perhaps a misprint for "R.C."), and the dedication to be to John Peirce ("I.P.").

with the Indians in the partly deserted settlement, near starvation, on the bounty of discarded scraps from the natives.

The ship's Captain told Standish that the people whom Sanders had left in charge while he went off to Monhegan were still hidden somewhere in the village, while the bulk of the population had made off in three parties into the woods.

Standish marched into the town with his eight men,

ignored the Indians and searched through the houses until he had unearthed the leaders of the settlers. He got them together, told them of his plan to frustrate the Indians and to drive them away, but warned them that however successful he might be the settlers would sooner or later have to learn to stand on their own feet, or would be at the mercy of the Indians until they were picked off one by one.

He offered to take the settlers, after he had made his attempt to kill Wituwamat, back to Plymouth with him, where the Pilgrim Fathers would do what they could to safeguard them and keep them from starvation until Weston's supply ship arrived to succour them – so long as they obeyed the rules and did their share of the work. The Wessagusset settlers, the few that could be found, were in such a state of hunger and fear that they were only too ready to accept any solution to their problems.

Standish then made some enquiries as to where in the woods the rest of Weston's settlers were likely to be found and, when he discovered one company of them, he ordered a runner to tell them to return at once to the settlement. But during those early days of April 1623 the weather was bad, and it was some time before Standish could concentrate the colonists in the village – with still about two-thirds of them in the wilds. He fed them from the stores aboard his shallop, then prepared to attempt to eject the Indians.

He posted the Wessagusset men at strategic points within the village and ordered them, when the time came, to hold the settlement at all costs with their swords and axes. He warned them solemnly to maintain absolute secrecy in the meantime as to his own whereabouts and plans, but so little did he trust the destitute, demoralized settlers that he made it clear to them that he would execute any who ventured more than a musket shot's distance from the town, or were seen talking confidentially to the Indians.

During all this time hordes of Indians wandered in and out of the settlement at will – but there was nothing left for them to take. One in particular caught the attention of the alert Plymouth contingent, Pecksuot, a Pines of the Massachusets Indians, who came into the town bringing furs with him ostensibly to trade with the settlers. It was too obvious that he had news of Standish's arrival and had been sent to find out how powerful and purposeful was his force.

Seeing that he was suspect, and having learned of the tiny force at Standish's disposal, Pecksuot openly went to Hobomok and told him that he knew very well that Standish had come to kill him and the rest of the Indians there. He challenged Hobomok to carry the message to the Captain that they were not afraid of him and that, if he dared, he could begin the battle as soon as he pleased.

Standish realized that it was out of the question to attempt a frontal attack with his eight men on the hundreds of Indians that wandered in and out of the settlement, nor could he expect any real help from the starving colonists, who had already sold all their weapons for food. He noticed, too, that the Indians were insultingly beginning to whet their knives on stones almost under his nose – and Wituwamat arrived to show his contempt in the same manner.

Pecksuot, who was considerably taller than Standish, sneered at the Captain's strength and physique, but the Plymouth leader was not to be provoked into precipitate action. He was well aware that unless he exercised the greatest restraint and caution every Englishman in the settlement – and in the region far beyond it – would be slaughtered.

He kept a tight rein over his own men, too, while the Indians wandered about in small parties, any one of which could easily be overwhelmed – although the result when the rest retaliated would have been disaster for the Englishmen. The Indians moved about the village freely and made what use they liked of the English houses – and Standish was quick to note that Wituwamat and his closest associates were in the habit of using one in particular. He saw his opportunity, and set a trap.

Next day he and four of his men took up their positions in the house unnoticed and waited to see who would walk into it. Wituwamat, Pecksuot, a third Indian and an 18-year-old Indian youth were the victims – the very ones with whom Standish hoped to settle accounts. He slammed the door as soon as they stepped inside and, while he attacked Pecksuot and after a short struggle killed him, his men used their finely honed knives to dispose of Wituwamat and the third Indian. Immediately thereafter, he had the youthful Indian hanged where everybody could see him and the corpses of the Indian leaders.

The shocked Indians fled, but they left behind their womenfolk, who were promptly held as captives. Standish freed only one of them, to carry a message to the terrified men, threatening to kill the women if any one of them carried word of what had happened to

Tab. 6.

Pipe of peace w.ch I have Seen.

Lahontans Calumet of peace. p. 82.

a Birchen Canoe

or Canoe of Bark.

S.G. Scul.

The wife and daughter of a Virginia Indian chief. This drawing by John White shows also typical bark canoes of these Indians and two ceremonial pipes.

Sachem Obtakiest. Then he sent a runner to the nearest company of Wessagusset settlers in the woods, ordering them to kill the Indians among them, in the hope of preventing the news of the attack being spread too far and too fast. But, whether through weakness, fear or sheer ineptitude, they killed only two; to make matters worse, Standish's own party allowed one of a pair of Indians they came across to escape into the woods to spread the alarm.

Treachery by some of the Wessagusset settlers was perhaps the worst feature of Standish's attempt to aid the settlement. Before the Plymouth leader could consolidate the position he had won by clearing the village of natives, three of the local Planters, who had some standing among the Indians because of their ability to build canoes, quietly deserted the settlement with the intention of making their way to the wigwam of Obtakiest, the Sachem of the Massachusets Indians, to offer information – and their services – in exchange for food. They took with them bows and arrows, the only weapons they now possessed, saying that they were going hunting in hope of finding a deer. But the older of the trio became alarmed as they passed beyond the musket-shot limits set by Standish, and tried worriedly to persuade his companions to return with him. But the thought of

food at the hands of Sachem Obtakiest was too much for them and they refused. The old man escaped from them during the night and, using unfrequented paths through the woods, succeeded in making his own way back to the settlement, where he reported what had happened to the Captain.

In the morning, Standish took four of his men and one or two from the settlement and, using Hobomok as a guide, he made a cautious sortie out of the town. The party soon encountered a file of Indians and gave battle, both sides striving to capture a small but commanding hill. The Indians slowly retreated until they took up defensive positions behind some trees, from which they could discharge their arrows in comparative safety. But a double shot from Standish and one of his men caught one of the Indians as he stretched his bow arm out from behind a tree, and broke it. The Indians promptly fled into the swamp.

The Indian Pines leading them was killed, and Hobomok, holding the title of Pines himself, suddenly burst from cover and raced towards the Indians as they sheltered in the swamp. Fearful of him because of his rank, they raced off and disappeared.

Returning to the settlement, Standish ordered the release of the Indian women, refusing to allow the settlers to rob them of their furs or molest them in any other way before they left. He then made his plans for a return to Plymouth, having accomplished all he could in the defence of Wessagusset.

While his tiny force stood guard around the outskirts of the village, he gathered together the demoralized settlers and pointed out to them, in obvious contempt, that with eight men he had cleared the town, scattered the Indians and perhaps frightened them away for good. It was now their turn, with fifty men, to hold what he had secured for them. He then reminded them of Bradford's offer to care for those who returned with him to Plymouth; alternatively, he proposed to leave a good part of the shallop's store of corn for those who preferred to stay behind.

Some few did elect to return with Standish's party to Plymouth, but the majority preferred to take the food offered to them, after which they proposed to sail in the *Swan* to Monhegan where their leader had gone, and where they hoped to contact some fishing vessel's Master who would be willing to transport them back to England.

That was the end of Weston's colony. Tragically, within a year sixty healthy men, unencumbered by women and children, had been so indisciplined and incompetent that the whole enterprise had deteriorated into a rabble of destitute, dishonest blundering men.

Shortly afterwards Thomas Weston, who had financed the project, arrived in a fishing vessel to see what profit had accrued to his venture. Shocked by the news of its utter failure, he went ashore in a shallop with a couple of men to discover if the stories were true. But the men were unskilled in managing a boat and the shallop was cast away near the mouth of the Piscataqua River – in New Hampshire – and Weston barely escaped with his life. He fell into the hands of some Indians who robbed him of everything he had, including every item of his clothing – leaving him entirely naked. More by luck than because of his own resourcefulness, he reached Piscataqua (now Portsmouth), where he succeeded in obtaining a suit of clothes – from whom, we do not know – and so found his way to Plymouth. We cannot imagine how

he made such a journey without being captured and killed – after the Indians had failed to take Wessagusset they had taken to the bush in fear of reprisals and, having abandoned their homes and supplies, were starving and vengeful.

Report has it that Weston was a travesty of the man known to the Pilgrim Fathers before they left England. Bradford also leaves it on record that out of pity, and despite the Pilgrims' poverty, they loaned him 170 lb of beaver pelts when he finally sailed back to England later that year. Rumours current in the years that followed ascribed the fortune that Weston undoubtedly made to the skins he carried with him from Plymouth – but the settlers there were never repaid for their generosity.

Standish and his men returned to Plymouth in triumph, bringing with them Wituwamat's severed head, which was promptly impaled over the entrance to the fort for all to see – as was the practice in Europe in those robust but cruel times. Then the Indian prisoner who had been held in chains was handed over to the Captain. Catching sight of the spiked head of Wituwamat as he was taken from the guardroom, he confessed the details of the plot that had been hatched against the settlements of both Wessagusset and Plymouth. He told Standish that there had been five leaders of the enterprise, and that these five had provoked Obtakiest into lending his authority to the attack on the Englishmen. Two of the principal organizers were Wituwamat and Pecksuot, both now dead, and the other three were Powows known to Standish – one of whom was wounded.

The prisoner denied any involvement on his own part – and the Governor, being inclined towards mercy and seeing in him the ideal courier to send with a stern message to Obtakiest, agreed that he should be freed. He was sent back to his Chief with instructions to tell him that he had only himself to blame for his defeat, and to warn him that any repetition of such a plot would result in him and his people being utterly destroyed. Further, Obtakiest was to send to Plymouth the three Englishmen he held – the two canoe-builders who had deserted Wessagusset and one other known to be there. The prisoner was also to warn the Sachem not to destroy the palisade around Wessagusset or to damage the homes inside it in any way. He was then ordered to return with the Englishmen – or the Sachem's reply – under the safe conduct of the word of the Governor

The fort in the Plymouth Colony; detail of a drawing by M. J. Jeffries.

of the Pilgrim settlement.

No reply was received for some considerable time, and when it did arrive it was brought by an Indian woman. She told the Governor that the three Englishmen had been killed on the orders of Obtakiest before the message had reached him – and that the prisoner released to carry the message had been too scared to return with the news. The squaw messenger went on to say that Obtakiest was now sorry for what had happened and was anxious to be on friendly and peaceful terms with the Plymouth settlers, but had been too afraid to make contact with them. In fact, so fearful was he that he had abandoned his wigwam to move from place to place in order to keep out of reach of any pursuit by Standish.

In the final outcome, the plot ended in disaster for the Indians far beyond the expectation of either side. The execution of Wituwamat and Pecksuot, even though it had been in a fair fight, so shocked all the tribes involved in the conspiracy that they abandoned their wigwams and villages, terrified of possible reprisals, and took to the woods and swamps. So hurriedly did they decamp that they left behind their stores of corn, much of their possessions and, often, their weapons. Without food or shelter they quickly became destitute, as had the settlers at Wessagusset. Disease broke out among them and quickly reached epidemic proportions. Many hundreds of them died – among them Sachems Cawnacome of Manomet, Aspinet of Nauset and Iyanough of Mattachiest.

Nothing seemed to stem the disaster: one Sachem sent a canoe manned by three terrified warriors with presents for Governor Bradford in the hope of establishing friendly relations with him again, so that those of his tribe who still survived dared return to their homes and their hidden reserves of grain – but the canoe was overwhelmed in a sudden, wholly unpredicted storm. Two of the Indians were drowned and the third found his way back to his stricken tribe, convinced that the wrath of the English God lay over them and was beyond any pacification.

21 The *Anne* and the *Little James* Arrive

The Indians were not to know that the Pilgrim Fathers had now, in April 1623, no time to spare for further moves against – or negotiations with – the local tribes. Their whole attention was necessarily being given to attending their crops, hunting and fishing. The last of their grain stocks had been exhausted, except that required for seed, and no supply ship had arrived from England – nor, of course, had they any news of one.

Strangely, one of the side-effects of the acute shortage of food was the mutual independence of the settlers. Each family began to provide for itself, exclusively, guarding with intense jealousy all that was obtained by their own labour. The more successful and better organized households took advantage of their strength and will to enlarge their homes, to improve the amenities attached to them and to plan for the future. Others, sadly, proved themselves to be little better than inactive, despondent drones, dependent on the good will of their neighbours for food. They made little shift to improve their dwellings or to prepare for the rigours of the still distant but inevitable winter, and begged for more than their fair share from the common reserves of corn.

Quarrels began to break out between the families as it became more and more evident that only certain members of the community were still doing anything towards improving the settlement and its defences, and as even these began to withdraw their labour in disgust all semblance of communal interests and welfare began to break down.

It soon became a certainty that very shortly the idle and thriftless among them would begin to batten on the industrious, and there were already signs that, as the drones dropped below the subsistence level needed to keep them alive, warm and contented in their idleness, they would begin to steal from one another.

Bradford and the members of his council were quickly alive to the changing spirit and acted determinedly to protect the industrious majority from the idle minority. They allocated an acre of land to each Planter – which, for the following year, he must plant, cultivate and harvest for his own good, relying on no other source of corn. But, not being blind to the need to support certain officers, such as the surgeon, fishermen and others, as and when it was necessary to employ them for the public good, the Governor and the Elders would claim a portion of every man's crop to support them. In all other duties the settlers would be required to work for the public good, and to keep their bargain with the Company of Adventurers who had financed them.

Because of the variations in the quality of the soil – the natural drainage, the distance from water, the extent to which it had already been cleared and its situation – it was decided that lots would be drawn for each plot, which would be held for a single year only, and that there would be no law of inheritance, so that death would not increase anyone's holding.

The allocation of privately held land to each of the families proved itself an instant success. From the moment the settlers felt that they had land of their own, almost every member of each family gave enthusiastic time and energy into obtaining from it as much corn as it could possibly yield, knowing that, except for the levy for public employees, everything they produced would be for their own use – to be shared with no other. Even the women stopped complaining that their children were too weak to work in the fields, or that they were being exploited – and took them along to help on their own plots of land. And the men who had battened on the common stocks and those of their neighbours, realizing now that their future welfare depended entirely on their own efforts, regretfully and perhaps a little fearfully bestirred themselves into some sort of activity.

Long before the end of April every plot was properly planted out and, while food was desperately short, there was a new feeling of confidence and hope among the Plymouth settlers.

Virginia Indians "sitting at meat"; engraving by Theodore de Bray after a drawing by John White.

Only one shallop was now left to the Pilgrims, but under this new paternal discipline those available to man it were divided up into companies of six or eight and sent out in turn to the fishing grounds, spending days at sea, to catch what they could to keep the community fed. Others were set to work to dig for shellfish, and hunting parties succeeded in bringing back an occasional deer.

Hearts were higher than they had ever been, helped by the fine weather, some successful fishing expeditions, the prospects of a not-too-distant harvest – and a feeling of certainty that the arrival of a supply ship from England could not be delayed much longer.

And then, with unexpected cruelty, drought parched the land, dried up the creeks and rivulets, and took its toll of the growing crops. The early planted corn began to sprout ears before it was half grown and the later plantings hung dejected and lifeless. The beans were too weak to spread and much of the crop was parched to destruction.

From 1st June to 15th July the drought persisted, and the new spirit among the settlers began to wilt again as fears for the future began to tease their minds once more. And to intensify their worry, no supply ship had yet reached them and they began to wonder if they had been abandoned by those at home – by the Company of Adventurers who had a financial stake in their well-being and success, and by the brethren of the Pilgrim Church at Leyden and in Southwark, from whom they had long expected reinforcements and encouragement. Then the wreckage of a ship was found on the coast and, after a close examination of the flotsam, there seemed no doubt that it was all that was left of an English ship – probably the supply ship they had long awaited.

The Pilgrim Fathers decided that their ill fortunes were the act of an angry God; so convinced were they of the fact that they held a council to consider what they could do to appease the wrath of the Almighty. The solution was simple enough, they believed: a day should be set aside when everybody, regardless of their employment or any other cause, should join together in a mass Day of Prayer.

The day chosen was 16th June 1623, and was destined to be spent in eight hours of non-stop supplication. When it dawned the skies were cloudless and hazed with heat, and the drought was at its deadliest. By the time the last prayer had been said, clouds were drifting overhead, full of the promise of rain. And next morning the rain came down, mistily, gently, but with a steady persistence that continued until the end of the month. The jaded crops revived, the streams and brooks ran freely again, and the spirits of the Planters lifted high in tune with the vastly improved conditions.

The Indians, who had suffered severely under the drought, took note of the result of the Day of Prayer held by the Pilgrim Fathers; Hobomok pointed out that generally, when the rain fell at that time of the year, there had always been the danger of the crops being flattened by the weight of water that descended – but, at the earnest request of the Pilgrims to their God, it had fallen gently and richly. (Unfortunately this is the last reference to Hobomok in any of the chronicles of those days and we know nothing of his later life or of his end.)

More good news was to follow within a matter of days – news of supply ships at last, and the story behind their delay.

Standish, returning from a trading expedition at the beginning of August, brought back with him David Tomson, a Scotsman who had been sent out only a few weeks earlier, by Sir Ferdinando Gorges, to found a plantation at Smith's Isle – now the Isles of Shoals, Portsmouth, New Hampshire. He told the Plymouth settlers that John Peirce, the titular head of the Company of Adventurers, had chartered the *Paragon* with its Captain, Francis West, in the autumn of 1622 and had sailed from London with supplies and passengers for New England in accordance with the charter.

Unfortunately the ship had been so badly damaged by storms before it even cleared the Downs in the Channel that, after fourteen days spent striving to force a passage to the west, it had been compelled to return to London for repairs – where it had lain for six or seven weeks before being made fit for sea again.

On 22nd December the *Paragon* left London for the second time, carrying supplies and 109 passengers and crew, bound for New Plymouth. But after struggling through 900 miles of continuous winter gales the vessel had become so leaky and unmanageable that by mid-February, after it had been held for a fortnight by nonstop gale-force winds, had the upperworks ripped from the decks and thrown to the waves, and the mast cut away to release the tangled rigging, the Captain was forced to put about and head for England. Only by masterful discipline and brilliant seamanship had he succeeded in getting the hulk and his desperately weak and unhappy passengers back to Portsmouth.

When John Peirce learned of the extent of the damage to the *Paragon* and the fact that it would not be fit to venture out into the Atlantic unless it had some unwarrantably expensive repairs, he decided that he had had enough of the enterprise – and resigned his patent to the Company of Adventurers.

The directors of that company immediately started negotiations to acquire a stouter and more suitable vessel – and, before David Tomson had left England, he had learned that such a ship had been obtained and was even then being prepared for its Atlantic voyage.

The *Anne*, a fine ship of about 140 tons and commanded by William Pierce, arrived at Plymouth during August, followed within a few days by the *Little James*, a pinnace designed to stay with the settlers to serve as a trading and communications craft around the Bay and along the coast.

The *Anne* brought with her some sixty members of the Pilgrim Churches in Leyden and London, and not a few members of the families of those who had already pioneered the settlement in New England. Fear and Patience Brewster, accompanied by Experience Mitchell, arrived to join their parents who had come over in the *Mayflower* almost three years earlier; Francis Cooke's wife with their children and the family of Richard Warren; Alice, the widow of Edward Southworth who was so soon to marry Governor Bradford; and the wives of William Hilton, Robert Hickes, Thomas Flavell and William Palmer. Bridget Fuller, the widow of Edward Fuller, who had died during the epidemic of 1621, arrived too to become, in time, the second wife of Miles Standish.

But among the passengers there were a few who

owed no allegiance to the Pilgrim Church and had made the passage to New Plymouth under separate financial arrangements with the Adventurers. John Oldham was perhaps the leader of these "outsiders" who were not incorporated in the "general" company on the same terms as the Pilgrim Fathers and who, although they were offered the friendship of the original settlers and the opportunity to integrate themselves into the colony, mostly chose to complain about the conditions and the lack of the "sacraments", and to make themselves so much of a nuisance that most of them were encouraged to return to England in the following year.

One name from Leyden was, unhappily, not included on the passenger list of any of the main parties to arrive from Europe: John Robinson, still regarded by the Pilgrims as their pastor. It was said that, because he remained in Holland, the Pilgrim Church in New England was without any spiritual guidance, nor had they anyone possessed of the authority to baptize the children and perform other essential offices – unaware that the Pilgrims required no such "authority", and were content, while they waited for Robinson to arrive, to heed the teachings of William Brewster as their Deacon.

Even yet there was a great deal of opposition to any such nonconformist beliefs as his in England, and the Adventurers, who needed to pay some heed to both the king and the Anglican Church at home, found it expedient to neglect him.

The *Anne* sailed for England on 6th September 1623 carrying as passenger Edward Winslow, appointed by Governor Bradford to carry despatches and reports to the Old Country. So convincingly good were those reports that an upsurge of interest in the colonization of the New World followed, starting up a scramble for grants and patents that, however, failed to touch the settlement at New Plymouth.

On 1st January 1624 Lord Sheffield granted to Edward Winslow and Robert Cushman a patent for the Plymouth Colonists in their own right, empowering them to erect a town and to enact such laws as they saw fit; and on the 24th Cushman sent word to Bradford to say that he was sending out to him a carpenter to build ships, a person to make salt and a preacher.

But the preacher was not to be their own pastor, John Robinson, but a certain John Lyford. He arrived in Plymouth in the company of Edward Winslow aboard the *Anne* on its second round-trip, in March. Winslow had used the full weight of his strong personality to obtain and bring with him also some substantial supplies – including three heifers and a bull, the first cattle to be put ashore in New England.

Lyford was never, however, to take the place of Robinson in the affections of the Pilgrim Fathers in New Plymouth, although they did their best to make him welcome and at home. Perhaps, aware of this, the new pastor stepped ashore so full of reverence and humility, bowing so low and cringing so humbly, that it was difficult to accept his sincerity. He wept as he begged the settlers to accept him, and with some caution, and being advised that he should consult with Brewster, who had acted as their Deacon in the absence of Robinson, he was received into the community as its pastor.

Lyford very soon became a close friend of John Oldham who had arrived aboard the *Anne* on its first voyage to the New World, as "leader" of the dissidents among the passengers, and from the moment the pair got together they both assumed the leadership of the Church. Oldham was already at loggerheads with the Pilgrims because of his incessant complaints, but they were shocked to see how Lyford developed a totally unexpected arrogance.

Between them they soon split the Pilgrim Church into factions – those who accepted the sometimes profane, always bombastic "Anglicism" of Lyford, and those who rejected his malignant outpourings as being contrary to the promptings of conscience that had caused them to leave England for the New World.

Whispered hole-in-the-corner meetings began to take place, destructive character-blacking campaigns unsettled those against whom they were directed, and so much time did Lyford spend in writing letters that the suspicions of many were aroused concerning their content. Indeed, so secretive did he become that, when the ship that had brought him to Plymouth was preparing to return to England, Bradford boarded it with some assistants and demanded that Captain Pierce, the Master of the *Anne*, should hand over to him all the correspondence put aboard by both Lyford and Oldham.

Pierce, having heard much of the rantings of the new pastor against those in authority and the conduct of the Church in the settlement, did not hesitate to comply. The writings were found to contain whole series of lying accusations, some of them so seriously prejudicial to the well-being of the settlement and its elected officers that they could not be allowed to pass unchallenged. And even more criminal was the taking of copies of letters written between Robinson in Leyden and Brewster in America, and from Winslow to Robinson, that had obviously been done while the ship was on its outward-bound voyage, and then their annotation with scurrilous comments before they were readdressed to a minister, John Pemberton, in England.

But the most startling of the letters was one written by Oldham, stating the intention of Lyford and himself to reform the Church in Plymouth as soon as the *Anne* sailed, and to restore the sacraments of the Anglican form of worship.

Bradford returned ashore with the offending letters secreted in his pockets. He then sent Standish to bring Oldham before him, but the man drew a knife, called the Captain a knave and a rascal, and raved against his right to carry the commands of the Governor. Hearing the noisy argument Bradford intervened, but receiving no better treatment than had Standish he ordered Oldham imprisoned until his temper improved.

The Governor made no reference to the letters he had removed from the *Anne*, nor did he produce them when Oldham was finally brought before him to receive some mild punishment for refusing to obey the order conveyed to him through Standish. He preferred to allow the pair sufficient rope to hang themselves.

On the Sunday following his release, Oldham and Lyford convened a public meeting for worship apart from that of the Pilgrim Church, having informed neither the Governor nor any of the Elders of their intention. The Governor immediately set up a court and charged the two men with failing to respect the ordinances of New Plymouth and the settlers who had created it. Then, as both Lyford and Oldham denied the charges out-of-hand, they were further accused of plotting to introduce religious and civil matters into the community that denied the liberty of conscience – the whole reason for the existence of the colony.

Lyford continued to deny each charge in turn and demanded proof of them. His letters were produced – and for the moment he was shocked into silence. But not so Oldham; he began to rave and rant, and cried out for those who supported Lyford and himself to rebel against the leaders of the community and to

demand that they conform to the doctrines as laid down by the Church of England. He was silenced in his turn – when it dawned on him that not a single voice was raised on his behalf. Bradford then made some attempt to reason with Lyford, although he held him convicted of hypocrisy and treachery. Lyford broke down and wept with all the humility and fervour that he had displayed so unconvincingly when he had first arrived in the settlement. He confessed his guilt and prayed to God to forgive him.

The sentence of the court was that both men should be expelled from Plymouth: John Oldham at once, although his wife and family were to be allowed to stay all next winter if necessary until he could make proper provision for them elsewhere; Lyford was to be given six months' grace before leaving the settlement, and it was hinted that it might be prolonged if he behaved himself.

Lyford confessed again publicly to the scandalous nature of the charges he had made in his writings, and to having been overwhelmed with pride, vainglory and self-love. He repeated his confessions yet again at a meeting of the Pilgrim Church, proclaiming in tears his repentance and his great fear that God would never forgive him for such deadly sins – and two months later wrote a second letter to the Company of Adventurers in London reiterating all his previous charges.

Edward Winslow received news from England that Lyford had been forced to leave Ireland because of his relations with other women than his wife and his persistence in calling God to witness his innocence, despite the proven facts and at least one bastard child. This information, coupled with news of the letters he had written to England since his "confessions", decided Bradford to banish Lyford from the settlement at once. Lyford went to Nantasket, then moved on to Salem and finally drifted to Virginia, where he died.

John Oldham returned to Plymouth during the annual election of the Governor in March 1625 – and again did his best to raise a storm of revolt against the leaders of the community and the Pilgrim Church. When he failed to find a single supporter he reviled them all as rebels and traitors in the most outrageous terms – until he was, for the second time, committed to imprisonment in the guardroom until he could control his maniacal temper. Once he had calmed down, he was taken out and made to run the gauntlet of a double row of musketeers wielding the butts of

The expulsion of Oldham from Plymouth in 1625; he was
eventually to be murdered by Indians in 1636.

their weapons, then taken to the harbour and put aboard a boat that was just about to depart for the fishing grounds to the north.

The activities of Lyford and Oldham had considerable impact on the Plymouth settlers. A tiny measure of prosperity was coming to the plantation but the benefits were being garnered by the industrious, the better trained and the more intelligent families, leaving the less energetic and the slower witted to drift along only just above the poverty level. This had created resentments and divisions in the community which threatened to bring about a growing rivalry and hostility between the factions. But, when the two sides saw how Lyford and Oldham had attempted to drive them so far apart, they had reacted by coming closer together instead – and the "outsiders" became so ostracized that they made up their minds to leave Plymouth at the first opportunity. At the same time Bradford, procuring the election of more assistants, took the opportunity to encourage and even to enforce the labour and land regulations that ensured at least a modicum of prosperity to even the least enthusiastic families.

But that tiny measure of prosperity was soon to be put in jeopardy. The Company of Adventurers in London had gained little from its enterprise and began to break up. Most of its members finally withdrew their support, leaving the settlement in New England to stand on its own. At first, nothing seemed lost to the Pilgrim Fathers – the harvest had been good, providing them with not only sufficient Indian corn to see them safe until the next harvest but enough and to spare to trade with the Indians.

Having two shallops, they decked in one amidships to keep the corn dry and then sent it out on a trading expedition. It brought back a fine return of beaver and other pelts, and these were promptly casked and loaded into a little ship, the *James*, for the voyage to England.

Although the Atlantic crossing was made in exceptionally fine weather and the English Channel entered in almost record time, when the crew in the rigging were expecting to sight Plymouth soon the vessel was suddenly overhauled and captured by a Turkish warship. The Master and crew of the *James* were taken to Turkey and sold into slavery, and most of the eight hundredweight of valuable furs were sold at the ridiculous price of fourpence apiece.

Standish had sailed to England at the same time as the *James*, by a larger and slower vessel, to act as agent for the Plymouth settlers, and he returned in April 1626 with much sad news. He told the story of the loss of the *James* and its valuable cargo – so precious to the community. He told, too, of the

John Endicot or Endecott, the zealously Puritan Governor of the
Massachusetts Bay Colony.

disastrous plague that had ravaged England during 1625; in London and Westminster alone, over 40,000 were said to have died in the epidemic of that year – among them many friends and relatives of the Pilgrims.

Standish also carried the news that John Robinson, their pastor and probably the most earnest and devoted of all their leaders, had died at Leyden in Holland on 1st March 1625. Although he had never succeeded in joining his flock in the New World, John Robinson had never ceased to keep in touch with them as their spiritual leader, and they, in their turn, had done all they could to overrule the objections of the financiers to provide him with a passage. Perhaps the best picture of the esteem in which Robinson was held by the Pilgrim Fathers on both sides of the Atlantic is to be gained from the following extract from a speech made by Bradford: "Mr John Robinson, was pastor of the Church of Leyden, in Holland; a man not easily to be paralleled

for all things, whose singular virtues we shall not take upon us here to describe. Neither need we, for they so well are known by both friends and enemies. As he was a man learned and of solid judgement and of quick and sharp wit, so was he also of a tender conscience and very sincere in all his ways, a hater of hypocrisy and dissimulation, and would be very plain with his best friends. He was very courteous, affable and sociable in his conversation, and towards his own people especially . . ."

And on 27th March 1625 King James had died at Theobalds, to be succeeded by Charles I.

In 1627 it was Isaac Allerton's turn to visit England on behalf of the Pilgrim Fathers, where he made a compact with what remained of the Company of Adventurers; on 15th November 1626 the Company had gone into voluntary liquidation.

In the same year a start was made on a permanent allocation of land to the settlers in New Plymouth.

Until then the Planters had owned but one acre each, and that had been subject to redistribution every year – the rest of the plantation being the property of the Adventurers under the Seven Years' Agreement. Care was taken to see to it that this new allocation should not be on such a vast scale as to stultify the growth of the settlement through lack of reinforcements; each person was given twenty acres, no more, whatever his or her status, four acres (along the water front) by five acres. Land in this way was preserved for the Pilgrim Fathers yet to come to the New World, thirty-five of whom arrived in August 1629, in company with a number of settlers bound for Neumkeak – now Salem – where John Endicot had started a new settlement a year earlier.

The Neumkeak settlers held similar religious convictions to those of the Pilgrim Fathers, and as their plantation was within the confines of Massachusetts Bay, to the north of Boston Bay and no more than fifty miles' sailing distance from Plymouth, they brought with them a new hope of companionship for the lonely Pilgrims of the older settlement.

The link between the two Christian communities quickly blossomed, particularly after an infection, carried from a ship, spread among the Planters of Neumkeak. Endicot sent to Plymouth for help, at the beginning of May 1929, even before the arrival of the new colonists, and Bradford immediately despatched Surgeon Fuller to render what aid he could: his ministrations were entirely successful and gratefully acknowledged, and from that day forward there was much coming and going between the two groups of settlers.

22   Together in the New World

In May 1630 the *Handmaid* dropped anchor in Plymouth harbour, New England, and from it there disembarked sixty passengers from Leyden, Holland – the last of those to arrive in the New World under the mantle of the Pilgrim Church and entitled to style themselves as the "Pilgrim Fathers of New England".

In the ten years that had passed since the *Mayflower* had sailed from Plymouth, Devon, 292 members of that Church had arrived in Plymouth, New England – 52 to die within six months of the first landing in the New World. But, through the incidence of births and deaths during that decade, the population of the settlement was now around 300.

Fortunate indeed were these "last arrivals", for the "Forefathers" had never forgotten the solemn compact into which they had entered with every member of the Pilgrim Church in April 1620, before the first of them sailed from Leyden to join the *Mayflower*, the fourth and last clause of which declared:

"If the Lord should frown upon our proceedings, then those that went to return; and the brethren that remained still there, to assist and be helpful to them. But if GOD should be pleased to favour them that went, then they also should endeavour to help over such as were poor, and ancient, and willing to come."

As this last company of the Pilgrim Fathers stepped ashore, their eyes and hearts must have been gladdened by the sight of the houses that had been built for them and the ground that had been prepared for their use, and by the knowledge that provisions for sixteen months were being held in reserve for them, until such time as they could harvest their own first crops.

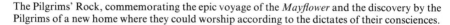

The Pilgrims' Rock, commemorating the epic voyage of the *Mayflower* and the discovery by the Pilgrims of a new home where they could worship according to the dictates of their consciences.

Appendix

(a) Indian Names

(As there were, of course, no written Indian languages in the seventeenth century, Indian words are spelt here, phonetically, as interpreted by the author.)

Agawam – Ipswich, N.E.
Agawaywam – Wareham, N.E.
Aspinet – Sachem of the Nauset Indians.
Canonicus – Sagamore of the Narragansetts.
Cantaugcanteest – Strawberry Hill (1623), now Watson's Hill in New Plymouth.
Cawnacome – Sachem of the Manomets.
Corbitant – a Sachem of the tribes at Mattapoist and Namaschet.
Cummaquid – Barnstable harbour, N.E.
Hobomok – a Wampanoag Pines who lived with the settlers at New Plymouth.
Isle of Capawack – Martha's Vineyard, N.E.
Iyanough – Sachem of the Mattachiest Indians.
Kietitan – Indian God.
Manamoick – Chatham, N.E.
Manomet – Sandwich, N.E.
Massachusets – Indians domiciled in northern Boston Bay area.
Massasoit – Sagamore of the Wampanoag Indians.
Massasoit's Spring – Warren, N.E.
Mattachiest – district around Barnstable, N.E.
Mattapoist – Gardner's Neck, Swansea, N.E.
Monchiggan – Monhegan, N.E.
Namaschet – Middlesborough, N.E.
Nanepashemet – a deceased Sagamore of the Boston Bay Indians.
Narragansetts – Indians based chiefly in Rhode Island, N.E.
Nauset – Eastham, N.E.
Neumkeak – Salem, N.E.
Obtakiest – Sachem of the Boston Bay Indians.
Packonokik – Bristol district of Rhode Island.
Pamet – Cape Cod.
Patuxet – New Plymouth.
Pecksuot – Pines of the Boston Bay Indians.
Pemmaquid – Bristol, N.E.

Pines – a Councillor under a Sachem.
Powow – Medicine Man, healer or adviser.
Quadequina – a Wampanoag Sachem and brother of Sagamore Massasoit.
Sachem – a local chief.
Sagamore – a paramount chief.
Samoset – Sagamore of the Pemmaquid tribes.
Sowans – Massasoit's "capital" in Packonokik.
"Squanto" – Tisquantum, an Indian resident with the settlers in New Plymouth.
Squaw Sachem – chief's wife.
Succonet – Falmouth, N.E.
Tarrantine Indians – domiciled along the Penobscot River, in Maine, N.E.
Tisquantum – see "Squanto".
Tokamahamon – Indian interpreter loaned to the settlers by Massasoit.
Wampanoag Indians – particularly domiciled in and around Rhode Island.
Wassapinewat – Sachem, brother of Obtakiest.
Wessagusset – Weymouth, N.E.
Wituwamat – a Pines of the Boston Bay Indians.

(b) Officers of the Plymouth Plantation

Governors

1602	John Carver
1621–1632	William Bradford
1633	Edward Winslow
1634	Thomas Prence
1635	William Bradford
1636	Edward Winslow
1637	William Bradford
1638	Thomas Prence
1639–1643	William Bradford
1644	Edward Winslow
1645–1657	William Bradford
1658–1672	Thomas Prence
1673–1680	Josiah Winslow
1681–1686	Thomas Hinckley

Secretaries

1636–1644 Nathaniel Souther
1645–1684 Nathaniel Morton
1685–1686 Nathaniel Clarke
1687–1692 Samuel Sprague

Treasurers

1636–1651 William Paddy
1652–1655 Miles Standish
1656–1658 John Alden
1659–1679 Constant Southworth
1680–1686 William Bradford the younger

Ruling Elders

at Amsterdam 1608–1609 William Brewster
   Leyden   1609–1620 William Brewster
   Plymouth   1620–1643 William Brewster
              1649–1691 Thomas Cushman

Pastors

at Gainsborough 1606–1607 John Smith
   Scrooby   1607–1608 Richard Clifton
   Amsterdam   1608–1609 Francis Johnson
   Leyden   1609–1625 John Robinson
   Plymouth   1624   John Lyford
             1628   Rogers
             1629–1636 Ralph Smith
             1636–1654 John Reyner
             1659   James Williams
             1665   William Binstead
             1669–1697 John Cotton the
                          younger

Deacons

at Amsterdam 1608–1609 Christopher Bowman
   Leyden   1609–1625 Robert Cushman
   Plymouth   1620–1633 Samuel Fuller
            1617–1621 John Carver
            1629–1633 Richard Masterson
                    and Thomas Blossom
            1634–1644 John Doane
            1634–1651 John Cooke
                    and William Paddy
            1652–1687 Robert Finney
            1669–1693 Ephraim Morton

Teachers

at Scrooby   1607–1608 John Robinson
   Amsterdam 1608–1609 Henry Ainsworth
   Plymouth   1631–1643 Roger Williams
            1636   John Norton
            1638–1641 Charles Chauncy

Assistant Governors

1621–1632 Isaac Allerton
1624–1635 Captain Miles Standish
1624–1632 Edward Winslow
1624–1636 Stephen Hopkins
1624–1628 Richard Warren
1629–1635 John Howland
1631–1639 John Alden
1633–1634 William Bradford
1633   W. Gison
1633   J. Doane
1634–1635 Edward Winslow
1634–1637 William Collier
1635–1637 Thomas Prence
1636   William Bradford
1636   Timothy Hatherley
1636   Peter Browne
1637–1641 Captain Miles Standish
1637–1638 Edward Winslow
1637–1640 John Jenney
1637   Timothy Hatherley
1638   William Bradford
1638–1645 Peter Browne
1638   Henry Atwood
1639   Thomas Prence
1639–1640 Timothy Hatherley
1639–1651 William Collier
1640–1646 E. Freeman
1640–1657 Thomas Prence
1641–1643 Edward Winslow
1641–1657 Timothy Hatherley
1642–1644 William Thomas
1645–1656 Captain Miles Standish
1645–1647 Edward Winslow
1647–1650 William Thomas
1647–1655 Peter Browne
1650   Edward Winslow
1651–1672 John Alden
1661–1665 Thomas Willet
1652–1653 Thomas Southworth
1654–1665 William Collier
1656–1657 J. Cudworth
1657–1672 John Winslow
1658–1681 William Bradford Jr.
1658–1659 Thomas Southworth
1665–1666 J. Brown
1666–1673 N. Bacon
1666–1686 J. Freeman
1670–1678 Constant Southworth
1673–1680 J. Cudworth
1673–1683 J. Brown
1679–1686 D. Smith
1681–1686–B. Lothrop
1682–1686 J. Thatcher
1684–1686 J. Walley.

No fewer than four one-time presidents of the United States are said to have been descendants of the Pilgrim Fathers:

Zachary Taylor, who was President 1849–50 had among his ancestors both William Brewster and Isaac Allerton.

Ulysses Simpson Grant, President 1869–77, was descended from Richard Warren.

William Howard Taft, President 1909–13, had among his ancestors Francis Cooke.

Franklin Delano Roosevelt, President 1933–45, claimed relationship with no fewer than six of the Founding Fathers: Francis Cooke, the Allertons, Warrens, John Howland, John Tilley and the De la Noye family.

The Pilgrims are ferried from the shore at Delfshaven to the *Speedwell*.

Select Bibliography

Note: The books listed here are in the main fairly popular works designed for the reader who wishes to learn more about the Pilgrims' story or about the background of the period. Some, particularly the earlier ones, will differ in detail from the account given in this book: the reader should bear in mind that all contemporary sources are unreliable and often conflicting, since both the Pilgrims and their adversaries quite naturally tended to colour their accounts according to their opinions, much as, I am sure, there are interpretations in this present work with which others would disagree.

Arber, Edward: *The Story of the Pilgrim Fathers 1606–1623; as told by themselves, their friends and their enemies*, Boston, 1897.

Bartlett, W. H.: *The Pilgrim Fathers*, Nelson, Edinburgh, 1863.

Belden, Rev. Albert (Minister of the Pilgrim Fathers' Memorial Church, Great Dover Street, London): *Prison Church and Pilgrim Ship*, recent pamphlet, n.d.

Bradford, William: History of the Plimouth Plantation, ed. J. A. Doyle, Boston, 1896.

Burgess, Walter H.: *John Robinson, Pastor of the Pilgrim Fathers*, n.d.

Caffrey, Kate: *The Mayflower*, Deutsch, London, 1975.

Churchill, Winston S.: *History of the English-Speaking Peoples*, Vol. 2, *The New World*, Cassell, London, 1956.

Davies, Godfrey: *The Early Stuarts, 1603–1660*, Oxford University Press, 1959.

Gebler, Ernest: *The Plymouth Adventure* (a chronicle novel of the voyage of the *Mayflower*), Doubleday, New York, 1950.

Godfrey, Dennis (Pastor of the Pilgrim Fathers' Memorial Church, London), recent pamphlets.

Hubbard, William: *General History of New England*, 2nd edn., 1848.

MacKennal, Alexander: *Homes and Haunts of the Pilgrim Fathers*, 1899.

McManus, Blanche: *The Voyage of the Mayflower*, Boston, 1901.

Masefield, John: *Chronicles of the Pilgrim Fathers*, Everymans Library, London, 1917.

Morton, Nathaniel: *New England's Memorial*, 5th edn., 1826.

Plumb, A. H.: *William Bradford of Plymouth*, 1920.

Robinson, John: *Collected Works*, 1851.

Steele, Ashbel: *Chief of the Pilgrims: of the Life and Times of William Bradford*, Philadelphia, 1857.

Usher, Roland: *The Pilgrims and Their History*, 1918.

Windsor, Justin: *Elder William Brewster of the "Mayflower"*, 1887.

Young, Alexander: *The Chronicles of the Pilgrim Fathers*, 2nd edn., 1844.

The Pilgrim Society, Plymouth, Massachusetts.

Western Morning News, Plymouth, UK – especially the *Mayflower* supplement of 6th September 1920, the tercentenary of the sailing of the *Mayflower* from Plymouth.

Acknowledgements

The publishers have used their every endeavour to trace the owners of copyright material used in this book; anyone who feels that they have a copyright claim to press should, in the first instance, approach Webb & Bower (Publishers) Ltd., 33 Southernhay East, Exeter, Devon EX1 1NS, UK.

Acknowledgements for black-and-white illustrations are as follows:

Barnaby's Picture Library: pages 16, 22, 35, 124, 162

J. Allan Cash: pages 29, 55

Devon Library Services: page 177

Mary Evans Picture Library: pages 8, 10 (right), 11, 12, 13, 15, 17, 18, 19, 26 (lower), 33 (lower), 34, 37, 39, 40, 41, 45, 46, 53, 57, 58, 59, 78, 99, 122, 125, 132, 142, 145, 153, 155, 160, 187, 188, 193

Fotomas: pages 9, 10 (left), 14, 28, 30, 33 (upper), 43, 44, 48, 60, 95, 96, 107, 157, 179

Robert Harding Associates: pages 168, 190

Vernon Heaton: pages 21, 25, 26 (upper), 32, 38, 42, 62, 64, 67, 68, 73, 77, 93, 124, 130 (upper), 139, 143, 148, 154, 173

E. J. Jane: pages 80 (lower), 82, 126, 165, 181

Mansell Collection: pages 71, 75, 105, 116, 117, 120, 146

Peter Newark's Western Americana: pages 49, 72, 92, 98, 101, 103, 109, 112, 123, 127, 128, 137, 147, 170, 172, 183

The Pilgrim Society, Plymouth, Massachusetts: pages 20, 24, 54, 56, 69, 70, 79, 89, 90, 130 (lower), 135, 140, 149, 161

Acknowledgements for colour illustrations are as follows:

Barnaby's Picture Library: pages 83 (upper), 151 (lower)

Mary Evans Picture Library: page 134

Fotomas: page 65

Robert Harding Associates: page 84

E. J. Jane: page 133

National Portrait Gallery, London: page 66

Peter Newark's Western Americana: page 151 (upper)

Spectrum Colour Library: pages 83 (lower), 152

Index